DANGEROUS GIFTS

DANGEROUS GIFTS

GENDER *and* EXCHANGE
in ANCIENT GREECE

DEBORAH LYONS

UNIVERSITY OF TEXAS PRESS

Austin

This book was supported in part by Alice Lynch in honor of Joanna Hitchcock, former director of the University of Texas Press.

Requests for permission to reproduce material from this work should be sent to:
Permissions
University of Texas Press
P.O. Box 7819
Austin, TX 78713-7819
utpress.utexas.edu/about/book-permissions

♾ The paper used in this book meets the minimum requirements of
ANSI/NISO Z39.48-1992 (R1997) (Permanence of Paper).

LIBRARY OF CONGRESS CATALOGING-IN-PUBLICATION DATA
Lyons, Deborah J.
Dangerous gifts : gender and exchange in ancient Greece / by Deborah Lyons.
   p.   cm.
Includes bibliographical references and index.
ISBN 978-0-292-75433-1
1. Gifts—Greece—History.   2. Ceremonial exchange—Greece—
History.   3. Barter—Greece—History.   4. Sex role—Greece.
5.   Greece—Social life and customs.   I. Title.
GT3041.G8L96   2012
394—dc23   2011038884

First paperback printing, 2013

Dedicated to my brothers, Benjamin Lyons and Jonathan Lyons, and to the memory of my father, Will Lyons

CONTENTS

CHAPTER SEVEN

CONCLUSION: THE GENDER OF RECIPROCITY

LIST *of* ILLUSTRATIONS

FIGURE I

Polyneikes offering a necklace to Eriphyle. Attic red-figure Oinochoe. Schuwalow Painter, c. 450–400 BCE. 31

FIGURE 2

Polyneikes offering a necklace to Eriphyle. Attic red-figure Oinochoe. Schuwalow Painter, c. 450–400 BCE. 32

FIGURE 3

A man offering gifts to a woman. Attic red-figure Oinochoe. Attributed to the Berlin Painter, c. 490–480 BCE. 32

FIGURE 4

Paris abducting Helen. Attic red-figure Skyphos, Side A. Painter: Makron, c. 490–480 BCE. 34

FIGURE 5

Menelaos reclaiming Helen. Attic red-figure Skyphos, Side B. Painter: Makron, c. 490–480 BCE. 35

ACKNOWLEDGMENTS

Because this book has taken quite a long time to write, I find myself in the awkward position of having to acknowledge more debts than I can hope to remember. I implore the many friends and colleagues whose insights have so often pointed me in the right direction or opened up a new way of thinking to forgive me if I have neglected to give them credit.

The writing of this book has benefitted from a Mellon fellowship at Harvard University, supported by the Andrew W. Mellon Foundation; a fellowship at the Center for Hellenic Studies; and a year at the National Humanities Center, supported by the Lilly Endowment and the Research Triangle Fund. I thank the fellows and staff of these institutions for all their help and encouragement. Particularly warm mention is due to Deborah Boedeker and Kurt Raaflaub, directors of the Center for Hellenic Studies, for their intellectual example and the amazing hospitality they offered those fortunate enough to be in residence during their tenure. Thanks are also due to Miami University for summer research support.

The associates of the Susan B. Anthony Institute for Women's and Gender Studies at the University of Rochester provided much-needed support. The Classics Department of the Johns Hopkins University offered a welcoming berth for the five years I was there. The Classics Department of Miami University has provided me with a permanent home and a grateful end to the life of the itinerant scholar.

I owe a debt for their many helpful comments to audiences at Wesleyan University, SUNY Buffalo, Amherst College, Duke University, University of North Carolina—Chapel Hill and Greensboro, Feminism and Classics Conferences III and V, Union College, Rice University, University of Chicago, the University of Michigan, the University of Iowa, and the Johns Hopkins University. Portions of this book appeared in *Classical Antiquity* 22 (2003) as the article "Dangerous Gifts: Ideologies of Marriage and Exchange in Ancient Greece." I thank the editors for permission to reuse this material, much of which forms the nucleus of Chapter Five.

I owe great thanks to Jim Burr, my patient editor for this project, and to Joanna Hitchcock, my first editor ever, and former director of the University of Texas Press. Her retirement, although well deserved, is nonetheless a great loss to the field of Classics. Silvia Montiglio and James Redfield made invaluable comments on the manuscript in their capacity as readers for the Press. Sherry Wert, copyeditor extraordinaire, saved me from countless errors. Ayham Ghraowi's cover design captures the essence of this book more brilliantly than I had any right to expect.

Friends and colleagues who deserve mention include Carla Antonaccio, Bradley Ault, Karen Bassi, Fred Bohrer, Mary Baine Campbell, Rick Griffiths, Debra Hershkowitz, Nick Humez, Michele Longino, Irad Malkin, Lisa Maurizio, Laura McClure, Lynette Mitchell, Deborah Modrak, Sarah Morris, Gregory Nagy, Steve Nimis, Robin Osborne, Matthew Roller, Peter Rose, Alan Shapiro, Moshe Sluhovsky, Benjamin Sutcliffe, Hans van Wees, and David Weinstock.

Although I never succeeded in convincing him that Melanesia was sufficiently near ancient Greece to be of any use, I owe much to Raymond Westbrook, who read my drafts and argued amiably with me about many points in this volume. His untimely death is a great loss to scholarship and to all who knew him.

Michael Herzfeld, my *cicerone* to the world of anthropology, has been unfailingly helpful, but is wholly blameless for the inevitable lapses of a nonspecialist. None of those thanked are to be faulted for the failings of this book. Had I only heeded their advice more completely, it would undoubtedly be better.

In a heroic display of sibling reciprocity, Jonathan Lyons read and commented on the entire manuscript in one day—as luck would have it, only a few weeks after I had done the same for him. Benjamin Lyons, always a challenging interlocutor, also called my attention to the invaluable work of David Graeber. My mother Evelyn Lyons commented on drafts and provided much-needed encouragement. My father Will Lyons, an economist, listened patiently to my accounts of economic behavior that defied all his models. The love and support of my family has meant more to me than I can say.

This book was always going to be dedicated, as is appropriate to the subject matter, to my brothers. Sadly, I must add to this a dedication to the memory of our father.

NOTE TO THE READER

In spelling Greek names I have resorted to a by-now familiar expedient: the most familiar names appear in their Latinized forms (e.g., Aeschylus, Sophocles, Helen). All others are transcribed according to their Greek spelling. I use *k* to indicate the Greek letter *kappa*, but *ch* for the letter *chi* (e.g., Klytemnestra, Chryseis).

All unattributed translations from Greek, Latin, and other languages are my own. Where indicated, I have modified the translations of others, making only minor changes to bring out the meaning of the original Greek more clearly.

DANGEROUS GIFTS

INTRODUCTION

ἐκ γάρ δώρων πολλὰ κακ' ἀνθρώποισι πέλονται.

For many evils come to human beings from gifts.

———

ANTIMACHOS OF TEOS, CITED BY
CLEMENT OF ALEXANDRIA, *STROMATA* 6.12.7

Deianeira sends her husband Herakles a poisoned robe. Eriphyle trades the life of her husband Amphiaraos for a golden necklace. Atreus' wife Aerope gives the token of his sovereignty, a lamb with a golden fleece, to his brother Thyestes, who has seduced her. In all of these examples, drawn from Greek myth and its tragic elaborations, precious objects of metal or textiles enter into circulation because of women. And in each case, disaster follows. Many cultures view all exchange as potentially dangerous, but in the ancient Greek imagination women and gifts appear to be a particularly deadly combination.[1]

This book explores the role of gender in structuring relations of exchange in ancient Greece, and specifically the representation of women as both objects and agents of exchange. The anthropological concept of reciprocity is central to this investigation of gender and exchange in ancient Greek thought. I approach the Homeric epics, Attic tragedy, and other mythic material in light of ethnographic accounts detailing the social organization of other traditional societies marked, like those of ancient Greece, by both an interest in exchange and a high degree of sexual dimorphism. As will become clear, my debts to anthropology go far beyond theories of reciprocity, extending to kinship and other features of social organization.

The theme of reciprocity in the ancient world has recently received significant attention in the work of Walter Donlan, Richard Seaford, Leslie Kurke, and others.[2] That I owe much to these scholars will be obvious, although my focus is generally rather different. Similarly, I have learned a great deal from those who have explored the theme of "the traffic in women" in tragedy, among them Victoria Wohl, Kirk Ormand, and Nancy Sorken Rabinowitz.[3] As I am in general sympathy with these readings, I have tried only to acknowledge where I build on their ideas, rather than to indicate every point of agreement or disagreement. Although "the traffic in women" is also central to my own conception, it is the point of departure for a consideration of a gendered system of exchange in which women's economic agency is ultimately as important as their objectification. In this, my approach overlaps most with that of Wohl, despite a very different trajectory. What distinguishes my project from those I have mentioned above is its attempt to construct an "economics of gender" by examining gendered exchange in ancient Greece from a cross-cultural perspective. In so doing, I also offer a new interpretation of ancient Greek conceptions of sibling relationships as seen through the lens of reciprocity.

My interest is in exchange marked by gender difference. Exchanges between two partners of the same gender are not central to my argument, except when a woman is the object of the exchange. I use the word "gender" rather than "women" in my title in order to make explicit the notion that women's roles in relations of exchange, whether as subject or object, rely for their meaning on their place within a coherent system of exchange that is necessarily inflected by gender.[4]

My purpose in analyzing this material is neither to demonstrate once again the subordination of ancient Greek women, nor to offer an "optimistic" account of occasions for female autonomy.[5] Rather, I am interested in the complex specificities of the place of women in ancient Greek thought. Given the difficulty of determining social realities in ancient Greece, my aim is instead to elucidate some aspects of gender ideology by examining the social and economic role of women (and consequently of men) as represented in some of the central literary and artistic documents of the archaic and classical periods. I do in some instances draw on historical evidence, but I use it to elucidate ancient Greek thinking about gender, rather than to make a historical argument.[6]

A persistent theme of this book is the danger attendant on the participation of women in exchange and the role of exchange in the breakdown of the marital relationship. I argue that since wives as a general rule come from outside of the immediate family, the suspicion with which they are regarded is born of the tension between the ideal of self-sufficiency and the need to engage and exchange with others.[7] The necessity of bringing a wife from outside the *oikos* (household) also creates a certain ambiguity, since in most other respects, "outside" is coded as male, whereas "inside" is the province of women.[8] As I will show, the persistent association of women's infidelity with the loss of household wealth is closely related to these concerns.

In analyzing patterns of ancient Greek mythic thought about gender and exchange, I use Homeric epic and Attic tragedy, as well as other repositories of myth from Greek antiquity. For my purposes, fragments of the Cyclic epics may be as illuminating as the canonical Homeric poems, and ancient handbook versions may be as useful as those found in the works of the great tragedians. Of course, no mythic version is an unmediated transmission from the past; each author shapes the tradition to his or her own purposes. At the same time, the authors of these versions had an intuitive feel for the protocols of exchange and the ideology of gender as expressed in their time and place. This is true even when it is clear that the author—and this is especially true of the tragedians—is deliberately working against the grain of tradition. I use the word "author" here in its broadest possible sense: in addition to literary texts, I also rely upon mythic versions transmitted in the images of Attic vase painting.

The arrangement of the texts under consideration, starting with Hesiod and Homer, then moving to Attic tragedy, might suggest a chronological argument about change in attitudes toward women and exchange. This is, however, not the nature of my undertaking, and the arrangement is more thematic than chronological. Although there are clear differences in the treatment of women from one text to another, the paucity of comparable data does not allow a full historical analysis. Texts representing different historical periods, different locations, and different genres can be compared, but it is hard to draw definitive conclusions about historical change from these comparisons. Rather, I analyze a series of texts that emerge from different moments in time and very different generic conventions, in hopes of elucidating some overarching patterns in ancient Greek thinking about women, gender, and exchange. In this I follow the approach recently taken by Jeremy McInerney: "The charge of anachronism is too easily used as an excuse not to look for the threads of culture that bind the practices of one age to another, and to impose sterile boundaries between different times. Certainly Homer's Achaians are not identical to Pericles' Athenians, but neither are they unrelated."[9]

In one respect, of course, it is impossible to escape from chronology, nor would I wish to try: the intertextuality betweeen earlier and later texts inevitably affects our reading of them. It is because of this that Homer and Hesiod can be read profitably in tandem with tragedy. The earlier texts never lost their relevance to the poets and audiences of later periods, among whom we must count ourselves.

A few remarks are in order about the status of the Homeric poems as evidence. The battle over the historicity of the epics rages on, but I do not intend to engage it here.[10] As already noted above, my argument is not a historical one, but rather concerns ideology and representation. Quite apart from the contentious question of whether the *Iliad* and *Odyssey* correspond to any particular Greek society in any distinct historical period is the question of whether the institutions described form a coherent system. It is my assumption that, for the most part, they do present a coherent representational and ideological system. Of course, that is not necessarily the same as a coherent social system.

Much has been made of the inconsistencies in Homeric institutions, where seemingly incompatible practices like cremation and inhumation, or bridewealth and dowry, appear to exist side-by-side.[11] We know, however, that such disparate practices may be found within a single society. Archaeological evidence from Athens, for example, shows the coexistence of cremation and inhumation. Furthermore, as anthropologists frequently remind us, people are always breaking the rules.[12] Not only that, but people frequently disagree about what those rules are, as even a casual reader of Miss Manners knows. Institutions depicted in the Homeric poems may be in flux, or even at times in crisis, but they nonetheless belong to a recognizable system built on shared assumptions. In Richard Seaford's phrase, Homer presents us with the "ideological image of a historical society."[13] Finally, whether coherent or not, Homeric epic exerted so powerful an influence for centuries throughout the Greek-speaking world that the representations it offers are of continuing ideological significance for ancient Greek culture of later periods. Whatever the value of the Homeric epics as historical evidence in the narrowest sense, they provide insight into the ideological assumptions not only of the age from which they emerged, but also to some extent of later centuries, in which they continued to function as cultural touchstones.

The first chapter of this book lays out the anthropological concepts that have guided my analysis of the Greek material. Among these are the structures of kinship and marriage, sibling intimacy or cooperation, the gendered division of labor, and the concept of wealth as a gendered category. Here, using examples from ethnographies of small-scale traditional societies, I argue for a code or protocol governing exchange that is applicable to the Greek texts to be discussed throughout this book. Thereafter, the ethnographic data play only a supporting role before returning to center stage in the final chapter. In the intervening pages, the reader will glimpse them working behind the scenes.

The second chapter explores Greek thinking about the *oikos*, specifically how it is shaped and at times distorted by the cherished ideal—one might even say ideology—of *autarkeia*, self-sufficiency. This is nowhere more evident than in the Hesiodic treatment of the creation of woman, the ultimate dangerous gift of the gods. This figure highlights the tensions between the requirements of exogamy and the desire for self-sufficiency, which result in the devaluing of women's economic contributions to the household.

Chapter Three deals with the traffic in women, which pervades the myths of the Trojan War, and which in some ways underwrites attitudes toward women throughout much of ancient Greek myth and literature. Here I discuss the operation of this dynamic within the *Iliad* and other myths associated with Troy, placing it within a larger context of corrupted reciprocity that affects the exchange of men as well as women.

In the fourth chapter, I argue that the *Odyssey* introduces a degree of agency for women not found in the *Iliad*, presenting them as actors in exchange more often than as objects of exchange. These exchanges are shown to be positive, and indeed, Odysseus would not be able to return home without them. Nevertheless, a lingering unease about women as treacherous exchange partners surfaces in several glancing references within the poem to women who betray men in exchange for gifts.

The anxiety about exchanging women emerges in full bloom in Attic tragedy, the subject of Chapter Five. In this genre, any exchange with a woman, whether she is virtuous or not, ends up being fatal. The tragedies treated in greatest detail here, Aeschylus' *Agamemnon* and Sophocles' *Trachiniai*, are those that most clearly show the operation of dangerous and perverted exchanges between men and women—specifically husbands and wives.

The sixth and final chapter takes up the one exception to the idea that exchanges between men and women are inevitably fraught with negative consequences. Unlike other male-female dyads, the sibling relationship is exempt from the fear of divided loyalties so often projected onto women. Here I show how the economics of gender is represented as benign when used in the service of familial solidarity, while remaining in tension with the need to engage with the outside world, as in marriage. At an opposite pole from Pandora—the divinely created object of desire who comes from outside for the ruination of the *oikos*—is the sister who evokes the fantasy that exchange can be avoided, that self-sufficiency is an attainable ideal.

In what follows, I bring the tools of anthropology to an examination of the relationship between women, men, and gifts in Greek myth and literature. In so doing, I hope to broaden our understanding of the gender ideology—as well as some of the central texts—of archaic and classical Greece.

CHAPTER ONE

GENDER *and* EXCHANGE

In a footnote to his fundamental article on "the mythic idea of value" in ancient Greece, Louis Gernet noted "the significance of the theme of the woman's role in the transfer of a talisman or other precious object from one person to another."[1] Gernet, however, was less interested in the agents of these exchanges than in the objects exchanged: precious and highly wrought tripods, weapons, and jewelry that fall under the category of *agalmata*. In Gernet's view, these objects carried not only economic and social value in a premonetary economy, but also, in a line of thought owing much to Marcel Mauss, a kind of sacred charge.[2] The original meaning of the word *agalma* is "adornment."[3] Its metaphorical use in Aeschylus' *Agamemnon*, where Iphigeneia is called the *agalma* of her father's house (*Ag.* 208), suggests that she herself is potentially an object of exchange.[4] To quote Gernet:

> The word *agalma*, in its earliest usage, implies the notion of "value." It can be used of all kinds of things, even, on occasion, of human beings thought of as "precious." It usually expresses some idea of opulence, and above all of aristocratic wealth (horses are *agalmata*). . . . The word *agalma* is used especially in relation to a class of movable objects which concerns me here. . . . The objects I am concerned with are "industrial objects": but it must be stressed that they are products made for a luxury market.[5]

The mythic examples used by Gernet to elucidate the meaning and power of the *agalma*, such as the tripod of the Seven Sages, the necklace of Eriphyle, and Atreus' lamb with the golden fleece, are prestige objects with complex genealogies and fateful histories. Although Gernet was primarily interested in the circulation of *agalmata* and the sources of their power, these very examples can be used—as he noted—to illuminate the role of women in that circulation.

The connection between women and the circulation of precious objects can be even more precisely delineated than Gernet's formulation suggests. For in the myths he treats, as in many others, it is only in the context of a marital crisis that a woman is allowed to transcend her usual role as *object* of exchange and to become instead an *agent* of exchange. These myths locate fears about women and exchange within the context of marriage—or rather, its failure—showing how completely these fears are entwined with concern about the fidelity of wives. The exchanging woman is assimilated to the adulterous woman, while her involvement in the circulation of objects is tied to the potential for the illicit circulation of her own person. As if to stress the fundamental inability of women to act as legitimate exchange partners, these myths play out against a backdrop of perverted reciprocity characterized by the violation of established codes governing the economic and social spheres of women and men.

Further examination of this theme reveals a complex and nuanced system in which not only the givers but also the objects they give are conceived of as gendered. The gendering of exchange objects and the rules governing the separate spheres of men's and women's exchanges can be better understood with reference to the anthropological categories of "male wealth" and "female wealth." These categories are closely related to the roles of men and women in the production of the kinds of objects in question. Thus we must take into account the gendered division of labor as conceptualized in archaic and classical Greek thought.

Closely related to the gendered division of labor and production is the spatial opposition between inside and outside, which distinguishes not only types of wealth, but also the different (and differently gendered) spheres of wealth-producing activities encompassed by the Greek *oikos*.[6] This domestic economy exists in opposition to the outside world of trade and artisanal production. It is my contention that much of the anxiety about women as exchangers is related to tension between the ideology of self-sufficiency (*autarkeia*) of the *oikos* and the frequent necessity of importing wives from outside.

———

The methodological and conceptual underpinnings of this study have emerged from a reading of ethnographies from a wide range of cultures.[7] The anthropological concepts on which I rely are among the staples of traditional anthropology, such as kinship and exchange, which are associated with giants in the field from Lewis Henry Morgan to Claude Lévi-Strauss, and Marcel Mauss to Bronislaw Malinowski. I have drawn on classic texts of anthropology as well as relatively recent work, some of it critical of the earlier texts.[8] I have particularly taken into account feminist challenges to traditional anthropological analyses of marriage and other institutions.[9]

———

The degree to which the study of single societies can lead to the formulation of general laws of human society has long been a matter of debate among anthropologists.[10] Anthropology nonetheless offers a set of tools for analyzing a culture, and these I make use of unapologetically. Not only theoretical models but also specific data from anthropology can be valuable, if handled carefully. Ethnographies provide material for comparisons that may elucidate issues common to many cultures (e.g., the divided loyalties felt by women caught between their natal families and the families into which they have married), but it is important not to overstate the epistemological power of these apparent parallels. Isolated similarities have little explanatory power. It is only in comparing systems, or significant parts of systems, that parallels can be anything more than suggestive. Alternatively, parallels that are found across a wide range of cultures can support more ambitious hypotheses than those found in only a few contexts. To the extent that these parallels produce illumination, we require either *depth* of similarity from culture to culture, or *breadth* of similarity across many cultures.

I have found the greatest correspondence between ancient Greece and the cultures of the Pacific, especially Melanesia, which are famous in the anthropological literature for their highly elaborated systems of exchange, introduced to the world through the work of Malinowski. In this I am not alone. To give only one notable recent example, Hans van Wees made excellent use of this material in a 2002 article entitled "Greed, Generosity and Gift-Exchange in Early Greece and the Western Pacific." In addition, I have used ethnographies from other cultures equally characterized by highly elaborated rituals of gift exchange. These are all small-scale preindustrialized societies, most of which can be described as "Big Man" societies, in which political power is maintained through the ability to stage suitably magnificent feasts or acquire a particularly famous shell arm-band. In other words, these societies share with that depicted in the Homeric poems an ethos requiring those who wield political power to continue to demonstrate their superiority in order to keep it.

The mythic accounts and the historical record do not tell quite the same story. If exogamy were considered risky or undesirable, we might expect to find a high level of endogamy. In fact, documents mostly from fourth-century Athens detail various kinds of endogamous marriage, including that between half-siblings.[11] Where we have sufficient evidence to judge, as in the Athenian case, the evidence shows that marriage to close kin was an available but not a preferred option.[12] The one exception was when the survival of the patriline was at issue. In this case, an endogamous marriage was more or less obligatory. In the institution known as the epiklerate, the daughter of a man who dies without a male heir (*epiklēros*) is married to her nearest available male relative.[13] Their son becomes heir to the deceased father of the *epiklēros*, his own grandfather. The term itself indicates that the woman comes with the allotment of land (*klēros*) belonging to her father, or that she is "upon the estate."[14] This institution had analogues in other Greek cities, such as the Spartan *patrouchos* (Hdt. 6.57.4) and the *patroiokos* in the Code of Gortyn (Willetts 1967). But endogamy, although an available marriage strategy, was not practiced all that frequently in the periods for which we have adequate data, nor does this possibility seem to have allayed all fears associated with marriage: the *epiklēros* is sometimes portrayed as a household tyrant to her husband.[15] Here, as in many other instances, the concerns expressed in myth are not a precise reflection of social practices, but they do suggest the anxieties these practices may stir up.

Related to these concerns about endogamy is the treatment of sibling relations in Greek myth. Unlike other female-male dyads in the myths, such as mother-son and wife-husband, which so often end in betrayal, the sister-brother relationship is nearly always positive. In this relationship, the woman sides with her brother and may use gifts, usually textiles, to express her allegiance to him. In a more sinister angle on the sibling relationship, a woman may be induced by a gift to side with her brother and thereby betray her husband, as in the myth of Eriphyle, who trades her husband's life for a gold necklace.

As I argue in Chapter Six, the sibling relationship raises the issues of exogamy and the incest taboo. If marriage with women from outside the family is a necessary evil, how tempting is the fantasy embodied in the bond with the sister, that marriage exchange can be avoided altogether? I do not argue for explicitly incestuous relationships between male and female siblings, which are only rarely articulated in Greek myth and literature. Rather, I argue that the dream of the avoidance of marriage brings sisters to the fore and emphasizes the benign quality of their dealings with brothers. The fantasy of avoiding marriage exchange valorizes the sister, the woman who originates inside the *oikos*, and—at least potentially—allays the anxieties attendant on the exchange of and with women.

KINSHIP STRUCTURES AND THE STATUS OF WOMEN

It is an anthropological commonplace that the status of women tends to be higher in matrilineal societies. Many of the cultures discussed in this chapter are matrilineal, while those of classical Greece were decidedly not, with notable consequences for women's status. Some scholars have noted that

Greek myth reveals traces of an older matrilineal inheritance system.[16] This might explain the sometimes forgotten fact that descent in Athens was not purely patrilineal but bilateral.[17] Foley (2001: 61) suggests that in Athens, bilateral inheritance and the dowry were together responsible for placing women "in a difficult role mediating between two households." Both institutions are, however, also potential sources of protection for women, as they signal the continuing interest of the natal family in its married daughters. Even in Homer, where the dowry does not appear to exist, attitudes toward daughters are not radically different.[18] Despite Foley's claim that in Homeric marriage the woman is transferred to her husband's family, the involvement of Penelope's family in her future and the frequent use of the patronymic "daughter of Ikarios" (kourē Ikariou) throughout the Odyssey suggest something quite different.[19] To make sense of the consequences for women of the different systems of descent discussed here, I suggest that we treat forms of social organization such as matriliny and patriliny not as a set of polar opposites but as endpoints along a continuum. This can be illustrated with reference to two works on the status of women in Africa.

Karen Sacks' groundbreaking 1979 book, Sisters and Wives: The Past and Future of Sexual Equality, has been foundational for much later work in anthropology on the status of women in the family.[20] Sacks distinguished between women whose social role is defined as sister and those whose role is defined as wife. Women in kin-corporate societies have rights to the land as sisters through their natal lineage, and consequently higher status, while those in class-based societies, whose access to land is only as the wives of men who have such rights, are in a subordinate position. Yet Cunningham, building on Sacks, shows that the distinction between the two kinds of society does not tell the whole story: "While women in most kin-corporate societies do indeed have the rights as sisters that Sacks describes, only when they are in their natal villages can they fully exercise those rights. Once they leave for their husbands' villages they become wives [my emphasis]."[21]

This example shows the usefulness of thinking of social organization—and specifically the status of women—in terms of a continuum. The same woman can be treated more as a sister or as a wife, depending on her physical proximity to her natal family. In a matrilineal society, women do tend to have higher status, but even in nonmatrilineal contexts, the closer a woman remains to her natal family—whether through affective ties, geographical proximity, or legal rights to the wealth of the natal family—the higher her status is likely to be. To the extent that she is not completely subsumed under the category of wife, she retains rights gained from her position in her natal family.[22]

These examples show that women's status is greatly affected by whether they are regarded as members of their natal family or the family of their husband.[23] Despite their subordinate status, it is clear that in classical Athens, women were regarded as members of their natal family for life, and preserved their claim on the protection of that family. Although smaller than a son's share of the inheritance, the dowry of an Athenian woman could be sizable and was thought of as the daughter's share of the inheritance, in the form of a *pre mortem* distribution.[24] In the event of divorce or death of a husband, a woman had the right to reclaim the dowry and return to the paternal or fraternal roof until (potential) remarriage.[25] This ongoing connection with the natal family seems at times to have created an ambiguity that may have negatively colored the view of wives as outsiders to the marital family. On the other hand, when women are considered from the perspective of their natal families—in other words, as sisters—they are represented not as dangerous exchangers but as benign figures whose assistance is essential to their brothers. The significance of this principle will be highlighted in the analysis that comprises my final chapter.

Of course, no one is ever entirely subsumed by only one of her social roles. In the words of Janet Hoskins (1998: 24), "As fathers, daughters, husbands, sisters, wives, brothers, sons, and mothers, men and women are always complexly related. The question of how gender dualism is actually lived requires an ethnographic answer, using the particularities of individual lives to understand how they negotiate their own identities against the backdrop of paired cultural categories." For the ancient material, this is frequently impossible, dealing as we do with often fictional and always mute subjects; hence the usefulness of ethnographic comparanda.

THEORIES OF RECIPROCITY AND THE GIFT

Theories of exchange have been a mainstay of ethnographic literature since its beginning, but for many classicists, the study of exchange begins with the *Essai sur le don* (1925) by Marcel Mauss, who himself had a classical education and used comparative material from antiquity. This deeply evocative and highly influential work has enjoyed great success among classicists, partly through Gernet, but it has not gone without criticism and revision. Among the critiques that have had the most impact on the present work are those of Sahlins, Weiner, Godelier, and Graeber.[26] The work of Gregory (1982) has also been fundamental in systematizing recent thinking about the gift. I direct the reader to these texts for a more extensive treatment.

I have relied throughout on the notion of a continuum of reciprocity. As laid out by Sahlins (1972: 191–96), types of exchange can be classified based on the social distance of the participants and the time elapsed between exchanges. Central to this classification is the idea that reciprocity creates and maintains social relationships and networks of relationships, but only when the gift or service given has at least the appearance of generosity or altruism. In this kind of exchange, known as "generalized reciprocity," partners give without the expectation of immediate or equal return. In the Greek context, we may think of *xenia* (usually translated as "guest-friendship"). In Homeric epic, a hero might entertain a visitor and give him lavish guest-gifts (*xeneia*) without any prospect of a return visit, but with the knowledge that a (hereditary) relationship has been created. In the case of Glaukos and Diomedes in *Iliad* 6, the fact that their fathers were *xenoi* (guest-friends) is sufficient for a cessation of hostilities and an exchange of armor.

"Balanced reciprocity," on the other hand, refers to exchanges in which the debt is quickly discharged, and in which the norm is near equivalence of value of the objects given. It does not create much of a relationship, since whatever debt might have been incurred is immediately cancelled out. In the terminology of Sahlins (1972: 195), it is less personal and more economic.

Sahlins' scale of reciprocities ends with "negative reciprocity," a term I have found especially useful in thinking about the acquisitive practices of Homeric heroes. Sahlins defines it as "the attempt to get something for nothing." He places along the continuum of negative reciprocity everything from "haggling" or barter to cheating and theft, but for my purposes I prefer to place barter at the low end of sociability encompassed by balanced reciprocity, and to reserve the term "negative reciprocity" for those instances in which benefit accrues only to one party in the transaction. This seems more in keeping with Sahlins' own reference to "cunning, stealth, and violence" as hallmarks of negative reciprocity (1972: 185).

I omit from this brief summary those forms of economic and social behavior not encountered in the sources used in this study. One additional point should not go unmentioned, however. Although this summary conveys the idea of a continuum from greatest goodwill to least goodwill between participants, there are exceptions to this rule. Generalized reciprocity can take the form of competitive generosity, with potentially hostile intent—"fighting with gifts." Mauss was particularly taken with the idea of the North American potlatch, a kind of formalized competitive giving.[27] Although this kind of competition is not explicit in our sources, it is possible to read the unequal exchange of armor between Glaukos and Diomedes or the gifts offered by Agamemnon to Achilles in *Iliad* 9 in these terms.[28]

Usually called the "sexual division of labor" (e.g., Errington and Gewertz 1987) in works written before the mid-1990s, the gendered division of labor is a concept familiar to anyone who has ever shared lodgings with a member of the so-called opposite sex.[29] Even a society in which there is something like equality between men and women is apt to have some idea of which tasks are appropriate to men and which to women. Most obviously, women are traditionally associated with the tending of children. This is the only task for which there is any biological justification for the gendered division, and even this disappears once the child is weaned from the breast. Other tasks usually marked as female are closely associated with nurture, such as cooking and feeding members of the household or tending to them when they are sick. Food gathering, another predominately female task, is once again clearly linked to nurture; moreover, it is a task easily integrated with childcare.[30]

Other tasks usually assigned to women are those connected with clothing the body. In most societies worldwide, the production of all woven objects—including those not used as clothing—is considered women's work. In some cases, although the basic activity might appear the same—sewing or weaving, for example—the gendered division depends on the nature of the material or the purpose for which the item is made. For example, among the Inuit, the sewing of fur garments is men's work, while in classical Athens, the weaving of canvas for sails was a male activity.[31] Sanday (1981: 79) emphasizes distinctions based on the nature of the materials to be worked rather than the function of the objects produced:

> Raw materials that are hard or tough are processed strictly by males. Soft and pliable raw materials are more often (although not exclusively) processed by females. Only men work metal, stone, bone, and wood. Women, more often than men, make baskets and mats, do loom weaving, make pottery, and spin.

Since the origins of their discipline, anthropologists have attempted to explain the sources of these divisions, which most consider to be cultural phenomena rather than natural ones.[32] Ernestine Friedl (1975) suggests that women do work that can be frequently interrupted without loss or damage to the product. As she admits, this holds true for many kinds of female tasks, but does not explain them all.[33] In many cases, pragmatic reasons for the division of labor are overlaid with symbolic associations that mesh with, and make visible, ideological assumptions about gender in the society in question.

RANKED AND GENDERED WEALTH

Many societies privilege certain of their cultural productions, placing them in separate categories according to their purposes. Such objects, although not always of obvious material value to an outsider, are nonetheless considered wealth in these societies, as they are repositories of much purposive effort and are used in important exchanges, frequently of a ceremonial nature. Some of these objects are intended for purely ritual use in communication with the divine sphere; others are used to create and maintain the social network among human beings. These objects are differentiated from more quotidian items such as bowls of food, which are frequently exchanged in an informal way among family members and neighbors. In the Trobriands, the constant exchange of cooked yams among neighboring households can be contrasted with the much more infrequent movement of high-status objects among distant partners of the elaborate multi-island ceremonial exchange circuit known as the *kula*. No amount of yam can discharge an obligation incurred by the receipt of a precious shell valuable. Conversion or interchange between the two orders of gifts—one humble and ephemeral and the other prestigious and durable—is unthinkable.[34] Nor would one usually engage in both kinds of exchange with the same partner. Ranked spheres of exchange have been of particular interest to classicists, in part because most of the objects exchanged in ancient Greek myth and epic belong to the category of high-ranked or prestige items.[35]

Complicated systems of exchange such as the Maori *taonga* or the highly ritualized *kula* are fascinating to study, but it is important not to mystify them. It would not be hard for most North Americans to list kinds of gifts appropriate to a couple getting married; to a woman having her first child; or to a religious institution of which one is a part. Hand-knit booties (even if destined for charity) would look peculiar in a church collection basket, while in some circles, gifts of cash to a newlywed couple would be considered crass and in others *de rigueur*. This last example is particularly germane, since even within a single country, there is considerable variation among different classes and ethnic groups. Much ethnographic effort goes into untangling the subtleties of categorization of the kinds of wealth that circulate in the culture under study, and a full account of early twenty-first-century North American gift-giving practices would be no different.

Besides distinctions in exchange terminology having to do with destination or occasion, other distinctions concern the nature of the relationship between the partners, such as the Trobrianders' differentiation (which Mauss, following Malinowski, makes much of) between *vagyu'a*, the valuables traded in the *kula*, and *gimwali*, objects of commercial barter with outsiders.[36] There is an explicit hierarchy based on both the nature of the objects exchanged and the relationship between exchange partners. A barter relationship is highly perishable by design, while the connections formed through the *kula* may be handed down from father to son. Similarly, *kula* valuables have genealogies known to all in the trading circle.

A classificatory system may also use gender to distinguish among kinds of wealth, and especially among objects intended for giving. It is important to note that although objects are assigned a gender in many cultures (and here I do not refer to purely grammatical gender), these assignments vary widely in significance. The categories may be mainly pragmatic or purely symbolic, although the symbolic component is never entirely lacking. For example, different terms may distinguish objects according to whether they are produced, possessed, or used by women or men, but these distinctions may also point to ideological and symbolic differences between the genders. For example, in many societies, hard durable male wealth such as metal or stone is distinguished from soft ephemeral female wealth such as textiles. The two categories are distinguished by the gendered division of labor, but also by ideological constructs about the nature of the genders. Indeed, women's wealth tends to be textile wealth across a wide variety of cultures. (The association of women and textiles is so widely generalized that Sigmund Freud in his 1932 lecture "Femininity" went so far as to suggest that the invention of weaving was the sole female contribution to the history of civilization.[37])

Among the Trobrianders, male wealth, consisting of shell and stone valuables, is the object of the high-status exchanges of the *kula*. Like the *agalmata* of Gernet, many of these are famous and valuable objects, which carry their own genealogy of ownership.[38] Trobriand women's wealth is quite different in kind as well as in purpose, consisting mainly of fiber skirts and banana-leaf bundles, used principally in mortuary distributions by the family of the deceased but also recognized as wealth for its own sake.[39] Unlike the prized objects of the *kula*, whose temporary possession confers great prestige, in the case of women's wealth, the prestige consists instead in giving the objects away.[40] Some forms of women's textile wealth may be quite old, but they are not as durable as men's wealth. Men's wealth and women's wealth circulate in sharply differentiated contexts, although both kinds of wealth are clearly distinct from exchanges of food and other household items, which belong to a lower transactional order. The exact nature of male wealth may change from one society to another, but the dichotomy between hard male wealth and soft female wealth is widespread, if not quite universal.[41]

Access to goods and the freedom to dispose of them are at least partially related to production. As Friedl has observed, "Those who work to produce goods have a greater chance to be assigned the control of distributing them, but do not automatically gain the right to do so." She proposes that "it is the right to distribute and exchange valued goods and services to those not in a person's own domestic unit (extradomestic distribution) which confers power and prestige in all societies" (1975: 8–9). I would add that the greater the prestige of the objects produced and controlled, the greater the power conferred. In ancient Greek contexts, although cloth could at times achieve the status of *agalma*, for the most part—when not further embellished—it occupies a more humble place.[42]

In other cases, however, the distinctions concern not the objects that men and women make or own, but those that represent them: "Although net bags are the symbol of wombs, there are occasions when net bags filled with male objects symbolize male *and* female concerns."[43] In many of the societies of Melanesia and Polynesia, certain kinds of wealth are traditionally considered suitable for use in marriage negotiations, while others are reserved for exchanges like the *kula*, which are traditionally male contests of prestige. Marriage is certainly part of the search for prestige and preeminence, but it nonetheless has its own economy. In some cases, the objects employed in this economy are considered to bear resemblance to, or stand in for, the women who are to be exchanged as wives.

As long as production and use are the primary categories governing the gender of objects, the equation of female wealth with soft materials, usually textile, and male wealth with hard materials holds true. It is my contention that this distinction can be found throughout Greek literature, where it can be used to explain a number of mythic episodes.[44] A clear example of this dichotomy in the Greek material can be seen in Book 4 of the *Odyssey*, where Menelaos' guest gift to Telemachos is a silver bowl, and Helen's is a beautifully woven *peplos*.[45] A similar schema is found in *Odyssey* 8, where Alkinoos calls on his wife to give Odysseus a chest with a cloak and tunic in it, while he himself offers a gold cup (8.424–25, 430–32).[46]

Many other factors can affect the assignment of gender, including the specific context of the exchange.[47] As Hoskins notes: "Exchange valuables in Eastern Indonesia are complexly gendered. . . . In formal exchanges, they may be marked as male or female gifts. Because such exchanges are hierarchically coded, an object that is 'female' in one context (such as women's jewelry) may be 'male' in another (when all 'male' metal objects are opposed to 'female' cloth)."[48] In another example, according to Chowning's account, the Kove of Papua New Guinea "divide most goods into men's and women's but assignment to these categories is made in different ways which do not wholly coincide: how they are (or were) obtained, who uses them for everyday purposes, and their role in exchange." This is followed by a disclaimer: "In no case is direct gender symbolism involved; goods are not male and female in themselves."[49] On the other hand, Mauss (following Malinowski) speaks of gendered objects in the *kula* (discussed by Godelier [1996] 1999, 80–81). Godelier discusses ritual objects handled only by men among the Baruya of New Guinea, but which come in male and female versions ([1996] 1999, 114).[50]

Marilyn Strathern, in her influential 1989 book, *The Gender of the Gift*, adapts Erik Schwimmer's use of metaphoric and metonymic to distinguish different ways in which exchange objects can be gendered. In a metonymic assignment of gender, the giver gives of him- or herself (i.e., an object associated with the giver's gender), while in a metaphoric exchange, the gift is gendered according to the gender of the intended recipient.[51] The ambiguity created by the co-existence of these two opposed systems is exploited in an episode of the *Odyssey* discussed in detail in Chapter Three, in which Penelope accepts gifts of gold jewelry from the suitors. Gold objects can be generally classed as male wealth, and they are both produced and controlled by men. On the other hand, women are expected to have and wear jewelry, as is illustrated by the formula *himatia kai chrysia* (clothing and gold jewelry), a technical term for the things a woman brings with her into her new husband's house—her paraphernalia or trousseau—considered her personal property and not part of the dowry or bridewealth.[52] Such gifts might be appropriate in the context of a true marriage negotiation, but Penelope's status as a wife (however uncertain) calls to mind other, less wholesome narratives of adultery and betrayal, and makes of them something potentially sinister.[53]

The creation of the first woman, as recounted by Hesiod, demonstrates that the division of labor among the gods follows the lines of gender roles among mortals. Hephaistos, the smithy-god, uses ceramics and metalworking to create the female object, and the goddesses adorn her. Most notably, Athena teaches her the art of weaving or adorns her with cloth.[54] Interestingly, a prayer among the Kodi of Indonesia (Hoskins 1998: 19) takes this division even further, invoking a divine creator who is called *Mother who bound the forelock. Father who smelted the crown*, "suggesting that people were formed by a combination of women's work in binding threads (for weaving) and men's work in smelting metal (for tools, weapons . . . or the hard human skull)." Thus in the Kodi view, the hard and soft parts of the human body are the work not of two distinct deities expert in the roles determined by their gender, but of one doubly gendered creator-god.

The proper use of gendered categories of wealth, in all the possible ways this can be read, is central to ethnographic accounts of myths in societies from South America to Melanesia. I have also found it to be an invaluable tool in the interpretation of Greek myths. Nowhere and in no way do I argue for universality. Nevertheless, among cultures in which both the exchange of gifts and the pursuit of prestige are central and bound up with the exchange of women, there are important correspondences with Greek mythic thinking.

WOMEN IN MARRIAGE EXCHANGE

The notion of the circulation of women among groups of men has been the subject of much anthropological investigation, perhaps most notably in Lévi-Strauss' *Elementary Structures of Kinship* (1949). Complicated protocols of exchange govern this circulation, and although they differ from culture to culture, there are many common elements. Lévi-Strauss, as his critics have noted, neglected to consider other possibilities—societies in which sisters exchange brothers, rather than the other way around. (Nor do these two options exhaust the possibilities.)

For Lévi-Strauss, marriage was the original exchange and women the original exchange object. But he was careful to stipulate that women are not only objects of exchange:

> The emergence of symbolic thought must have required that women, like words, should be things that were exchanged. . . . But woman could never become just a sign and nothing more, since even in a man's world she is still a person, and since in so far as she is defined as a sign she must be recognized as a generator of signs.[55]

The contradiction with which Lévi-Strauss appears to struggle in this passage goes to the heart of my project. As much as men may define women as exchange objects, there is always the possibility that women will find a way to express their own agency—in the Greek mythic context, usually by giving themselves away again. In so doing, they often are responsible for the circulation of wealth as well as their own persons.[56]

To give an idea of a highly systematized exchange of women, I cite the following example. Among the Kodi, women "are exchanged among houses, traded against livestock and gold, and travel along with pigs, cloth, and ivory," according to Hoskins (1998: 59), but she also discusses other groups in which direct sister exchange (including the exchange of "classificatory sisters") is the only acceptable form of marriage: "No other object is exchangeable for a woman." Only the contracting of another marriage can reciprocate the original gift of a woman. In this context, a woman is an exchange object of inconvertible rank. Because nothing else but a wife will do, in some cultures the debt incurred by marriage is only discharged when it is paid off in a later generation.[57]

In my discussion of the traffic in women in Chapter Three, I consider a distorted form of the exchange of women in which both the nature of the relationship (involuntary concubinage) and the method of exchange (kidnapping) are a far cry from the harmonious workings of a society in balance. The *Odyssey* presents a wide range of marriage types, from those by capture, to the compromised union of Helen and Menelaos, to the endogamous marriage of Alkinoos and Arete, and the incest of the children of Aiolos, before ending with renewal of the extraordinary marriage of Penelope and Odysseus, which is uniquely predicated on reciprocity between the two principals.[58]

Through an examination of recurring mythic themes of exchange between men and women in epic and later literature, I aim to show that in archaic and classical Greek culture, the anxiety connected with exchange—an anxiety that cross-cultural analysis reveals to be present in nearly all societies—is focused to an extraordinary degree on women.[59] Moreover, as the examples discussed above indicate, this anxiety is tied most closely to women in their role as wives, and to the institution of marriage. It is no coincidence that each of the deadly exchanges enumerated by Gernet takes place in the context of a disruption or crisis in a marital relationship. In a society founded on the idea of the circulation of women, the possibility that a woman's circulation will not end with her marriage remains an ever-present threat.[60] At the same time, the theme of perverted protocols of exchange suggests concern about the additional economic (and affective) power to which the sexually mature woman may lay claim once she is established as wife and mother in her husband's household.

How does the state of affairs in the myths correspond to historical realities? Paradoxically, despite the recurrent theme of deadly gifts to and from women, a wealth of literary and historical documentation from the archaic and classical periods represents women as having little or no economic power. A literary tradition going back to the *Iliad* portrays women not as economic actors—*agents* of exchange—but as the *objects* of exchange: gifts to be traded among men, prizes to be won in war or in an athletic contest, daughters to be given in marriage.[61]

It has long been assumed that women were completely excluded from economic influence throughout the classical period, almost everywhere in Greece, and particularly in Athens.[62] In fact, Aristotle went so far as to point to the exceptional number of female landowners in Sparta as the cause of that society's decline.[63] This assumption about the economic exclusion of women, based largely on literary representations, has recently been challenged by social historians of classical Athens who argue that a degree of power was available to some aristocratic women through the institution of the dowry.[64] This power—to the extent that it existed—would, however, have found its expression entirely within the domestic sphere, without in any way threatening the official gender ideology of classical Athens, which does not differ greatly from that expressed in the earliest Greek texts.[65]

The case for the economic power of women has been made by social historians relying on nonliterary sources, particularly orations delivered in court cases, and their conclusions are highly contested. Although the orations serve different purposes from those of Athenian drama, they are not unmediated transcriptions of social realities, but rather *representations* of social realities every bit as ideologically conditioned as the scenes presented onstage.[66] Nor is the difference between Athenian drama and forensic oratory as neat as it might seem. In both instances, a text was composed for competitive public performance with the aim of pleasing an audience and achieving victory. Although the orations are an indispensable body of evidence, we should not expect to find them free from theatrical exaggeration, distortion of the evidence, or special pleading.[67] My use of them, as of the mythic material, is intended not to establish the "facts" of daily life, but to provide evidence for the ideological constructs surrounding women, marriage, and exchange.

In the mythic examples with which I began, the locus of anxiety about women and their powers, economic and otherwise, is marriage, and the role of the wife. Becoming a wife was the expected *telos* of women, as is reflected in the fact that a common word for wife in ancient Greek (as in many other languages) is the same as the word for woman: *gunē*. An indication of the fundamental nature of this association can be seen from the archaic tradition in which the creation of woman and the invention of marriage are one and the same (evil) thing.

CHAPTER TWO

MARRIAGE *and the* CIRCULATION *of* WOMEN

The codes governing women's (and men's) economic behavior form part of what may be called the "economics of gender." By this phrase, I mean a whole range of valuations and transactions conditioned by the different statuses of men and women. Primary among these transactions is marriage and, as a consequence, the production and reproduction in which women engage as wives. In many cultures, the role of wife encompasses a woman's identity far more than that of husband does for a man, with the result that whatever a woman produces from the time she marries is conceived of as part of her wifely role. Marriage in ancient Greece is not symmetrical— ideologically, functionally, or even linguistically—for the two sexes. When a man marries a woman, he does so in the active voice, while the same transaction places a woman in the middle voice.[1]

Marriage transactions almost always involve a complex series of exchanges, whether of bridewealth or dowry or some combination of both.[2] Sometimes the bride herself is regarded as the most valuable of the gifts that change hands between two families connecting themselves through marriage. In Greek, the verb *didōmi* (give) is regularly used with the meaning, "give in marriage," as when Telemachos says that he will give his mother to a husband (*aneri mētera dōsō, Odyssey* 2.223).[3] Although the woman is sometimes thought of as being given to her husband, the man is never thought of as a gift to his wife. There is an astonishing range of different marriage-related gift-giving practices across cultures, but certain basic principles are surprisingly widespread across time and space. Among these is the almost total inalienability of the dowry a woman brings into her marriage.[4] On the other hand, cultures differ greatly when it comes to the reckoning of a married woman as part of her natal family or of her husband's family. These differences may have profound implications for a woman's power, prestige, and even survival.

Once integrated into the new household, the Greek wife of any period was expected to bear legitimate children, to produce textiles (or oversee their production), and to guard the husband's possessions. This does not seem to have changed much over time, as can be seen from a reading of works as far apart in date as the *Odyssey* and Xenophon's treatise on household management, the *Oikonomikos*.[5] That the faithful execution of these duties was conceptually intertwined is clear from the words of Odysseus in the Underworld, when he asks his mother if his wife still remains with their son and watches over all his possessions (*menei para paidi kai empeda panta phulassei, Od.* 11.178). Penelope herself repeats this formulation when she describes herself as staying with her son and keeping everything safe (*menō para paidi kai empeda panta phulassō, Od.* 19.525), and honoring the marital bed (*eunēn t' aidomenē posios, Od.* 19.527).[6] In Semonides' misogynist account of the races of women, the only virtuous woman he acknowledges is the "bee-woman," whose household prospers and who bears handsome children of good repute.[7]

These conventional notions survived long past the archaic age. A fragment from Euripides' lost *Melanippē Desmotēs* (*The Captive Melanippe*) has the protagonist say that "women manage homes and preserve the goods which are brought from abroad. Houses where there is no wife are neither orderly nor prosperous."[8] Xenophon, writing in the early to mid-fourth century, represents Ischomachos as setting great store by training his inexperienced young wife to keep all the possessions of the household in order.[9] Similarly, the speaker of the oration *Against Neaira* in the Demosthenic corpus says that the function of wives (*gunaikes*) is "to bear children legitimately and to be trustworthy guardians of our possessions" ([Dem.] 59.122).

A similar pattern of thought can be found in Lysias' oration *On the Murder of Eratosthenes*. Here Euphiletos, the speaker, says that once his wife had borne him a son, he began to trust her more with the management of the household. This trust, however, has in his view merely provided her with the opportunity to take a lover:

Ἐγὼ γάρ, ὦ Ἀθηναῖοι, ἐπειδὴ ἔδοξέ μοι γῆμαι καὶ γυναῖκα ἠγαγόμην εἰς τὴν οἰκίαν, τὸν μὲν ἄλλον χρόνον οὕτω διεκείμην ὥστε μήτε λυπεῖν μήτε λίαν ἐπ' ἐκείνῃ εἶναι ὅ τι ἂν ἐθέλῃ ποιεῖν, ἐφύλαττόν τε ὡς οἷόν τε ἦν, καὶ προσεῖχον τὸν νοῦν ὥσπερ εἰκὸς ἦν. ἐπειδὴ δέ μοι παιδίον γίγνεται, ἐπίστευον ἤδη καὶ πάντα τὰ ἐμαυτοῦ ἐκείνῃ παρέδωκα, ἡγούμενος ταύτην οἰκειότητα μεγίστην εἶναι· ἐν μὲν οὖν τῷ πρώτῳ χρόνῳ, ὦ Ἀθηναῖοι, πασῶν ἦν βελτίστη· καὶ γὰρ οἰκονόμος δεινὴ καὶ φειδωλὸς [ἀγαθὴ] καὶ ἀκριβῶς πάντα διοικοῦσα· ἐπειδὴ δέ μοι ἡ μήτηρ ἐτελεύτησε,

πάντων τῶν κακῶν ἀποθανοῦσα αἰτία μοι γεγένηται. ἐπ' ἐκφορὰν
γὰρ αὐτῇ ἀκολουθήσασα ἡ ἐμὴ γυνὴ ὑπὸ τούτου τοῦ ἀνθρώπου
ὀφθεῖσα, χρόνῳ διαφθείρεται.

When I, Athenians, decided to marry, and brought a wife into my house,
for some time I was disposed neither to vex her nor to leave her too free
to do just as she pleased; I kept a watch on her as far as possible, with
such observation of her as was reasonable. But when a child was born to
me, thence-forward I began to trust her, and placed all my affairs in her
hands, presuming that we were now in perfect intimacy. It is true that in
the early days, Athenians, she was the most excellent of wives; she was a
clever, frugal housekeeper, and kept everything in the nicest order. But
as soon as I lost my mother, her death became the cause of all my troubles. For it was in attending her funeral that my wife was seen by this
man, who in time corrupted her. (Lysias 1.6–8, trans. Lamb)

The connection between offspring and possessions is not fortuitous.[10] In a
society that reckons descent through the male line, it is of the utmost importance that an heir be the legitimate son of his mother's husband. By taking a lover, a woman risks interfering with succession, potentially trans-
ferring her husband's goods to the descendant of another lineage.[11] This
anxiety about legitimacy, repeated in many ways in Greek literature, finds
expression also in the notion that the unfaithful wife may turn over not
only her own person, but even the keys to the storeroom. In fact, Euphiletos argues that a seducer is traditionally judged more harshly than a rapist,
for the rapist has presumably given in to a sudden passion, but the seducer
has gained the confidence of the wife, and with it, access to "the whole
house"—the husband's stores and possessions—as well as causing confusion about the paternity of the children. Euphiletos' claim is clearly a self-
serving rhetorical exaggeration, but nonetheless, the idea was presumably
one that might have sounded plausible to a jury.[12] These ideas, current in
late fifth- and early fourth-century Athens, can already be found in the earliest Greek texts we have, and figure prominently in the myths and tragic
dramas to which I will return.

If the integrity of household wealth was seen as bound up with a wife's
fidelity to her husband, this suggests that women had a great deal of in-
direct, or negative, economic power. On the other hand, their direct economic power was limited in a number of ways. In Athens, women did not
own property and could not contractually carry out any other than the
smallest financial transactions without the aid of the male relative acting as *kyrios* (guardian). This was not true in all Greek cities, and even in

Athens it is possible that these restrictions were sometimes honored in the breach. The existence of the "law of the medimnus," according to which women could not transact a sum larger than that needed to feed an average family for a week, has also recently come under question as an ideological construct.[13]

As Hunter and Foxhall have recently pointed out, some (usually wealthy) women may well have exercised considerable economic power in the context of the *oikos*.[14] Given the inalienability of the dowry, a woman with a large dowry might well have been treated with kid gloves. Were she to demand a divorce, the husband would have to return the money and property she brought into the marriage. The situation of the *epiklēros*, discussed in Chapter One, provides another example of a situation in which a woman might exercise unusual economic power within the family.

In the pre-monetary world of the heroes and heroines, restrictions on women's economic power express themselves quite differently. As discussed in Chapter One, many societies have rules about the types of objects that women may give and receive. A number of mythic examples will be discussed throughout this work, but a similar set of assumptions can be found to operate in a passage from Herodotos (4.162). Whether this anecdote is strictly historical or has been shaped by the historian's own understanding of the codes of which I have been speaking cannot be known, but the correspondence is striking. When Arkesilaos of Cyrene was deposed, his mother Pheretime went to Euelthon, who ruled Salamis in Cyprus, and asked for an army to put her son's faction back in power. Euelthon was unwilling to give her an army, although he gave her many other gifts. Each time, she thanked him for the lovely gifts, while adding that an army would be lovelier still. Finally he gave her a golden distaff and spindle, and when she once again said that an army would be nicer, he replied that he had given her gifts that were more suited to her sex.[15]

In the literary record, at least, a strict division of labor along gender lines prevails, according to which textile production—carding, spinning, and weaving—is women's work. This production of textiles is closely related to the role of women as providers for the needs of the household, and little effort is made to distinguish between "cloth" and "clothing," in part due to the unconstructed nature of most Greek garments. The historical record shows that "industrial" textile production, such as the making of canvas for sails, was carried on by men.[16] At the same time, there is some evidence that at least in classical Athens, women had a part in other kinds of manufacture, including the making and painting of vases.[17] The fact remains, however, that over the centuries, from Helen in the *Iliad* to the women on fifth-century vases, the one productive activity consistently associated with women, and especially with the aristocratic wives of myth and epic, is weaving.[18] Consequently, the few unmarked, and unremarkable, transactions in which mythic women take part are those in which they give gifts of cloth.[19] So tight is the association of women and textile production that in some contexts, weaving becomes a metaphor for marriage itself.[20]

The symbolism of textiles becomes part of the marriage ritual, when the new bride lifts her veil in the presence of her husband's family for the first time, in the gesture known as the *anakalyteria*.[21] The importance of the veil as a textile marker of women's status has been recently established by Llewellen-Jones (2002), who argues that adult women in ancient Greece were customarily veiled. Andromache's tearing off of her head coverings on the news of Hektor's death (*Il.* 466-70) shows the tight association of the covered head with married status (although maidens also sometimes wear head coverings). Another textile marker, the belt (*zonē*), serves as a marker of reproductive status: a series of belts mark a woman's transition from maidenhood to betrothal to marriage, and they are removed for consummation of the marriage and for childbirth.[22]

We encounter Helen at the loom in *Iliad* 3.121–28, weaving battles of the Trojan War, "endured for her sake" (*hous hethen heinek'*, 128). This is the first appearance of Helen and the first appearance of a woman weaving in surviving Greek literature. Although it is presented neutrally, and although the poet seems to be equating Helen's activity with his own, there is something unsettling about a woman celebrating by means of her handiwork the bloody war her own beauty has occasioned.[23] This helps to create an undertone of uneasiness about women and weaving that, despite its generally positive valuation, will be further amplified by Penelope's loom trick in the *Odyssey*.

Elsewhere in the same text, women and goddesses are shown frequently giving cloth and garments to Odysseus and to his son, and these gifts appear largely benign.[24] Meanwhile, Penelope is famous for her weaving—and even more for her unweaving.[25] She uses the cultural assumptions about women, weaving, and family obligations to concoct a delaying strategy:

ἡ δὲ δόλον τόνδ' ἄλλον ἐνὶ φρεσὶ μερμήριξε·
στησαμένη μέγαν ἱστὸν ἐνὶ μεγάροισιν ὕφαινε,
λεπτὸν καὶ περίμετρον· ἄφαρ δ' ἡμῖν μετέειπε·
κοῦροι, ἐμοὶ μνηστῆρες, ἐπεὶ θάνε δῖος Ὀδυσσεύς,
μίμνετ' ἐπειγόμενοι τὸν ἐμὸν γάμον, εἰς ὅ κε φᾶρος
ἐκτελέσω, μή μοι μεταμώνια νήματ' ὄληται,

Λαέρτῃ ἥρωϊ ταφήϊον, εἰς ὅτε κέν μιν
μοῖρ’ ὀλοὴ καθέλῃσι τανηλεγέος θανάτοιο,
μή τίς μοι κατὰ δῆμον Ἀχαιϊάδων νεμεσήσῃ,
αἴ κεν ἄτερ σπείρου κεῖται πολλὰ κτεατίσσας.
ὣς ἔφαθ’, ἡμῖν δ’ αὖτ’ ἐπεπείθετο θυμὸς ἀγήνωρ.
ἔνθα καὶ ἡματίη μὲν ὑφαίνεσκεν μέγαν ἱστόν,
νύκτας δ’ ἀλλύεσκεν, ἐπεὶ δαΐδας παραθεῖτο.
ὣς τρίετες μὲν ἔληθε δόλῳ καὶ ἔπειθεν Ἀχαιούς·
ἀλλ’ ὅτε τέτρατον ἦλθεν ἔτος καὶ ἐπήλυθον ὧραι,
καὶ τότε δή τις ἔειπε γυναικῶν, ἣ σάφα ᾔδη,
καὶ τήν γ’ ἀλλύουσαν ἐφεύρομεν ἀγλαὸν ἱστόν.

And she devised in her heart this guileful thing also: she set up in her halls a great web, and fell to weaving—fine of thread was the web and very wide; and straightway she spoke among us: "Young men, my wooers, since goodly Odysseus is dead, be patient, though eager for my marriage, until I finish this robe—I would not that my spinning should come to naught—a shroud for the lord Laertes, against the time when the fell fate of grievous death shall strike him down; lest any of the Achaean women in the land should be wroth with me, if he, who had won great possessions, were to lie without a shroud." So she spoke, and our proud hearts consented. Then day by day she would weave at the great web, but by night would unravel it, when she had let place torches by her. Thus for three years she by her craft kept the Achaeans from knowing, and beguiled them; but when the fourth year came as the seasons rolled on, even then one of her women who knew all told us, and we caught her unravelling the splendid web. (*Od.* 2.93–109, trans. Murray)

Here the wife's weaving has become a *dolos*, a trick, the same word that is used to describe another treacherous use of craft, the creation of woman, the "sheer hopeless snare" (*dolon aipun amēchanon*, Hes. *Works and Days* 83, trans. Evelyn-White). Penelope uses her female skills and her *dolos* in the service of her marriage, and does so while claiming to be using them on behalf of her husband's father and her marital *oikos*. She is in fact using them for the purpose of protecting her relationship to that *oikos*, but not at all in the potentially ill-omened way that she claims. Rather than preparing for the death of Laertes, she is playing for time until Odysseus can return and show himself to be still among the living. In so doing, she shows herself to be the female counterpart to the *polytropos* Odysseus. Feminine weaving and wiles are here praiseworthy and appropriately deployed.

Yet this trick, as Nicole Loraux has observed, is accomplished precisely by un-weaving, destroying the very work that would normally signal her specifically female contribution to the household wealth.[26] Papadopoulou-Belmehdi's analysis takes the ambiguity of weaving a step further. She argues against the idea that weaving is the sign of a good wife (1994b: 149) by showing the symbolic incompatibility of weaving and marriage (117). In her view, her constant weaving brings Penelope too close to the status of *parthenos* and the sphere of Athena. She notes that as long as Penelope weaves, she cannot marry, and that it is only when she has finished weaving that Odysseus returns (46-47). If Penelope's weaving, however stereotypically feminine an activity, does not lead to an increase in household wealth, conversely in Book 18, Athena inspires her to increase that wealth in a way that is not at all congruent with her wifely role—receiving gifts of gold from the suitors.

Although cloth, as a feminine—and domestic—product, can be given by women without constituting a scandal, not all gifts of cloth by women are "safe." To quote Laura McClure on textiles in tragedy, "Cloth helps women gain control over men, either by detaining, destroying, or seducing them; its presence in these texts represents the subversive potential of an ordinary, feminine activity to overturn the normal social order."[27] On the other hand, women's access to *agalmata* made of precious metals such as bronze and gold would normally be extremely limited. Men, however, frequently exchange metal objects, *agalmata*, for the most part without baneful consequences.[28] Since in many cases men also control the labor of women and its products, there is no taboo on male gifts of textiles, although these are less common.[29]

The gendered division of labor, as I have discussed, lends a distinct gender coding to the production of textiles and metals. As Ian Jenkins puts it, "Weaving in ancient Greece was a feminine art, while metal-working was a male preserve. This is true in the divine realm as well as in the mortal world" (1985: 121). Athena Ergane was patron of crafts, especially weaving, although she is also shown urging on the potter, while the arts of metallurgy were the realm of Hephaistos.[30] Interestingly, among the gods we find a "class" division between male and female production similar to that among mortals. Even goddesses are sometimes shown spinning or at the loom, but the only god ever to undertake the "banausic" activity of metalworking is Hephaistos, who is stigmatized as both a cripple and a cuckold, and thus is relegated to a lower status among the male gods of Olympos.[31] Although the sources discussed here, ranging from early epic to fourth-century orators, show women of all classes engaged in textile production, we see very little metalwork going on at all, aside from the activities of Hephaistos on Olympos. Unlike Helen or Penelope at their looms, few epic or tragic heroes and few Athenian citizens are seen putting a hand to any kind of domestic production.[32] Gernet speaks of the "industrial production" of *agalmata*: these are the work of specialists.[33] It seems that a separate work ethic existed for men and women of the aristocratic class.[34]

Sally Humphreys makes a direct connection between textiles and women's power: "Myths in which textiles play a prominent role seem to represent women in a position of power—fittingly enough, since weaving was the activity through which they autonomously produced wealth for the household."[35] The correspondence between production and the freedom to dispose of the product is not altogether straightforward, however. We recall that in Friedl's formulation, the ability to give away prestige objects itself confers prestige, although this ability is not automatically assigned to the producers. The code of exchange is represented as working along gender, rather than class, lines, but this obscures the fact that women's domestic production is taken for granted at all levels of the social hierarchy. (Equally obscured is the alienation of labor in the case of slaves and women of lower status.) Ultimately, the centrality of the male/female divide to the binarism so prevalent in Greek mythic thinking leads to a mapping of gender onto the division of labor, even in contexts where this may not reflect social realities. As textiles occupy a lower place in the hierarchy of values, they are consistently associated with women (even if historical evidence shows that not all textile producers were female). Within the logic of this system, then, textiles are shown as freely controlled by women, usually aristocratic ones.[36]

The gendered dichotomy between metal and textile wealth seems to have been reflected in ancient Greek women's religious practices. There is abundant literary evidence for organized public giving of garments to goddesses, beginning with the offering of a *peplos* to Athena by the women of Troy in Book 6 of the *Iliad*. Women's gifts to the gods were not restricted to textiles. Particularly in the Hellenistic period, women made well-documented monetary donations to religious sites and other public monuments, and they undoubtedly gave more modest mass-produced clay figurines and other votive objects throughout the centuries. The perishable nature of textiles may obscure the frequency of women's gifts of garments to the gods (Ridgway 1987: 403), but inscriptional evidence helps to fill the gap. The inscriptions from the temple of Artemis Brauronia show that women's textile gifts to the goddess were plentiful.[37] In this way, the gendered economics of ancient Greek life was reflected even in communication between the mortal and divine spheres.

In Chapter One, I noted that the circulation of mythic *agalmata* as discussed by Gernet often points to situations in which marriage relations have failed. Sometimes, the motif of the wife's seduction is explicit, as in the myth of the brothers Thyestes and Atreus, who fight over the throne. Thyestes gains possession of the lamb with the golden fleece, which is the symbol and guarantor of sovereignty, by seducing Atreus' wife, Aerope.[38] (As in the *Odyssey*, there is a nod to the motif of kingship acquired through marriage to the king's wife.[39])

Eriphyle's necklace, as Gernet has observed, illustrates what Marcel Mauss called the "coercive power of the gift" (Gernet [1948] 1981: 123). Adrastos, about to lead the expedition of the Seven against Thebes, must recruit his sister Eriphyle's husband, the seer Amphiaraos, if their attack on the city is to be successful; but Amphiaraos knows that all who take part are fated to die. In order to compel Amphiaraos' participation, Polyneikes is sent to give a gift or bribe (the Greek word *dōron* covers both meanings) to Adrastos' wife—a golden necklace that was originally a wedding gift from the gods to Harmonia, wife of Kadmos, founder of Thebes. Eriphyle is seduced by means of the golden gift, and induced to betray her husband on behalf of her brother Adrastos, who will head the expedition.[40] Her power to determine her husband's participation is the result of a prior agreement that she would adjudicate any disagreement between her husband and brother. Thus her actual perfidy consists in choosing to privilege her brother's interests over those of her husband, rather than in an act of physical infidelity.[41]

Although it is not an explicitly sexual seduction, the bribing of Eriphyle functions similarly in the myth, while illustrating the dangers associated with gifts, especially the wrong kind of gift, to or from a woman.[42] Certainly, jewelry was intended to be owned by women, and women's control of it is not inherently problematic.[43] What is problematic, however, is when women accept gifts of jewelry from outside the familial context, from men who are not husbands or kin. Such gifts never appear to be disinterested, and women are assumed to be powerless to resist the enticements they represent. The contexts in which such gifts appear, like Penelope's showing herself to the suitors in *Odyssey* 18, are those in which the fear, if not the reality, of female infidelity looms.[44]

The interpretation of the bribing of Eriphyle as a kind of sexual seduction may be confirmed by another kind of evidence. Two Athenian vases by the Schuwalow Painter from the second half of the fifth century depict the scene between Eriphyle and Polyneikes in ways that are remarkably simi-

Polyneikes offering a necklace to Eriphyle, Attic red-figure Oinochoe by the Schuwalow
Painter, c. 450–400 BCE. Ferrara, Mus. Nat. 3914 (T. 40A VP).

lar to contemporary depictions of erotic courtship. On these vases, a standing Polyneikes dangles a necklace in front of the seated Eriphyle (see Figs. I
and 2).[45] Comparison of these scenes with the many scenes often described
as "*Hetaira* with Customer" reveals a similar focus on the hands of the man
extending a gift and the woman reaching out to take it (see Fig. 3).[46] Com-

FIGURE 2
*Polyneikes offering a necklace to
Eriphyle, Attic red-figure Oinochoe
by the Schuwalow Painter,
c. 450–400 BCE. Ferrara,
Mus. Nat. 2309 (T.512 VT).*

FIGURE 3
*A man offering gifts to a woman.
Attic red-figure Oinochoe, attributed to
the Berlin Painter, c. 490–480 BCE.
San Antonio Museum of Art, gift of
Gilbert M. Denman, Jr. 86.134.59.*

mon to these scenes is the woman seated on her *klismos*, sometimes with the wool basket at hand. There has been much debate about the status of the women shown engaged in wool-working or with the wool basket at hand: they have been variously interpreted as *hetairai* (prostitutes) and as housewives.[47] If the small bags or purses that the men show or extend to the women are money-bags, as is usually maintained, the identification of the women as prostitutes is nonetheless up for grabs. Marion Meyer has argued that the purse is merely the attribute of a solid Athenian citizen.[48] This seems to hold for some of the images, but in others, the women reach out eagerly to take them, which suggests payment. For Lewis, these are associated with courtship, but Bundrick takes the purses and wool-baskets to represent the complementary contributions of a husband and a wife to the household.

Whether these scenes represent erotic courtship, or celebrate the reciprocity of marriage, the variants depicting Polyneikes offering the necklace to Eriphyle can still be read in opposition to the normative genre scenes. Depending on the identity of the women, the juxtaposition suggests either that Eriphyle is acting like a *hetaira* in accepting the necklace, or that she is violating the reciprocity between spouses by accepting a seductive gift from someone not her husband. Lewis (2002: 199) comments that the "gifts in themselves are not bad, but the addition of names to the characters in the scene converts it from the regular gift to the poisoned context of myth." I would argue that with or without names, the necklace, otherwise unusual in courtship scenes, is marked as a "bad" gift, and a clue that something is amiss.

In two of the scenes representing Eriphyle, the male figure holds a chest or basket from which he extracts the necklace. This detail is striking because in nearly all other scenes in vase-painting in which a similar chest appears, it is held either by the matron herself or by her maid. In fact, this would become a common iconographic detail on Athenian funerary stelai of the fourth century. The rare appearance of a man holding the chest, an object so thoroughly associated with women, and invading what was marked off as female space, reinforces the suggestion of seduction.[49] The congruence of these scenes, therefore, suggests that the persuasion directed at Eriphyle, and her responding complicity, could be conceptualized as seduction and adultery. This interpretation is further supported by a vase attributed to the Chicago Painter that shows Eriphyle on one side and an unambiguous scene of erotic gift-giving on the other.[50] Not only is it suggested in these images that Eriphyle's betrayal is analogous to adultery, but it is worth recalling that she meets with the same retribution as the faithless Klytemnestra, death at the hands of her son to avenge the death of his father.[51]

Another of Gernet's examples, the tripod of the Seven Sages, has particular resonance for the theme of the circulation of women. This tripod, destined for "the wisest," was given to Thales, who modestly passed it along to another sage, who in turn passed it along to another, and so on, until it came back to Thales. He in turn dedicated it to the god Apollo (Diogenes Laertius 1.28–29).[52] This tripod, which according to one version was originally made by Hephaistos as a wedding present for Pelops, turns out to have an even more complicated history, as it was among the possessions stolen by Paris from Menelaos' house when he abducted Helen. According to Diogenes Laertius (1.32), "It was thrown into the Coan sea by the Laconian woman [i.e., Helen], for she said that it would be the cause of strife" (*rhiphēnai eis tēn Kōian thalassan pros tēs Lakainēs, eipousēs hoti perimachētos estai*).

Although Diogenes' narrative emphasizes the peaceful circulation of the tripod from one sage to another until it had come full circle, the Helen of Diogenes' account sees in it a cause of strife, as it was soon to be.[53] In Helen's description of the object as *perimachētos*, Diogenes suggests a certain sympathy between the object and the woman who will soon be the

FIGURE 4

Paris abducting Helen, Attic red-figure Skyphos, Side A. Painter: Makron, c. 490–480
BCE. Museum of Fine Arts, Boston. Francis Barlett Donation of 1912, 13.186.

cause of strife.[54] Her abduction will soon provoke the Trojan War, and she herself—like the tripod—will be passed from hand to hand until she is returned to her original "owner," her husband Menelaos.[55]

Indeed, the same word *perimachētos* is applied in a later context to Helen herself, or rather to an image or phantom of her, an *eidōlon*. Plato uses this same word in a reference to this episode in the *Republic* (586c). Quoting from the palinode of the lyric poet Stesichoros, he says that the armies at Troy actually fought around not the real Helen, but only a phantom image of her. Thus it was, in Plato's paraphrase, that the image of Helen, not the real Helen, caused the Trojan War and was fought around (*perimachētos*) by armies ignorant of the truth.

A visual analogue for the circulation of Helen is provided by a skyphos by Makron.[56] This skyphos is unusual in depicting the abduction and return of Helen on two sides of the same vase.[57] On one side is Paris' abduction of Helen, with Aphrodite and Peitho (Persuasion) attending the bride (Fig 4). On the other side is her reclamation by Menelaos. He draws his sword intending to attack her, but is restrained by his desire, represented again by Aphrodite and her entourage (Fig. 5). Norbert Kunisch stresses the

FIGURE 5

Menelaos reclaiming Helen, Attic red-figure Skyphos, Side B. Painter: Makron, c. 490–480 BCE. Museum of Fine Arts, Boston. Francis Barlett Donation of 1912, 13.186.

way in which Makron's composition emphasizes continuity, linking two critical episodes in Helen's life by means of the power of the goddess Aphrodite.[58] Several features of the vase decoration reinforce the idea of the circulation of Helen.[59] The two scenes seem almost to flow into one another, without any framing devices that might isolate them.[60] Under the handles, additional figures fill out the gap between the two scenes. The figures, looking intently to the left or the right, occupy most of the space in a dynamic arrangement suggestive of movement. The composition seems designed to provoke in the viewer a desire to turn the vase, trying to follow the sight lines and see what the figures see. Depending on which side the drinker preferred to have facing him, those viewing the cup would see either a scene of seduction or one that emphasized the husband's authority.[61] Finally, the two handles on the skyphos suggest a correspondence between the very form of the vase, one that could be passed hand-to-hand, and the theme depicted on its sides. Thus the user would reproduce the circulation from man to man of the figure of Helen as depicted on the vase itself, in a gesture that mimics the circulation of the tripod of the Seven Sages as told by Diogenes Laertius.[62]

So many of the precious objects whose circulation brings grief were originally divine gifts. Gifts of the gods in Greek myth are famously ambiguous, but impossible to refuse. To quote Paris, a notorious beneficiary: "The glorious gifts of the gods are not to be refused, whatever they give, even if no one would take them willingly" (*ou toi apoblēt' esti theōn erikudea dōra, / hossa ken autoi dōsin, hekōn d' ouk an tis heloito, Iliad* 3.65–66). Whether beautifully wrought objects or equally attractive—and deceptive—intangible rewards, more often than not they lead to disaster for the mortals who receive them. Admetos, the hospitable king of Pherae, is rewarded for his gracious treatment of Apollo with the boon of avoiding death if he can find someone else to go in his place. This seemingly generous gift becomes the source of his greatest sorrow, as elaborated in Euripides' *Alkestis*.[63]

More tangible gifts, like the necklace given to Harmonia upon her marriage to Kadmos, have a history, even a genealogy, which allows us to trace their baneful influences as they are passed down from one generation to the next. Harmonia's necklace is harmless in her hands, as she is the immortal daughter of Ares and Aphrodite. But when handed down to her mortal descendants, it becomes an instrument of destruction, inducing Eriphyle to betray her husband and ultimately leading to her own death. Even the glorious armor made by Hephaistos for Achilles, although not the cause of his death, is a necessary link in the chain of events that will bring it about.[64] As Brillet-Dubois has noted, "The gifts of the gods distinguish certain mortals, while at the same time they may play a fatal role in their destiny."[65]

The intense interest in precious "heirloom" objects in the Homeric epics is shown by the number of these objects that have their own genealogies.[66] Seaford (2004: 152) notes the uniqueness conferred on valuable objects in Homer by a permanent association with their divine origin. As it happens, many of these are the same objects that figure in myths of exchange and betrayal. One of the most extended genealogies belongs to Agamemnon's scepter:

ἔστη σκῆπτρον ἔχων, τὸ μὲν Ἥφαιστος κάμε τεύχων.
Ἥφαιστος μὲν δῶκε Διὶ Κρονίωνι ἄνακτι,
αὐτὰρ ἄρα Ζεὺς δῶκε διακτόρῳ ἀργεϊφόντῃ·
Ἑρμείας δὲ ἄναξ δῶκεν Πέλοπι πληξίππῳ,
αὐτὰρ ὁ αὖτε Πέλοψ δῶκ' Ἀτρέϊ, ποιμένι λαῶν,
Ἀτρεὺς δὲ θνήσκων ἔλιπεν πολύαρνι Θυέστῃ,
αὐτὰρ ὁ αὖτε Θυέστ' Ἀγαμέμνονι λεῖπε φορῆναι,
πολλῇσιν νήσοισι καὶ Ἄργεϊ παντὶ ἀνάσσειν.

[Agamemnon] stood holding the scepter that Hephaistos had labored
   to make.
Hephaistos then gave it to King Zeus son of Kronos,
Zeus then gave it to the messenger Argeiphontes,
Lord Hermes gave it in turn to Pelops the charioteer,
and Pelops then gave it to Atreus, shepherd of men,
and Atreus when he died left it to Thyestes, rich in flocks,
and Thyestes left it to Agamemnon to carry,
so that he might rule over many islands and all of Argos.
   (*Iliad* 2.101–8)

Like most gifts from the gods, the scepter was made by Hephaistos. Somewhat more unusually, it was originally intended for Zeus but passed on
to his son Hermes, who gave it to Pelops. From there it passed down to
Pelops' grandsons, first Atreus and then Thyestes, and then to Atreus' son
Agamemnon. This bland account of the scepter's transfer to Thyestes on
the death of Atreus is peculiar in that it makes no mention of the hostility between the two brothers.[67] The scepter that Atreus "left" to his brother
Thyestes is a sign of the very kingly power over which they fought with
such deadly effect.[68] This passage is the only one in the *Iliad* in which Thyestes appears.[69] As in many other cases, the Homeric poet chooses to avoid
the more sensational details of the history of the house of Atreus. The dispute over the kingship of Argos results in a number of notable crimes, including the transfer of the golden lamb from Atreus to Thyestes when he
seduces Atreus' wife Aerope. These incidents lead to the horrific banquet at
which Thyestes' own children were served to him in revenge by Atreus, and
ultimately to the death of Agamemnon, which has such great thematic importance for the *Odyssey*. The golden lamb is an example of the alienation
of wealth caused by a wife's infidelity, and combines the categories of male
and female wealth.[70] The phallic and kingly scepter, by contrast, is of an ir-
reproachable masculinity. It is thus presented as being passed from man to
man, in a narrative that suppresses any hint of trouble—especially trouble
caused by women.

   The first recorded divine gift to mortals is "Woman" (called Pandora in
the *Works and Days*, one of the two earliest accounts of her creation). She,
like Harmonia's necklace or Achilles' armor, is created by the artisan god
Hephaistos. Unlike these other gifts, which are presented with good in-
tentions, she is expressly made to be a baneful gift for mortals. Not only is
her jar the source of all the evils known to man, but with her also comes
the troublesome institution of marriage, which Hesiod characterizes in the
most negative terms possible.[71] Hesiod's bleak view erases the contributions

of a woman to the *oikos* and sees her only as a drain on resources, rather than as a partner in the toils of existence.

An echo of Pandora can be seen in a second deadly gift of a woman, in this case one who did not need to be created because she already existed: Helen of Sparta, wife of Menelaos, the most beautiful woman in the world. Offered as a gift to the unwary Paris, in return for selecting Aphrodite as the most beautiful of the three goddesses competing for Eris' golden apple, she is not free to be given. Thus begins the most glorious, but also the most destructive, of all ancient Greek heroic exploits, the Trojan War. Many men are killed in battle, including Paris himself, a great city is sacked, its women enslaved, and its children murdered. In the figure of Helen can be seen the greatest fears about the behavior of women in marriage. They may be unfaithful, cause alienation of the household wealth, and continue to circulate among marriage partners long after they are assumed to be safely settled in one particular household.[72]

Whether as deadly creations who let loose untold evils into men's lives, or as *femmes fatales* whose possession is to be gained at great cost, these irresistible women allow us to glimpse the anxieties associated with women and marriage that are played out in ancient Greek myth. Brought into the household, they threaten its ruin, either by squandering resources from within or by allowing them to be plundered from without. Their potential for faithlessness threatens the very fabric of the household itself. What goes unsaid in these myths is that women are necessary for the constitution of the household. Furthermore, without them there can be no continuity of the *oikos*. The myths explored here obscure these basic truths about women's contributions, all the while projecting onto them anxieties about scarcity and survival.

WOMAN AS THE ORIGINAL DANGEROUS GIFT

The very origin of Woman, according to Hesiod, is traceable to an act of deceitful and treacherous gift-giving.[73] In the words of Pausanias, before the creation of Pandora, there was no *gunaikōn genos* (1.24.7). Vernant has analyzed both Hesiodic versions of the conflict between Zeus and Prometheus, of which the creation of woman is a part, as a series of deceitful gifts given and refused, or withheld and taken by stealth.[74] Prometheus has given the secret of fire to men, despite Zeus's desire to withhold it. In a retaliatory gesture aimed not directly at Prometheus but at his beloved mortals, Zeus creates a trap in the form of a lovely maiden. The woman Pandora—"All-gifts"—brings not gifts but troubles to men, specifically through the institution of marriage (*Works and Days* 81). Moreover, the account in the *Theogony* (590–612) essentially conflates the origin of women with the origin of human marriage.[75] Among the Greeks, the existence of men apparently required no explanation.

In Hesiod's treatment of women and marriage, concern about wives' potential misuse of household goods is very much in the forefront. In this context, it is worth noting that in the *Works and Days*, it was from a large storage jar (*pithos*, *Works and Days* 94) of the sort used to store grain, rather than a box, that Pandora, the archaic Greek prototypical woman, released evils into the world of men. Later versions attribute her act to a stereotypically destructive female curiosity, but Hesiod does not provide a motivation. Pandora's attribute of the jar and her release of its baneful contents in the *Works and Days* connect the origin of women to concerns about the use and control of scarce resources.[76] That her jar contains evils, including famine, rather than sustenance, goes hand in hand with Hesiod's repeated insistence that women consume household resources rather than contributing to them. Hope (*elpis*, *Works and Days* 96) alone remains trapped inside, a detail that has remained puzzling to most interpreters: Is Hope an evil that has not been released, or a good thing withheld from—or thus potentially available to—men?[77] As several scholars have shown, the theme of the retention or release of the jar's ambiguous contents also points to a related anxiety about reproduction.[78]

The Hesiodic texts spare no effort to present the gods' gift of "Woman" as an unmitigated disaster: "a beautiful evil," "a pain for men," "an inescapable trick."[79] Like so many other gifts of the gods that are joyously received but later prove to be the source of misery, this dangerous creature is the work of Hephaistos. Although she is made of earth (*Theogony* 571; *Works and Days* 70), she is clearly a divine artifact, and further divine contributions—fine garments, golden necklaces, or a golden crown—turn her into something of a luxury object (Brown 1997). In the *Theogony* account, after molding Woman out of clay like a potter making a vase, the god forges a splendid gold headdress for her and decorates it with images of animals of land and sea, so marvelously crafted that they seem to be alive.[80] The elaborately worked head-covering (*daidaleēn kaluptrēn*, 574–75) is described as a *thauma idesthai* (575, 581: "a marvel to be seen"). As Raymond Prier has observed in another context, an object described as a *thauma idesthai* is balanced between gods and men and "clearly 'other' in origin."[81] The woman is thus sent forth like a radiant mistress of animals, and a figure of reproductive fertility.[82]

γαίης γὰρ σύμπλασσε περικλυτὸς Ἀμφιγυήεις
παρθένῳ αἰδοίῃ ἴκελον Κρονίδεω διὰ βουλάς·
ζῶσε δὲ καὶ κόσμησε θεὰ γλαυκῶπις Ἀθήνη
ἀργυφέῃ ἐσθῆτι· κατὰ κρῆθεν δὲ καλύπτρην
δαιδαλέην χείρεσσι κατέσχεθε, θαῦμα ἰδέσθαι·
ἀμφὶ δέ οἱ στεφάνην χρυσέην κεφαλῆφιν ἔθηκε,
τὴν αὐτὸς ποίησε περικλυτὸς Ἀμφιγυήεις
ἀσκήσας παλάμῃσι, χαριζόμενος Διὶ πατρί.
τῇ δ᾽ ἐνὶ δαίδαλα δεινὰ τετεύχατο, θαῦμα ἰδέσθαι·
κνώδαλ᾽ ὅς᾽ ἤπειρος δεινὰ τρέφει ἠδὲ θάλασσα·
τῶν ὅ γε πόλλ᾽ ἐνέθηκε, χάρις δ᾽ ἐπὶ πᾶσιν ἄητο,
θαυμάσια, ζῴοισιν ἐοικότα φωνήεσσιν.

The famous lame smith took clay and, through Zeus's counsels,
gave it the shape of a modest maiden.
Athena, the gray-eyed goddess, clothed her and decked her out
with a flashy garment and then with her hands
she hung over her head a fine draping veil, a marvel to behold;
Pallas Athena crowned her head with lovely wreaths
of fresh flowers that had just bloomed in the green meadows.
The famous lame smith placed on her head a crown of gold
fashioned by the skill of his own hands
to please the heart of Zeus the father.
It was a wondrous thing with many intricate designs
of all the dreaded beasts nurtured by land and sea.
Such grace he breathed into the many marvels therein
that they seemed endowed with life and voice.
(*Theog.* 571–84, trans. Athanassakis)

The *Works and Days* account focuses not only on the woman's adorn-ments but also on the arts and skills imparted to the first woman by the gods: Athena teaches her to weave, and Hermes to lie and cheat. As pre-viously noted, the Hesiodic tradition discounts even those feminine skills such as weaving that are culturally valued elsewhere in Greek culture.[83] In the *Odyssey* (7.109–11), for example, Athena imparts knowledge of weav-ing, along with good character, to the Phaiakian women. Hesiod's pairing of weaving and lying, on the other hand, suggests a more sinister associa-tion: textiles are part of the deceitful but attractive outer form that makes of Pandora a gift that is both treacherous and irresistible.

Ἥφαιστον δ᾽ ἐκέλευσε περικλυτὸν ὅττι τάχιστα
γαῖαν ὕδει φύρειν, ἐν δ᾽ ἀνθρώπου θέμεν αὐδὴν

καὶ σθένος, ἀθανάτης δὲ θεῆς εἰς ὦπα ἐίσκειν
παρθενικῆς καλὸν εἶδος ἐπήρατον· αὐτὰρ Ἀθήνην
ἔργα διδασκῆσαι, πολυδαίδαλον ἱστὸν ὑφαίνειν·
καὶ χάριν ἀμφιχέαι κεφαλῇ χρυσῆν Ἀφροδίτην
καὶ πόθον ἀργαλέον καὶ γυιοβόρους μελεδώνας·
ἐν δὲ θέμεν κύνεόν τε νόον καὶ ἐπίκλοπον ἦθος
Ἑρμείην ἤνωγε, διάκτορον Ἀργεϊφόντην.

Then he ordered widely acclaimed Hephaistos to mix earth with water
with all haste and place in them human voice
and strength. His orders were to make a face
such as goddesses have and the shape of a lovely maiden;
Athena was to teach her skills and intricate weaving,
and golden Aphrodite should pour grace round her head,
and stinging desire and limb-gnawing passion.
Then he ordered Hermes the pathbreaker and slayer of Argos
to put in her the mind of a bitch and a thievish nature.
(*Works and Days* 60–68, trans. Athanassakis)

αὐτίκα δ' ἐκ γαίης πλάσσε κλυτὸς Ἀμφιγυήεις
παρθένῳ αἰδοίῃ ἴκελον Κρονίδεω διὰ βουλάς·
ζῶσε δὲ καὶ κόσμησε θεὰ γλαυκῶπις Ἀθήνη·
ἀμφὶ δέ οἱ Χάριτές τε θεαὶ καὶ πότνια Πειθὼ
ὅρμους χρυσείους ἔθεσαν χροΐ, ἀμφὶ δὲ τήν γε
Ὧραι καλλίκομοι στέφον ἄνθεσιν εἰαρινοῖσιν·
πάντα δέ οἱ χροΐ κόσμον ἐφήρμοσε Παλλὰς Ἀθήνη.
ἐν δ' ἄρα οἱ στήθεσσι διάκτορος Ἀργεϊφόντης
ψεύδεά θ' αἱμυλίους τε λόγους καὶ ἐπίκλοπον ἦθος
τεῦξε Διὸς βουλῇσι βαρυκτύπου· ἐν δ' ἄρα φωνὴν
θῆκε θεῶν κῆρυξ, ὀνόμηνε δὲ τήνδε γυναῖκα
Πανδώρην, ὅτι πάντες Ὀλύμπια δώματ' ἔχοντες
δῶρον ἐδώρησαν, πῆμ' ἀνδράσιν ἀλφηστῇσιν.

Without delay the renowned lame god fashioned from earth,
through Zeus's will, the likeness of a shy maiden,
and Athena, the gray-eyed goddess, clothed her and decked her out.
Then the divine graces and queenly Persuasion
gave her golden necklaces to wear, and the lovely-haired Seasons
stood round her and crowned her with spring flowers.
Pallas Athena adorned her body with every kind of jewel,
and the Slayer of Argos—Hermes the guide—through the will
of Zeus whose thunder roars placed in her breast

lies, coaxing words, and a thievish nature.
The gods' herald then gave her voice and called this woman
Pandora because all of the gods who dwell on Olympos
gave her a gift—a scourge for toiling men.
(*Works and Days* 70–82, trans. Athanassakis)

Is she merely an inescapable trap, or does the figure of Pandora conceal a double meaning? Not only the headdress and the *pithos* with its enigmatic Hope hiding inside, but also the name of this beautiful creature, suggest ambivalence, raising questions about her degree of agency, her nature, even her existential status, questions that the text of Hesiod seems to beg.[84] The woman created by the gods is not only a divine artifact, but possibly also herself a hidden divinity. Rather than "all-receiving," her name can be interpreted as "all-giving," which would make of her an active giver of benefits rather than a passive recipient of gifts.[85] This epithet would more properly apply to the earth goddess Gaia than to a mortal woman. In fact, Hesiod's explanation is unique, as this is the only place where the epithet *pandora/pandoros* or the related form *pandoteira* bears a passive meaning, that is, *receiving* gifts.[86] All other uses of these terms in Greek are clearly active, as in "all-bounteous, giver of all," epithets applied to the life-giving Earth.[87]

Whether or not we see Pandora as "Gaia reborn," the pictorial record suggests a close association between the two figures.[88] Two separate traditions taken together reinforce the connection, as Hurwit has shown. In the first, scenes that conform to the Hesiodic account center on a figure labeled "Anesidora"—"she who sends up gifts"—a less ambiguous variant of the name. In the second, a figure labeled Pandora emerges from the earth like an incarnation of Gaia.[89] We recall that in both Hesiodic accounts she is made of earth (*gaiēs gar sumplasse, Theog.* 571; *ek gaiēs plasse, Works and Days* 70), although Loraux rightly emphasizes that "woman" is never assigned an autochthonous origin.[90] Pandora's hollowness contains and conceals, like Hope held inside the jar, an alternative version of woman's nature in which her connections with fertility are wholly positive, and liken her to Gaia, the bountiful earth. In Hesiod's account, however, she is not an earth goddess, but a mortal creature of earth, who causes not plenty but scarcity.[91] Her arrival introduces misery to men's lives, in part because of her threatening and destructive fertility, which keeps them enslaved to agricultural labor to feed growing families.[92]

In the account in the *Theogony* of the same episode, the "gift" the woman brings with her, inasmuch as she is the ancestor of all women, is not the evil she releases from the *pithos* in the *Works and Days*, but the ambiguous institution of marriage (589–612). The lines that follow once again reveal ambivalence about this institution in the admission that a man who does not marry has a miserable old age—the so-called misogynist's dilemma.[93] Although Hesiod grudgingly admits the possibility of a man's finding a good wife "suited to his mind" (*kednēn . . . akoitin arēruian prapidessi, Theog.* 608), he nonetheless insists that a wife will consume precious resources without making any contribution to household wealth.[94] The likely role of a wife as producer is suppressed, hidden like the gifts of the earth or like Hope in the jar.

What becomes of women's weaving? In the *Theogony*, Hesiod makes no mention of it at all. The phrase *erga gunaikōn*, "the works of women," in other archaic texts almost always refers to the garments women weave, which are characterized as *lipara*, soft, shining, graceful, and beautiful.[95] Hesiod, on the other hand, couples the phrase *erga gunaikōn* with the word *mermera*, "baneful, anxiety-producing" (*Theog.* 603). For him, the "works of women" are not textile contributions to household wealth but the source of undefined troubles, probably sexual in nature. Marilyn Katz (Arthur 1982) takes the phrase to be an oblique "rendering of the pressure of sexual need."[96] The phrase *mermera erga* evokes—only to dismiss—another positive aspect of women's role. It is not only women's production that is devalued, but also their roles as sexual companions.

What is more, the wife's reproductive potential elicits a similar ambivalence. Women's contributions to the *oikos*, aside from the production of textiles, would be expected to include the bearing of children—necessary both as hands on the farm and as future inheritors of the *oikos*. But the *Works and Days* recommends strictly limiting the number of offspring to one son (*mounogenēs . . . pais*, 376) to preserve the inheritance. Women's reproductive potential is thus a double-edged sword.[97] Several later authors also recommend leaving a single heir, advice that is less obviously suited to an agrarian life.[98] The poet seems aware of this contradiction, as he follows up immediately (379–80) with the apparently conventional observation that having many children allows one to amass more wealth.[99] His ambivalence on this point is part and parcel of the ambivalence about women, marriage, and reproduction that runs throughout the poem. One might venture to suggest that the unclear status of Hope, left in the jar, corresponds to the ambiguous status of the offspring in a woman's uterus. Are children merely a burden, or are they the hope for the future? And might that hope prove illusory? All of these questions are implicit in the equation of the *pithos* with the uterus.[100]

Despite these few grudging admissions, the poet's precepts obscure the value of women as producers and limit them to highly dubious objects of exchange. Not merely a lousy trick, Pandora is also a bad bargain, not least because men cannot do without her. As Ferrari (1988: 52) puts it, she is "the very incarnation of bad exchange." This deadliest gift of the gods is one that cannot be refused.

If Pandora is a figure for the ambiguity of human existence, and if all the changes her arrival brings to men—marriage, children, and agricultural labor—signal, as Vernant has said, our difference not only from the gods, but also from the beasts, then surely she is not all bad?[101] Although her exterior is beautiful, Hesiod finds—or admits to finding—nothing good inside. Her role as bearer of children no longer strengthens the household but threatens to overwhelm it with unwanted progeny.[102] Her potential for agricultural labor is denied; instead, she lives off the labor of men. Her role as keeper of the household goods is reversed to that of devourer of its substance.[103] Even her *erga*, the paradigmatic work of women at the loom, are unraveled, transformed into a sexual threat. She stands—clothed in deceit but denuded of traditional female virtues—as a figure for the mystification of women's economic contribution. Hesiod's vehemence on this point shows how much is at stake. In the words of Cynthia Patterson, "Hesiod's 'misogyny' is a strong indication of the wife's significant economic role in a household in which she had a vested interest."[104] Created to be given in revenge for an act of "negative reciprocity," Prometheus' theft of fire, Pandora embodies the negation of every possibility of reciprocity between husband and wife.[105]

For all that she is troublesome, Pandora is also inevitable. She represents a necessary rupture with a former life—an impossible Golden Age existing outside of social networks of exchange, a life without production or reproduction. Were it not for a series of corrupted exchanges between Zeus and Prometheus, woman would not exist at all. She is created by Zeus in anger over Prometheus' trick of stealing fire for mortals, and with it (according to Plato's *Protagoras*), the arts of Hephaistos and Athena—metalworking and weaving respectively.[106] These two arts are then used against mortals in order to make woman irresistible. Apparently mortals cannot have production without reproduction, cannot have technology without also having sexual dimorphism and the division of labor. Even if this marked gendered division of labor is systematically written out of Hesiod's account, it sneaks back into the picture in the form of the *technai* (skills or crafts) of the gods Hephaistos and Athena. What Pandora takes with one hand, she gives back with the other. Man loses his freedom from toil, but gains thereby access to a new world not only of social interaction but also of creativity and invention. Made of clay and decorated with gold, Pandora is composed of the very raw materials on which that creativity is to be expended. Without the gift of woman (and the gifts of women), man cannot go forward, cannot fully experience what it is to be human. With her, he must progress, even if the journey is sometimes arduous and painful. Through the opening of the jar, with its ambiguous results—even the pessimism of Hesiod cannot fully disguise this—come not only the evils of mortal existence, but all of its possibilities as well.[107]

Hesiod is not alone among archaic Greek poets in his negative view of women's contribution to the household. Semonides (frag. 7) deals in some of the same stereotypes. The woman descended from a pig is useless as a housekeeper; the mare-woman only wants to sit around and look pretty and will waste a man's money on expensive hair products; and so on. Semonides' misogynist vision—if one can call it that—does, however, leave room for the prototype of the productive wife, the bee-woman.

> τὴν δ' ἐκ μελίσσης· τήν τις εὐτυχεῖ λαβών·
> κείνηι γὰρ οἴηι μῶμος οὐ προσιζάνει,
> θάλλει δ' ὑπ' αὐτῆς κἀπαέξεται βίος,
> φίλη δὲ σὺν φιλέοντι γηράσκει πόσει
> τεκοῦσα καλὸν κὠνομάκλυτον γένος.
> κἀριπρεπὴς μὲν ἐν γυναιξὶ γίνεται
> πάσηισι, θείη δ' ἀμφιδέδρομεν χάρις.
> οὐδ' ἐν γυναιξὶν ἥδεται καθημένη
> ὅκου λέγουσιν ἀφροδισίους λόγους.
> τοίας γυναῖκας ἀνδράσιν χαρίζεται
> Ζεὺς τὰς ἀρίστας καὶ πολυφραδεστάτας.

> One [comes] from a bee. The man is lucky who gets her.
> She is the only one no blame can settle on.
> A man's life grows and blossoms underneath her touch.
> She loves her husband, he loves her, and they grow old
> together, while their glorious children rise to fame.
> Among the throngs of other women this one shines
> as an example. Heavenly grace surrounds her. She
> alone takes no delight in sitting with the rest
> when the conversation's about sex. It's wives like this
> who are God's gift of happiness to mortal men.
> These are the thoughtful wives, in every way the best.
> (Semonides frag. 7.83–91, trans. Lattimore)

Of Semonides' types of women, the one who by virtue of her origins most calls to mind Pandora is not so much wasteful as stupid, too stupid in fact

to be the source of either good or evil, or even to know when to come in out
of the cold:

τὴν δὲ πλάσαντες γηίνην Ὀλύμπιοι
ἔδωκαν ἀνδρὶ πηρόν· οὔτε γὰρ κακὸν
οὔτ᾽ ἐσθλὸν οὐδὲν οἶδε τοιαύτη γυνή·
ἔργων δὲ μοῦνον ἐσθίειν ἐπίσταται.
κοὐδ᾽ ἢν κακὸν χειμῶνα ποιήσηι θεός,
ῥιγῶσα δίφρον ἄσσον ἕλκεται πυρός.

The gods of Olympus made another one of mud
and gave her lame to man. A woman such as this
knows nothing good and nothing bad. Nothing at all.
The only thing she understands is how to eat,
and even if God makes the weather bad, she won't,
though shivering, pull her chair up to the fire.
(Semonides frag. 7.21–26, trans. Lattimore)

Like Hesiod's two versions of the creation of Pandora, this text emphasizes
the woman's origin as an artisanal object, created by the gods. Unlike the
usual divine productions—elaborately wrought shields, necklaces of deadly
attractiveness, royal scepters—this one is made not of precious materials
but only of earth. Unlike Semonides' earth-woman, Hesiodic woman is
tricked out with the best handiwork and the best wiles the gods can offer.
Hesiod stresses the divine craft that goes into the adornment of the *kalon
kakon*: the headdress (*kaluptrēn*, *Theog.* 574) given her by Athena, and the
miraculous crown (*stephanēn*, *Theog.* 576) made for her by Hephaistos, on
which is represented every kind of living creature. For Hesiod, Woman is
clearly on a par with the other highly elaborated works that we expect from
the gods. And rather than a natural production, like the animals that the
land and sea bring forth, she is the work of an artisan.

But Woman (or Pandora) is not so easily placed on the gender grid.
Equipped with traditional female qualities, and clearly the ancestor of all
women, she is nonetheless an artisanal object, created by a male god and
adorned with gold. Although made of earth, not metal, she seems to fall
into the category of male wealth. Stored inside the house, as are other precious objects (*keimēlia*), she turns the model of domestic production on
its head by dispersing what was stored in the *pithos*, which should have
been grain but is instead evil of all descriptions. This myth of the origin of
woman exposes a flaw in the ideal of *autarkeia*: thanks to the incest taboo,
a wife must be sought from outside the immediate family. Both of the He-

siodic poems show women compromising the self-sufficiency of the *oikos*. What is not spelled out is that marriage of necessity involves men in exchange with the outside world. The paradox of women is that despite an association with the inside and domestic production, they must be acquired from outside the *oikos*, in a process that often includes the exchange of precious objects that can also only be made or acquired from outside.

This contrast between stability and mobility of goods replicates the ambiguity discussed by Vernant in his influential article on Hestia and Hermes.[108] His analysis points to a glaring problem. Greek mythic thinking assigns mobility to the male and stability to the female, who at least symbolically tends the home-fire. Yet this daughter of the *oikos* is also a potential bride, and must move to another household in order to fulfill her destiny. The economic stability of the *oikos* is often connected with the fidelity of the wife, as is clear from Odysseus' questions to his mother in the Underworld (*Odyssey* 11.178–79).[109] He wants to know if Penelope has stayed at home, respecting his bed and guarding his possessions. Keeping inside, keeping faithful, and keeping close watch on the household stores ideally all go together, but there are a number of threats to this ideal. The Hesiodic or Semonidean woman may stay in the house, but meanwhile she is consuming its stores from the inside out. In the case of Helen, it is her *mobility* that threatens the economic integrity of Menelaos' household. The potential for ongoing and illicit mobility of wives is always a threat to the integrity of the household. Both of these behaviors—overeating and running off with Trojan princes—represent serious threats to the ideal of the autarkic *oikos*, one from within and the other from without. Moreover, the acquisition of a wife involves one in exchange with the outside world, other *oikoi*, and the world of trade, and places one in conflict with the ideal of *autarkeia*.

THE GREEK *OIKOS* AND THE IDEAL OF SELF-SUFFICIENCY

The Greek word *oikos* covers a range of meanings, from the nuclear family with its ancestors and descendants, to the entire family and the property it controls.[110] For Aristotle, it is made up of parents and children.[111] Xenophon, in his *Oikonomikos*, on the other hand, regards it as "a unit of production, a unit of consumption, and . . . a unit of reproduction."[112] In what follows, I distinguish between the *oikos*, the intangible "house" (as in the phrase "the house of Atreus"), and the *oikia*, the physical building that houses members of the *oikos*. It is useful to keep in mind the contemporary as well as the original meaning of the word *economics*, from *oikos* and *nomos* (law or custom), in other words, the regulation of the household. And central to that concept is the ideal of *autarkeia*, self-sufficiency.[113]

The celebration of *autarkeia* is at the heart of the message of the *Works and Days*:

> οὐδὲ τό γ᾽ εἰν οἴκῳ κατακείμενον ἀνέρα κήδει.
> οἴκοι βέλτερον εἶναι, ἐπεὶ βλαβερὸν τὸ θύρηφιν.
> ἐσθλὸν μὲν παρεόντος ἑλέσθαι, πῆμα δὲ θυμῷ
> χρηίζειν ἀπεόντος, ἅ σε φράζεσθαι ἄνωγα.

> One does not worry about what lies stored in his home.
> Home is safer; what lies out of doors is harmed.
> To take from what one has is good, but grief comes
> with longing for what one lacks. Do think of all this.
> (*Works and Days* 364–67, trans. Athanassakis)

It is important not only to keep your stuff near to hand, but also to not want what you can't produce yourself. In the moral universe inhabited by Hesiod, anything not produced at home is not only unnecessary, but deeply suspect. Earlier in the poem, when he claims to give his brother Perses advice about sailing, the not-so-buried subtext is that sailing—and by extension trading—is a bad idea, and unnecessary if one learns how to farm properly:

> οὐδέ ποτ᾽ ἰθυδίκῃσι μετ᾽ ἀνδράσι λιμὸς ὀπηδεῖ
> οὐδ᾽ ἄτη, θαλίης δὲ μεμηλότα ἔργα νέμονται.
> τοῖσι φέρει μὲν γαῖα πολὺν βίον, οὔρεσι δὲ δρῦς
> ἄκρη μέν τε φέρει βαλάνους, μέσση δὲ μελίσσας·
> εἰροπόκοι δ᾽ ὄιες μαλλοῖς καταβεβρίθασι·
> τίκτουσιν δὲ γυναῖκες ἐοικότα τέκνα γονεῦσι·
> θάλλουσιν δ᾽ ἀγαθοῖσι διαμπερές· οὐδ᾽ ἐπὶ νηῶν
> νίσονται, καρπὸν δὲ φέρει ζείδωρος ἄρουρα.

> Men whose justice is straight know neither hunger nor ruin,
> but amid feasts enjoy the yield of their labors.
> For them the earth brings forth a rich harvest; and for them
> the top of an oak teems with acorns and the middle with bees.
> Fleecy sheep are weighed down with wool,
> and women bear children who resemble their fathers.
> There is an abundance of blessings and the grainland
> grants such harvests that no one has to sail on ships.
> (*Works and Days* 230–37, trans. Athanassakis, modified)

Throughout archaic Greek literature we find a tension between the desire for self-sufficiency and the need for contact and exchange with the outside world.[114] The household of the archaic period might have been largely self-sufficient, but this was only possible to the extent that imported metals or other luxuries were not desired or required. And although Homeric epic celebrates the beauty and workmanship of any number of intricate objects of artisanal production, the artisan in question is nearly always the god Hephaistos. The *Odyssey* (17.383, 19.135) does refer to *dēmioergoi*, traveling specialists, but the simple life described by Hesiod does not seem to have a place for them.

The Homeric poems show that despite an ambivalent attitude toward traders (e.g., *Odyssey* 8.162–64), the movement of precious goods was an expected part of economic life in the world of epic.[115] As Redfield has noted, in the *Odyssey* "there is a tendency to undervalue trade at the expense of agriculture, and yet to trade far more than one admits."[116] Nonetheless, traders are often mentioned in the same breath with pirates, and there is certainly a nagging suspicion that traders will cheat or even kidnap the unwary, as happened to Eumaios in the *Odyssey*.

Distrust of traders may be so much xenophobia, but the passage just cited from the *Works and Days* indicates some of what is behind this. A peasant prejudice dictates that the just man, or one who knows what is good for him, is capable of producing everything that he needs on his own plot of land, and conversely, of needing only that which he can produce. At the same time, a peasant caution would disapprove of sea voyages. The austerity advocated by Hesiod to his apparently spendthrift brother would mesh perfectly with the distrust of unnecessary luxuries and the sea voyages often necessary to acquire them.

This archaic ideal may offer a possible explanation for the pervasive negativity toward, and mystification of, women's labor expressed in Hesiod and Semonides, as well as the widespread concern with female mobility. If women involve one with exchange with the outside world, this idea attaches to them and leads to the idea that involvement with a woman exposes one to the risk of economic ruin. This explanation hangs on the tension between the ideal of household self-sufficiency, and the necessity of exchange with the outside world implicit in marriage. In order to demonstrate the gendered nature of this dichotomy, it will be necessary also to consider how it interacts with several others, each gendered in its own way. These involve the distinction between the inside and the outside of the *oikos*, as well as the source and location of the different kinds of wealth it holds.

Although feminist scholarship has done much to expose the limits of binary thinking, most ancient Greek philosophical and ideological discourse operates according to just these kinds of pairings. Familiar oppositions like male/female and outside/inside might seem to require no further discussion. In fact, these very polarities are at the heart of the economics of archaic Greek culture as represented in both Homeric epic and the Hesiodic poems.

First of all, the gendered division of labor in archaic Greece, with obvious parallels to many other cultures, places women and their work—indeed, nearly their entire lives—*inside* the house, while men are associated with work and other activities *outside* the house. David Cohen (1990; 1991) has done much to indicate the degree to which this is ideologically constructed. Cohen's work draws on ethnographic parallels to demonstrate that when women say they never leave the house, there is always an asterisk. In practice what they mean is that they never leave the house except in the performance of socially sanctioned activities.[117]

To make matters more complicated, the *oikos* itself can be conceptualized as divided between inside and out: the actual nonmetaphorical house (*oikia*) versus outside in the fields. This division operates at the same time as the larger division of the world into inside the *oikos* and outside the *oikos*, and they are sometimes elided. Both of these divisions are coded female = inside, male = outside, and are clearly marked in archaic and classical Greek texts, such as Xenophon's *Oikonomikos*. As discussed in Chapter One, the wealth of the *oikos* is conceptually divided between the things that are stored (*keimēlia*) and those that are on the hoof (*probata*), but although this set of distinctions can be mapped onto the categories of inside and outside, it does not map as neatly where gender is concerned. *Keimēlia* remain inside the house, like women, and may consist of textiles produced by women. They may also, however, include precious-metal objects that are coded as male wealth, usually the work of specialists and obtained from outside the *oikos*, whether through war, gift-giving, or occasionally trade. On the other hand, *probata*, herd animals, live outside and are tended mainly by men, but also provide the raw material for women's production of textiles.[118]

Closely related to the inside/outside dichotomy is that between artisanal and domestic production. This pair of opposites, like the others just mentioned, can be placed into ideologically positive and negative columns. But once again, it interacts with the other sets of oppositions in some unexpected ways. Because artisanal production is generally thought of as coming from outside the *oikos*, it challenges the ancient Greek ideal of *autarkeia*, self-sufficiency. It is thus assigned the negative valence, despite being associated with men, as opposed to domestic production, which is—to a large extent—associated with women.

Even when wealth is conceptually divided between that which is stored (*keimēlia*) and that which is on the hoof (*probata*), there is no reason why both of these forms of wealth could not be produced at home. Nor is it out of the question that goods produced within an *oikos* could also be exported articles of trade.[119] These possibilities, however, do not seem to fit into the ideological constructs surrounding the archaic *oikos*.

But the ideal of self-sufficiency is elusive, as even the *Works and Days* makes clear. The frequent references to those who must beg from their neighbors, and the clear preference for being the one who is able to give rather than the one who must ask, indicates that in hard times, it was sometimes necessary to throw oneself on the mercy of others. The positive valuation of *autarkeia* persists into the classical period, where passages in Plato's *Republic* and Aristotle's *Politics* reveal the contradictions it entails. Where archaic Greek ideology had suppressed the need for anything produced elsewhere and brought into the *oikos* by trade, these later discussions of *autarkeia* by Plato and Aristotle completely redefine it away from the strict Hesiodic ideal, while continuing to lay claim to its virtues. By now, the impracticability of doing it all yourself has become clear, with the result that *autarkeia* is redefined as the independence that comes from being able to provide everything for oneself and one's own, even if some of it is produced by others.

In the *Charmides*, Socrates makes fun of the idea that it is best for a man to make everything he needs for himself without regard to specialized skills:

τί οὖν; ἦν δ᾽ ἐγώ, δοκεῖ ἄν σοι πόλις εὖ οἰκεῖσθαι ὑπὸ τούτου τοῦ νόμου τοῦ κελεύοντος τὸ ἑαυτοῦ ἱμάτιον ἕκαστον ὑφαίνειν καὶ πλύνειν, καὶ ὑποδήματα σκυτοτομεῖν, καὶ λήκυθον καὶ στλεγγίδα καὶ τἆλλα πάντα κατὰ τὸν αὐτὸν λόγον, τῶν μὲν ἀλλοτρίων μὴ ἅπτεσθαι, τὰ δὲ ἑαυτοῦ ἕκαστον ἐργάζεσθαί τε καὶ πράττειν;

Well then, I went on, do you think a state would be well conducted under a law which enjoined that everyone should weave and scour his own coat, and make his own shoes, and his own flask and scraper, and everything else on the same principle of not touching the affairs of others but performing and doing his own for himself? (161d10–162a2, trans. W.R.M. Lamb)

In the following passage, Aristotle's distinction between trade and the sort of exchange that is merely a "replenishment of natural self-sufficiency" smacks of special pleading. As Seaford remarks of this passage, "Even the realistic Aristotle attempts, with inevitable difficulty, to set up an unrealistic ideal of the self-sufficient household, with all of its resources provided by nature, against the undesirability of artificial and unlimited money-making."[120]

ἐν μὲν οὖν τῇ πρώτῃ κοινωνίᾳ (τοῦτο δ᾽ ἐστὶν οἰκία) φανερὸν ὅτι οὐδέν ἐστιν ἔργον αὐτῆς, ἀλλ᾽ ἤδη πλειόνων τῆς κοινωνίας οὔσης. οἱ μὲν γὰρ τῶν αὐτῶν ἐκοινώνουν πάντων, οἱ δὲ κεχωρισμένοι πολλῶν πάλιν καὶ ἑτέρων· ὧν κατὰ τὰς δεήσεις ἀναγκαῖον ποιεῖσθαι τὰς μεταδόσεις, καθάπερ ἔτι πολλὰ ποιεῖ καὶ τῶν βαρβαρικῶν ἐθνῶν, κατὰ τὴν ἀλλαγήν. αὐτὰ γὰρ τὰ χρήσιμα πρὸς αὐτὰ καταλλάττονται, ἐπὶ πλέον δ᾽ οὐθέν, οἷον οἶνον πρὸς σῖτον διδόντες καὶ λαμβάνοντες, καὶ τῶν ἄλλων τῶν τοιούτων ἕκαστον. ἡ μὲν οὖν τοιαύτη μεταβλητικὴ οὔτε παρὰ φύσιν οὔτε χρηματιστικῆς ἐστιν εἶδος οὐδέν (εἰς ἀναπλήρωσιν γὰρ τῆς κατὰ φύσιν αὐταρκείας ἦν).

For the members of the primitive household used to share commodities that were all their own, whereas on the contrary a group divided into several households participated also in a number of commodities belonging to their neighbors, according to their needs for which they were forced to make their interchanges by way of barter, as also many barbarian tribes do still; for such tribes do not go beyond exchanging actual commodities for actual commodities, for example giving and taking wine for corn, and so with the various other things of the sort. Exchange on these lines therefore is not contrary to nature, nor is it any branch of the art of wealth-getting, for it existed *for the replenishment of natural self-sufficiency* [my emphasis]. (Arist. *Pol.* 1257a19–30, trans. Rackham)

Despite these ideological constructions, the problem remains. Like the object that can only be acquired because someone else, somewhere else, has made it, and that can only be acquired by trade or even seafaring, a wife must come from somewhere outside the *oikos*, must in fact be imported. A wife is something a man can't make for himself at home.

CHAPTER THREE

WOMEN *in* HOMERIC EXCHANGE

If the extreme pessimism of the Hesiodic view of women was not shared by the Homeric tradition, it nevertheless finds its analogues there and in the larger body of myths surrounding the Trojan War.[1] Like the woman created in the *Theogony* or the *Works and Days* to serve as a deceitful gift in a transaction between two gods, Helen is offered to Paris by Aphrodite as a bribe that allows the goddess to triumph over the other contestants in the divine beauty pageant.[2] In both cases, the gift is offered as part of a power struggle among immortals, whose price is, inevitably, paid by mortals.[3] Like Epimetheus' heedless embrace of Pandora, Paris' ill-fated abduction of Helen is only a means to a divine end to which he is largely irrelevant.[4] Starting with Helen's abduction as the cause of the war, the theme of the exchange or circulation of women pervades the *Iliad*, but with none of Hesiod's contempt.[5] The old men of Troy, and Paris himself, replay the part of Epimetheus, taking in the deceptively beautiful image of a woman, all the while unaware of the evil she will bring.[6] The poet of the *Iliad*, however, chooses to present Helen as a figure of some sympathy, a fully drawn character with her own subjectivity.[7] Other women whose mobility causes trouble, like Briseis and Chryseis, are treated by the poet with respect and compassion. On the other hand, the anonymous women skilled in handiwork (*amumona erga iduias*) offered as prizes or compensation are assigned no more moral value, and no more subjectivity, than a gold tripod or iron ingot.[8] Yet their economic worth—both use-value and exchange-value—is clearly reckoned as with any other object of exchange.[9]

THE VALUE OF A WOMAN AT TROY

What is a woman worth? The question is implicit throughout the *Iliad*. For Paris, is Helen worth the hatred of his fellow Trojans and the possible destruction of his city? For Agamemnon, is Chryseis worth the wrath of

Apollo and the death of his men from plague? For Achilles, is Briseis worth his alienation from his heroic destiny? Even the old men of Troy confront a version of this question.

The *Iliad* attempts to answer the question in a variety of ways. The first few books of the poem could almost be read as a textbook on the value of a woman in an elaborate economy based on tangibles (like cattle) and intangibles (like *kleos*, renown). Already in line 13 of the first book, an exchange for a woman is proposed as the priest Chryses offers ransom for his daughter, who has been carried off and given to Agamemnon as a prize of war. It is the decision to return her to her father that provokes the aggrieved Agamemnon to take Briseis, Achilles' captive, thus arousing his wrath and setting in motion the events of the poem.

The *Iliad* offers several systems for assigning value to women, each of which has its own ideological work to do. These systems for the most part suggest the interchangeability of all women, even the most noble or illustrious. The economic valuation of a woman expressed in terms of other objects of value, such as head of oxen, serves to highlight the idea of woman as property.[10] Comparison of one woman with another emphasizes the transience of male favor, and the degree to which women depend on it. Comparison to animals is a staple of the misogynist tradition going back to Hesiod and Semonides of Amorgos, and most likely beyond. Finally, women may be compared to goddesses. As we will see, this is usually, but not always, intended as a compliment.

At the high end of this scale of value are the immortal goddesses, comparisons to whom are a stock feature of epic compliments, such as that of Odysseus to Nausikaa (*Odyssey* 6.149–52), or, with more than a touch of irony in the *Homeric Hymn*, Anchises to Aphrodite (5.92–99). Achilles goes so far as to use this trope in his response to the embassy in *Iliad* 9, in order to make his refusal of Agamemnon's daughter all the more emphatic. He explains to the embassy that he would not marry her if she were as beautiful as Aphrodite, and as skilled in handiwork as Athena (9.388–91). The goddesses themselves, although not "women," are not immune to this sort of thing, as can be seen from the myth of the Judgment of Paris. For what is more clearly a contest of value than the beauty pageant staged for the benefit of the male gaze?

Aias' bemused response (*Iliad* 9.636–38) to Achilles' refusal of Agamemnon's offer brings things down to earth: why would his friend remain upset over "only one woman" when Agamemnon has offered seven by way of recompense? We find a similar coarseness in Book 1, when Agamemnon expresses his reluctance to return Chryseis to her father: he says that he prefers Chryseis to his own wife Klytemnestra. His comparison of the two women commodifies their attractions and serves to bring Klytemnestra down to the level of an enslaved woman:[11]

καὶ γάρ ῥα Κλυταιμνήστρης προβέβουλα
κουριδίης ἀλόχου, ἐπεὶ οὔ ἑθέν ἐστι χερείων,
οὐ δέμας οὐδὲ φυήν, οὔτ' ἄρ φρένας οὔτέ τι ἔργα.

I prefer her to Klytemnestra,
my own wedded wife, since she is in no way inferior,
neither in form nor stature, nor in intelligence nor handiwork.
(*Iliad* 1.113–15)

When Agamemnon demands a replacement for his *geras* (118–19), and then takes Briseis from Achilles' tent in recompense for the loss of Chryseis, he makes a similar equation, expressing the view that one woman—irrespective of rank or affective relations—is as good as another.

Finally, in a moral rather than an economic equation, women can be compared to animals. Helen repeatedly refers to herself as *kunōpis*, literally "dog-faced," that is, shameless. This brings to mind the long tradition of ancient Greek misogynistic poetry, like the previously discussed poem by Semonides of Amorgos, which catalogues the different types of women and the animals from which they descend.[12]

Women's status as commodities is emphasized by their frequent mention in the same breath with other objects of value. In Book 23 of the *Iliad*, when Achilles prepares for the funeral games of Patroklos, he assembles as prizes cauldrons and tripods, horses, mules and oxen, women, and iron (259–61). These—with the exception of the women—are what Marcel Mauss calls "high-rank gifts."[13] Their relative ranking is established a few lines later, when the prizes for the charioteers are set out: for the winner, a woman skilled in handiwork and a tripod; the runner-up receives an unbroken mare; third prize is a cauldron; fourth, two bars of gold; and fifth, a two-handled bowl.[14]

The figure of Helen in the *Iliad* is commodified to such an extent that she can scarcely be separated from the objects of value that Paris stole along with her from her husband Menelaos' house. Whenever there is an attempt to settle the dispute over Helen by negotiation, it is suggested that she be returned to Menelaos along with his other possessions. Approximately half the relevant passages link "Helen" and *ktēmata* (property) as two roughly analogous items.[15] Here we see that the woman, although she may temporarily rise to agent status, ultimately remains subordinated and objectified, even assimilated to other items in a man's household.

When Agamemnon's men lead the unwilling Briseis from Achilles' tent in Book 1 of the *Iliad*, they are reenacting on a small scale an event central to the experience of war for women in Homeric epic. Achilles, telling his mother of the origins of the dispute with Agamemnon, begins with a matter-of-fact account of a raid culminating in looting and abduction: "We went to Thebe, the sacred city of Eetion, and destroyed it, and brought back all the booty. The sons of the Achaians divided the spoils among themselves, but for the son of Atreus they selected Chryses' fair-cheeked daughter" (1.366–69). In a few short lines, we have the destruction of a city, the carrying off of the spoils, and the distribution of these spoils, in particular the women. For a large-scale enactment of this scenario, we need look no further than the Trojan War itself—a war fought over the abduction of a woman that ends with the entire female population of the city led off at sword-point.

As we know from later sources, the enslavement of women was a common feature of the conquest of cities throughout Greek history. In no other text, however, does this traffic have the structural importance that it bears in the *Iliad*, where the circulation of women underwrites the war against Troy and the interactions of the men who fight that war.[16] This circulation does not end with the arrival of female captives in the Achaian camp. Rather, it continues after the looting ends, as the women are distributed among the bravest heroes as rewards for valor. But this is not the end of the story. Resentment about inequalities in the distribution fester, even before the ransom of Chryseis further destabilizes the situation. As prizes awarded in contests and as gifts offered to make amends, the captive women become a way for Achilles and Agamemnon to express their relationships to one another, and to contest their relative status.[17]

The circulation of women is at the heart of a network of corrupted exchanges throughout the *Iliad* and other accounts of the Trojan War. Richard Seaford has written of a "crisis of reciprocity" in the *Iliad*, and I borrow that phrase here for my own purposes.[18] I find it an apt description of the corrupted exchanges of which I will be speaking, but I differ from Seaford in that I attempt to locate the problematic circulation of women at the heart of this crisis of reciprocity. The crisis has its roots in the abduction of Helen by Paris, an egregious violation of the sacred relationship between guest and host that starts the Trojan War. Within the poem, it manifests itself in Agamemnon's refusal to ransom Chryseis and in the fight between Achilles and Agamemnon over Briseis. In this way, the failure of reciprocity and the traffic in women are bound up together from beginning to end. The treatment of women as movable goods, in which a hero like Achilles engages without a moment's thought (at least until Agamemnon takes his own concubine Briseis), becomes not only a means of communication but also a source of trouble among men. Furthermore, the usual mechanisms for resolving conflicts fail, as ransom is refused, embassies are turned away, and agreements are violated. Ultimately the crisis of reciprocity finds a partial resolution in Book 24 with the ransom of Hektor, but even this will not prevent the death of Achilles, the destruction of Troy, or the enslavement of its female population. It is a resolution that takes place between men only.[19] In a world in which women function predominantly as objects of exchange, it is hard to imagine a resolution that could include them as agents in any meaningful sense.

RANSOMING CHRYSEIS: CRISES OF RECIPROCITY IN THE TROJAN WAR

As we have seen, the traffic in women—or rather a distorted version of it—makes its first appearance in the *Iliad* early in the first book, when the priest Chryses tries unsuccessfully to ransom his daughter. Agamemnon's refusal to return the woman to her father and his hasty reversal in the face of divine retribution—in the form of a plague sweeping through the Achaian camp—sets the stage for the next appropriation of a woman. When forced to return Chryseis to her father, the aggrieved Agamemnon indulges in a disastrous act of negative reciprocity when he takes the captive Briseis from her master Achilles in recompense for his loss.[20] Achilles' subsequent withdrawal from battle is so catastrophic for the Greeks that Agamemnon eventually offers his own daughter in marriage in hopes of calming Achilles' anger, an offer that is refused. In this way, one woman is exchanged, or offered in exchange, for another, as a war begun over the theft of a woman is almost lost over the theft of another.

The struggles over Chryseis and Briseis echo the abduction of Helen that started the war. Moreover, the raids that brought these women to the Greek camp as captives prefigure the fate that awaits Troy and its women. This fate is anticipated by Hektor in speaking with his wife Andromache in Book 6 as he imagines her led off in tears by an armed Achaian, to work the loom in Argos at the commands of a mistress or carry water from foreign springs (6.454–58). He delicately omits the sexual services that captive women could expect to have demanded of them. Later in the poem, Priam foresees a similar future. His prophecy in particular makes clear the humiliation involved in having one's daughters and daughters-in-law dragged off by the enemy (22.59–65).

The connection between women and war operates at a number of levels. A woman is the cause of the war, and her reclamation its stated aim, although the taking of the city quickly replaces this goal. (Even then, the metaphor latent in the use of the word *kredemna* for the towers of Troy, the same word used for a woman's headdress, hints that these two goals are not entirely distinct.[21]) Not only that, but the war can neither begin nor end without the sacrifice of a woman. Agamemnon's daughter Iphigeneia must die at Aulis before the fleet can sail to Troy to fight (Hesiod, *Catalogue of Women* Merkelbach-West 23a, where she is called Iphimede). At the end of the war, Priam's daughter Polyxene must be sacrificed to appease the angry spirit of Achilles before the Achaians can sail safely home. These sacrificed virgins form brackets to the Trojan War, and are mirror images of one another. Polyxene, daughter of the conquered king, can be seen as recompense or counter-gift for the sacrifice of Iphigeneia, daughter of the victorious general. Moreover, their sacrifices are equated with marriage, the more usual means by which women are exchanged. Iphigeneia is brought to Aulis under the pretext of marriage to Achilles, and Polyxene's sacrifice is represented as a kind of marriage in death to the dead hero.[22]

In the world of the *Iliad*, women are the cause of war, the propitiatory victims without which it cannot proceed, the prizes awarded for bravery, and the ultimate aim. On a more mundane level, they are similar to the provisions, such as wine or animals, that are captured along with them by raiding parties. The *Iliad* does not spend much time on women's work, but in a camp full of men, it is useful to have women around to provide food and sex—in short, to tend the bodies of the men who fight the war. When captives are taken back home to Greece, they perform similar duties. Agamemnon, in refusing to return Chryseis to her father, says that she will grow old in Argos, plying the loom and sharing his bed (*Iliad* 1.29–31). The brutality of his reply makes clear the reality that Hektor has glossed over in speaking to his wife of her probable fate.

The sacking of cities and the carrying off of women are prime examples of Sahlins' concept of negative reciprocity, discussed in Chapter One.[23] The three relations of exchange in his schema—generalized, balanced, and negative reciprocity—can easily be related to the activities of Homeric heroes. Generalized reciprocity includes hospitality, generosity, sharing, and other "putatively altruistic transactions," which may be repaid at some future time, and not necessarily by the same exchange partner. The Homeric institution of *xenia*, "guest-friendship," the ritualized and often hereditary relation of reciprocity between host and guest, is a good example of this.[24] Balanced reciprocity, direct exchange without delay or within a finite and narrow period, can be illustrated in the *Iliad* by the practice of ransoming a warrior or his body in exchange for gold or other precious goods (*apoina*). Negative reciprocity, in Sahlins' words, "ranges through various degrees of cunning, guile, stealth, and violence to the finesse of a well-conducted horse raid" (1972, 195)—all activities familiar to the average Greek hero.[25]

Within the *Iliad* are enacted a number of dramas of reciprocity, each centered on the attempt to gain the return of a woman. Yet none of them is successful. Chryses' attempt to ransom his daughter is arrogantly rejected by Agamemnon. Achilles makes no direct move to regain Briseis, but boycotts the fighting to protest Agamemnon's high-handedness. When Agamemnon, attempting to make peace with Achilles, does offer to return Briseis, along with many wonderful gifts, and even to give one of his own daughters in marriage to Achilles, he is angrily refused, and the embassy he sends to make his offer is rebuffed. The Greeks and Trojans negotiate a resolution of the conflict over Helen, arranging a general truce and a trial by duel between Paris and Menelaos. But the gods, with a view to the interests of their mortal protégés, intervene to break the truce, and the fighting resumes. Thus supplication, ransom, embassy, mediation, heralds, negotiation, truces, the settlement of differences by duel—all the customary mechanisms of resolution—fail to restore even one of these women, although each one will eventually be returned by other means.

Although Chryses' bid to ransom his daughter is rejected, this failure of reciprocity on the mortal level is met with a more satisfactory divine response. The priest calls on Apollo: "'If ever I built a temple that pleased you, or if ever I burned upon your altar fat thigh-pieces of bulls or goats, fulfill for me this prayer: let the Danaans pay for my tears with your arrows.' Thus he spoke, praying, and Phoebos Apollo heard him" (1.39–43). The mortal reminds the god of past services to him before asking for a favor, and the god, more mindful of the claims of reciprocity than most mortals, grants the prayer.

The theft of Briseis from Achilles sets in motion a complex chain of obligation. As the son of the goddess Thetis, Achilles does not need to pray to her. Once he has begged his mother for help, she goes to Zeus and grasps his knees and chin, employing the same gesture of supplication used by warriors begging for their lives later in the poem. In the language of prayer, she reminds Zeus of her previous services to him, and on the strength of these she puts forth her request for help for her son (1.503–10).[26]

The involvement of the gods in the case of Helen, as they become principal actors in the Trojan War, unfolds throughout the *Iliad*. Since it can be said that the gods bring about the fall of Troy, their involvement in Helen's return is considerable. The alienation of Helen, Briseis, and Chryseis, the three women whose circulation is so critical to the plot of the *Iliad*, sets in motion elaborate attempts to bring them back that implicate gods as well as mortals in networks of reciprocity and obligation.

Ultimately, each woman is returned. In the case of Briseis, of course, return means only going back to Achilles' tent, since he has killed most of her family (19.291–94) and there is no home to which she can return. The women cannot be ransomed, which is to say that they cannot be returned in exchange for precious metals and gifts. As they were taken away by violence or stealth, they cannot be restored by balanced reciprocity. (The *Iliad* mentions only one ransom of a woman—Andromache's mother—at 6.427.) Instead, they are returned only after the deaths of many men—Chryseis after a plague devastates the Achaian camp, and Briseis after scores of Greeks die in battle without Achilles to spur them on. What is more, they are returned, not in exchange for anything, but "with interest"—splendid hecatombs for the god Apollo, the countless gifts that Agamemnon offers as "amends." The interest on Helen is even more costly, and consists of the wealth and the women of Troy, not to mention the lives of its men.

The failure of the institutions of mediation in the cases of all three women mirrors a progressive breakdown of the practice of ransoming captive warriors throughout the poem. Everyone remembers the "old days" when a hard-pressed warrior could save his life by offering ransom. In fact, the good old days seem to have ended scarcely more than a week and a half before. Achilles himself alludes to the practice at *Iliad* 2.229–30, speaking of the gold that might be paid as ransom by a Trojan for his son. But when in Book 21 Lykaon begs for his life and reminds Achilles that he once before sold him into slavery, thereby allowing Lykaon to ransom himself, Achilles is no longer amenable.[27] Very little time has passed: Lykaon has been back in Troy a mere twelve days before finding himself once again in the clutches of Achilles; but since the death of Patroklos, Achilles plays by different rules. He is not, however, the only one to refuse supplication on the battlefield. As early as Book 6 (lines 55–60), Agamemnon stops Menelaos from accepting ransom from Adrastos, and he adheres to this practice throughout, although we know that it was previously his practice to accept such offers. As Donna Wilson (2002) has pointed out, all attempts at ransom fail during the dramatic time of the poem, from Chryses' appeal to Agamemnon until Priam's successful appeal to Achilles in Book 24.

Apoina may be given in exchange for freedom, in exchange for a life, or, more grimly, to redeem the corpse. In the course of the poem, the meaning shifts. By the time Achilles and Hektor meet in battle, there is no question that it is a fight to the death. In this context, it is no surprise that Hektor begs only for his body to be ransomed, and that Achilles refuses.

The verb most commonly used in the sense "to ransom" is *luō*.[28] A survey of the uses of this verb allows us to track the progressive crisis in the practice. In Book 1, where the word is used only in connection with Chryseis, it appears first in the future (*lusomenos*, 13), then in the mood of wished-for but unfulfilled events, the optative (*lusaite*, 20), as the old man makes his case, and then in the negative indicative (*ou lusō*, 29) as Agamemnon refuses. The true resolution of the episode is foreseen by the prophet Kalchas, who announces that in the end she will have to be returned "unbought and unransomed" (*apriatēn anapoinon*, 99). From then until the very end, all uses in the indicative are in the past, describing events that will not be repeated, or in the future of wishful thinking describing ransoms that will never occur (in one instance because the men in question are already dead).[29]

This does not change until another father approaches his enemy at the end of the poem, this time not to ransom a beloved child, but only to reclaim his body. At 24.501–2, Priam tells Achilles that he has come to ransom his son: "For his sake I have come to the ships of the Achaians to win him back from you, and I bear ransom past counting." Line 502, beginning with the same future participle *lusomenos*, echoes line 13 of Book 1, where Chryses makes his futile attempt to ransom his daughter: "He came to the swift ships of the Achaians to ransom (*lusomenos*) his daughter, bearing ransom past counting." This time, however, the attempt will be successful. This is eventually confirmed by Hermes when he comes to rouse Priam and take him out of the enemy camp: "You have ransomed (*elusao*) your son, and you gave a great price" (24.685). This is the final use of the word in the poem, and here it appears without markers of wish or negation, but rather in the aorist indicative, a *fait accompli*. It is not exactly the last word on the subject, however. Hermes goes on to warn Priam that if Agamemnon finds out he is there, his sons will have to pay triple *apoina* to free him again, thus overturning the natural order of things, in which fathers ransom sons.[30]

In the crisis of institutions of reciprocity and mediation, interactions are subject to more than one interpretation, even by those engaged in them. A prime example is the exchange of armor by Glaukos and Diomedes. Although it looks like balanced reciprocity, an exchange of armor for armor, it certainly is not successful as such. The poet informs us: "Zeus must have taken away his wits, for he traded gold armor for bronze" (6.234). There seems to be a discrepancy in the two actors' estimations of the transaction. Glaukos at least is acting according to the generalized reciprocity of guest-friends. The poet tells us that Diomedes has won, but according to the traditions of gift-exchange, Glaukos is the clear winner, for by his greater generosity he has put his partner under obligation to him. The poem suggests instead that Diomedes engages in sharp practice, getting more than his share, a form of negative reciprocity, and is thereby the cleverer one.[31]

This is not the only time in the history of the Trojan War that different kinds of reciprocity collide with or shade into one another. Throughout the poem, there are encounters between two parties who have different ideas about the rules. This happens at times among the Achaians, and particularly between Achilles and Agamemnon, but it is even more common in encounters between Greeks and Trojans—Chryses and Agamemnon, Glaukos and Diomedes, the various warriors begging for mercy, and especially Hektor pleading with Achilles to ransom his body. The same dynamic also occurs in the episode of the Trojan horse told in the *Iliou Persis* (and the *Ilias Parva*), when the Trojans assume that the Greeks have left behind a true gift for them, instead of a treacherous one.

Balanced reciprocity fails throughout the *Iliad*, until the end, with the ransom of Hektor's body. Even then, it does not last long but quickly turns into generalized reciprocity in the form of *xenia*, as Achilles and Priam sit down to a meal together. This instance of *xenia* is far from ideal. Each side engages in a breach of etiquette, as Priam (who hasn't realized that the script is one of *xenia*, since he is enacting one of *apoina*) attempts to leave without eating. Achilles' breach is even worse, detaining a guest against his will (and, what is more, with the threat of violence). But paradoxically, it is only his insistence that Priam stay and eat with him that transforms Priam, however briefly, into Achilles' guest, creating a fragile and transient relationship of *xenia* between them. We might wish to recall that although there is a history of negative reciprocity between Trojans and Achaians as peoples, there is none between Priam and Achilles. Achilles makes this point in refusing to fight: "The Trojans never stole my cattle or horses" (1.154). Since he was not one of Helen's suitors, he had no part in the pact to protect her, and was therefore also not a direct party to the injury inflicted by her abduction by Paris. It is only once the Trojans "steal" from him his dear friend Patroklos that he can once more be mobilized against them.

This celebration of reciprocity must be tempered by two considerations. First, the meal takes place almost literally over the body of Priam's son. Moreover, the old man shares a meal with his son's killer only under threat of violence. The violence on which this scene is predicated is somewhat softened by the brief moment of sympathy that the two men achieve, as the aged Priam reminds Achilles of his own father. Nonetheless, it would be too much to insist on the transcendence of generalized, or "positive," reciprocity at the end of the *Iliad*. After all, the war is not over, and soon Achilles will lead the charge once more against Priam's city. The restoration of reciprocity is temporary. But in narrative terms, we have come full circle from the negative reciprocity of the beginning to an act of *xenia*, however compromised, at the end.

A look beyond the limits of the *Iliad* reminds us that the Trojan War is caused in part by the action of two treacherous divine gifts. The first, recounted by Apollodoros and possibly a late accretion, is the apple, inscribed "to the Fairest," brought by the uninvited guest Eris (Strife or Discord) to the wedding of Peleus and Thetis.[32] The second is Helen, offered as a gift by Aphrodite to Paris in exchange for his awarding her the prize for beauty. Since Helen is already married, this gift is not unencumbered but must be taken by guile. Paris violates the hospitality of Menelaos in order to claim his gift, and the Trojan War is set in motion. Thus we have two offenses against hospitality and (one or) two deadly gifts as part of the background to the war. At the end of the *Iliad*, these offenses against *xenia* are briefly resolved by the meal shared by Priam and Achilles before the hostilities and the treacheries resume. But ultimately Troy will be taken by the exercise of another ruse—the deployment of a final treacherous gift, the Trojan horse.

With the fall of Troy, the traffic in women is renewed. To follow the path of only one woman: Kassandra is raped in Athena's temple by Lokrian Aias, son of Oileus, who drags her away from the image of the goddess. To expiate this sacrilege, the Lokrians were still sending two young girls every year to serve in the temple in historical times.[33] Kassandra is later taken home as Agamemnon's spear-prize, and is killed along with him by his wife Klytemnestra, who according to some versions is motivated to murder her husband in part by jealousy over his arrival with a concubine.[34] In this way, the fall of Troy brings the traffic in women home to Greece, with disastrous consequences.

GOOD GIFTS AND BAD FAITH: THE FIRST SACK OF TROY

The equation between war and the traffic in women at Troy predates—in narrative terms if not historically—the war with the Achaians. An episode from the first sack of Troy, which we know mainly from extra-Homeric traditions, replays the issues of negative reciprocity and its reconciliation. It also hints at the possibility of female agency. The *Iliad* alludes to the episode, brought about by the doubly manifest bad faith of King Laomedon, Priam's father and predecessor (5.638–42; 21.442–57); an account of the sack is found in Apollodoros (2.6.4).

This earlier sack of Troy occurred when Laomedon reneged not once but twice on his promises, with fatal results.[35] When Apollo and Poseidon built a wall around Troy, Laomedon refused them the agreed-upon wage, and threatened them with mutilation and enslavement. Poseidon retaliated by sending a sea monster to ravage the land. An oracle decreed that the king's daughter Hesione be sacrificed to placate the monster. In exchange for the rescue of his daughter, Laomedon offered Herakles immortal horses that had been given by Zeus in recompense for the abduction of Ganymede. The king, as was his habit, fulfilled the bargain dishonestly by giving him mortal horses instead. Herakles, as was *his* habit, came back with an army and wrecked the city. Or as Homer puts it, he "stormed Ilion and widowed the streets" (*Iliou exalapaxe polin, chērōse d' aguias*, 5.642). After the sack of the city, Herakles gave Hesione to his comrade-in-arms Telamon. She was allowed to choose one from among the captured Trojans to go free. She chose her brother Podarkes and ransomed him with her shawl (*kaluptra*; Apollodoros 2.6.4). He was henceforth known as Priamos, the ransomed one. As Anderson puts it, "Two corrupt transactions are here succeeded by an honest sale."[36]

Let us return briefly to the horses that Laomedon promised to Herakles. Zeus had originally given them as compensation (poinē, *Iliad* 5.266) to Ganymede's grieving father, Tros, the uncle of Laomedon. By giving them, Zeus tries to turn the rape of Ganymede into an even exchange, an example not of negative but of balanced reciprocity. But this is something not even Zeus can accomplish, for the horses continue to attract negative reciprocity. Not only does Laomedon renege on his promise to give the horses to Herakles as a reward for rescuing his daughter, but it is recounted that Aeneas' horses are descended from those of his father Anchises, who "stole a breed" from the horses of Laomedon by introducing his mares to them in secret (*Iliad* 5.268-72). The spirit of negative reciprocity seems to cling to these horses, recalling the act of negative reciprocity—the rape of Ganymede—that first led to their arrival in Troy.

This episode contains many elements seen in the *Iliad*—the sacking of cities associated with the capture and distribution of women, the negative reciprocity on the part of Laomedon eventually resolved by the "positive" reciprocity first enacted by Herakles and Telemon, and then, in a new development, by a woman—Hesione. For it is in the transition from object of exchange to economic actor, when she ransoms her brother, that the figure of Hesione hints at the possibility of female agency in exchange that will be so fully developed in the *Odyssey*. If the theme of negative reciprocity at Troy finds its resolution in the treacherous gift—the wooden horse that allows the Achaians to capture Troy—the problem of *xenia* (along with those of women and exchange) will require another poem to work out its dilemmas.

CHAPTER FOUR

WOMEN *and* EXCHANGE *in the* ODYSSEY: *From* GIFTS *to* GIVERS

As has often been observed, the *Odyssey* rewrites the *Iliad*, and never more than in its treatment of women. The later poem consistently calls our attention to the ways in which the earlier poem ignores or elides the work of women. That the *Iliad* describes an exclusively male world to a far greater extent than does the *Odyssey* cannot be disputed. Even allowing for this difference, however, given the number of captive women in the Greek camp it is striking how rarely any of them is shown at work. At the same time, the value of a woman is consistently defined in terms of her skill, mostly at handiwork.[1] The *Iliad* ascribes value to women on the basis of the work they know how to do, but the *Odyssey* shows women actually doing it, and even exchanging the products of their labor.[2]

The *Odyssey* presents us with a far more expansive picture of the social and economic roles of women than Hesiod, or even the *Iliad*. In so saying, I do not want to be misunderstood as positing a historical development. Although I accept the common assumption that the *Odyssey* was written down somewhat later than the *Iliad*, this is ultimately unverifiable. Moreover, I see no reason to regard the *Odyssey* as representing a tradition or period so far removed from that of the *Iliad* as to allow time for significant change in the status of women. Rather, it is the difference in the setting of the two epics that accounts for much of the difference in subject matter. Baldly put, the *Iliad* concerns itself with activities that are culturally defined as male, while the peacetime world of the *Odyssey* provides greater scope for the activities, and the agency, of women.

In the *Odyssey*, women's economic contributions are clear: female slaves are shown doing the work of the household, and even goddesses work at the loom. At the same time, the notion of women as objects of exchange or pieces of property so common in the *Iliad* is by no means foreign to this poem. Women are acquired by purchase, like Eurykleia, bought by Laertes for twenty oxen (1.430–31), or by capture, like Eurymedousa, given to Alkinoos from the spoils of her city (7.8–11). Meanwhile, the critical question of the potential exchange-value of Penelope is allowed to hang in the balance throughout the poem. The frequently repeated suggestion that she will go to whoever offers the best gifts obscures the complicated and ambiguous nature of the economic transaction being contemplated. It is unclear whether the decision is hers (or her son's) to make or whether her father will be responsible for giving her away again. It is similarly unclear whether the successful suitor can expect to receive not only Penelope but also the riches of Odysseus' household, which by rights should go to her son Telemachos.[3]

In stark contrast to the *Iliad*, however, the *Odyssey* represents women not only as objects, but also as participants in gift-exchange. Here we find an interesting dichotomy between foreground and background. In the body of the narrative, women like Arete and Helen give gifts to no ill effect.[4] But the *Odyssey* also makes explicit for the first time the notion that women and gifts are a combination deadly to men. Employing a rhetoric of ambivalence that so often attends the discussion of women, the poem contains several almost parenthetical allusions to women's treachery, inserted into the narrative as cautionary exempla. These brief narratives are twice signaled by mention of the dangers of "womanly gifts" (*gunaia dōra*), an ambiguous phrase to which I will return.[5] The association of women, gifts, and danger first suggested here will be played out in full in tragic drama, but to make sense of it, we will first need to consider how the gender of both persons and objects shapes the protocols of exchange.

First, let us briefly consider some unmarked gift-exchanges, some of the few that take place between women. When Telemachos visits Helen and Menelaos in *Odyssey* 4, Helen is the very picture of domesticity with her silver wool basket and gold distaff, which she received from the Egyptian woman Alkandre. The description of the gifts to Helen is motivated by the setting of the scene, but we are also, somewhat gratuitously, told of the gifts given by Alkandre's husband to Menelaos. Like the gifts to be given to Telemachos a few lines later, these are also presented in gendered opposition:

> Φυλώ δ' ἀργύρεον τάλαρον φέρε, τόν οἱ ἔθηκεν
> Ἀλκάνδρη, Πολύβοιο δάμαρ, ὃς ἔναι' ἐνὶ Θήβης
> Αἰγυπτίης, ὅθι πλεῖστα δόμοις ἐν κτήματα κεῖται·
> ὃς Μενελάῳ δῶκε δύ' ἀργυρέας ἀσαμίνθους,
> δοιοὺς δὲ τρίποδας, δέκα δὲ χρυσοῖο τάλαντα.
> χωρὶς δ' αὖ Ἑλένη ἄλοχος πόρε κάλλιμα δῶρα·
> χρυσέην τ' ἠλακάτην τάλαρόν θ' ὑπόκυκλον ὄπασσεν
> ἀργύρεον, χρυσῷ δ' ἐπὶ χείλεα κεκράαντο.

Phylo brought a silver basket, a gift from Alkandre
the wife of Polybus who rules in Egyptian Thebes,
where the greatest wealth is laid up in the houses;
Polybus gave Menelaos two silver basins
and two tripods and ten talents of gold.
Apart from these, his wife gave Helen beautiful gifts:
a golden distaff and a silver basket on wheels with a golden rim.
(*Od.* 4.125–32)

Here we notice that all the gifts are made of worked precious metals, aside from the gold talents, which are presumably unworked metal. What distinguishes the gifts to Menelaos from those to Helen is that the woman's gifts are related to textile-working—a distaff and a basket to hold the spun yarn. This is an interesting variation on the theme of male and female wealth: although according to the schema for which I argue, no danger attaches to exchanges even of metal objects between women, these metal objects are clearly marked as related to the production of female textile wealth and therefore are doubly "safe." As François Lissarrague notes, containers such as chests, caskets, and baskets on Greek vases indicate women's "role in managing material goods of the oikos and in domestic production, especially wool working. All these objects are almost exclusively branded as female, and the male is rarely part of this picture."[6]

There is one other gift that Helen was given in Egypt, however, and it is of a very different order.[7] This is a painkilling drug given her by the Egyptian Polydamna. The drug is introduced in the following terms:

ἔνθ' αὖτ' ἄλλ' ἐνόησ' Ἑλένη Διὸς ἐκγεγαυῖα·
αὐτίκ' ἄρ' ἐς οἶνον βάλε φάρμακον, ἔνθεν ἔπινον,
νηπενθές τ' ἄχολόν τε, κακῶν ἐπίληθον ἁπάντων.
. . . τοῖα Διὸς θυγάτηρ ἔχε φάρμακα μητιόεντα,
ἐσθλά, τά οἱ Πολύδαμνα πόρεν, Θῶνος παράκοιτις,
Αἰγυπτίη. . . .

Then Helen, born of Zeus, had a thought,
and at once put into the wine they were drinking
a drug to banish pain and anger, and make one forget all evils. . . .
Such clever and excellent drugs did Zeus' daughter have,
which Egyptian Polydamna, the wife of Thon, had given her.
(*Od.* 4.219–21, 227–29)

This gift is extraordinary for many reasons. First, as a *pharmakon* it is an object of great ambivalence.[8] A *pharmakon* may be, and is in fact more likely to be, a poison rather than a beneficial substance. Confusion about the nature of *pharmaka* underwrites many a tragic denouement. In Sophocles' *Trachiniai*, as discussed in Chapter Five, Deianeira's failure to recognize the deadly nature of the centaur Nessos' "gift" brings on the destruction of both husband and wife. As I argue there, this gift from male to female is marked in any number of ways as forbidden and dangerous. The nurse in Euripides' *Hippolytos* creates a deliberate ambiguity about the nature of the *pharmakon* she offers Phaidra as a "cure" for her disastrous passion for her stepson, allowing Phaidra to convince herself that it is a substance that will act beneficially on her. What the nurse offers is not a physical substance at all, but an ill-advised plan whose disastrous outcome is predictable, given the ambivalence with which *pharmaka* were regarded in Greek culture.

That Helen has received the substance from another woman is, however, less than remarkable, for women were generally considered experts in love potions, abortifacients, and other questionable substances.[9] Although there are few analogues in Homeric epic, there is one example of a male receiving a dangerous substance from another male. According to Athena, disguised as Mentor in *Odyssey* 1.259–65, Odysseus attempted to obtain poison (literally, a "man-killing drug," *pharmakon androphonon*) for his arrows from Ilos, who refused him, fearing the wrath of the gods:

> οἴχετο γὰρ καὶ κεῖσε θοῆς ἐπὶ νηὸς Ὀδυσσεὺς
> <u>φάρμακον ἀνδροφόνον</u> διζήμενος, ὄφρα οἱ εἴη
> ἰοὺς χρίεσθαι χαλκήρεας· ἀλλ' ὁ μὲν οὔ οἱ
> δῶκεν, ἐπεί ῥα θεοὺς νεμεσίζετο αἰὲν ἐόντας,
> ἀλλὰ πατήρ οἱ δῶκεν ἐμός.

> Odysseus went there on his swift ship
> seeking a murderous poison, so that he
> might smear it on his bronze-tipped arrows: but
> he did not give it to him, fearing the anger of the
> ever-living gods. But my father gave it to him.
> (*Od.* 1.260–64)

This story, while conveying a cultural distaste for *pharmaka*, is complexly distanced from the main narrative. Although it harmonizes with the tricky nature of Odysseus, it is unclear whether Athena is telling of some true incident or merely telling "lies that are like to the truth."

Helen's *pharmakon* seems to be entirely positive, until one considers the implications, fully spelled out in the lines I omitted from this scene above:

ὃς τὸ καταβρόξειεν, ἐπεὶ κρητῆρι μιγείη,
οὔ κεν ἐφημέριός γε βάλοι κατὰ δάκρυ παρειῶν,
οὐδ' εἴ οἱ κατατεθναίη μήτηρ τε πατήρ τε,
οὐδ' εἴ οἱ προπάροιθεν ἀδελφεὸν ἢ φίλον υἱὸν
χαλκῷ δηϊόῳεν, ὁ δ' ὀφθαλμοῖσιν ὁρῷτο.

Whoever drank once it was mixed in the wine bowl
could not that day drop tears down his cheeks,
not even if his mother or father should die,
nor if he saw his brother or his own dear son
run through by the sword right in front of him.
(*Od.* 4.222–26)

Since it is capable of preventing one from feeling an entirely appropriate grief at the loss of a close relative, perhaps we are meant to feel some ambivalence about the nature of Helen's "good drug."[10] What is more, one cannot help wondering if frequent doses of the *pharmakon nēpenthes* are required by both husband and wife to endure what must be a rather complicated marital situation.

THE DANGER OF "WOMANLY GIFTS"

In the *Odyssey*, the potential treachery of women in exchange relations is signaled in several passing allusions, which do not tally with the exchange activities of the female characters in body of the poem. In this way, the poem allows women entry into the network of exchange relations, but not without expressing a certain anxiety about their role. The sign of this anxiety is a phrase that appears twice, once to introduce Astyoche's betrayal of her son for a golden vine (*Od.* 11.521), and a second time to explain the treachery of Eriphyle, who betrayed her husband for a golden necklace (*Od.* 15.247), in each case by sending them off to war and certain death.

ἥρω' Εὐρύπυλον· πολλοὶ δ' ἀμφ' αὐτὸν ἑταῖροι
Κήτειοι κτείνοντο <u>γυναίων εἵνεκα δώρων</u>

The hero Eurypylos and many of his companions,
the Keteians, were slain around him, because of *womanly gifts*.
(*Od.* 11.520–21)

λαοσσόον Ἀμφιάραον,
ὃν περὶ κῆρι φίλει Ζεύς τ' αἰγίοχος καὶ Ἀπόλλων

παντοίην φιλότητ᾽· οὐδ᾽ ἵκετο γήραος οὐδόν,
ἀλλ᾽ ὄλετ᾽ ἐν Θήβῃσι <u>γυναίων εἵνεκα δώρων</u>.

Amphiaraos, whom aigis-bearing Zeus and Apollo loved in their hearts
with every sort of love: he did not reach the threshold of old age,
but perished in Thebes because of *womanly gifts*.
(*Od.* 15.244–47)

The phrase *gunaiōn heineka dōrōn* is difficult to translate, due to a linguistic ambiguity that makes the direction of the gifts unclear. It can mean on account of "a woman's gifts," "gifts to a woman," or "womanly gifts." Although there is no distinction between active and passive—womanly gifts could be presents from a woman—these particular gifts are eagerly received by faithless women who barter away the lives of sons or husbands in exchange. Robert Fitzgerald's translation spells it out: "A woman, bought by trinkets, gave him over to be cut down in the assault on Thebes." As with Pandora, a misogynist tradition predetermines the reading of ambiguous phrases as passive rather than active, casting women not as givers, but as receivers, in both instances to the detriment of men.[11]

The golden vine by which Astyoche was induced to send her son Eurypalos off to fight at Troy was in origin another divine gift. According to the *Little Iliad*, this vine, made by none other than Hephaistos, was given to Laomedon by Zeus in recompense for his abduction of his son Ganymede. It then passed to Priam, who sent it to Laomedon's daughter Astyoche.[12] The golden vine is twice called upon to induce a parent to part with a son.[13] Laomedon is not judged for accepting the gift, perhaps because it is after the fact, or because a mortal is powerless against the desires of the gods; but in the *Odyssey* aside in Book 11, the mother's acceptance of the gift is clearly interpreted as sinister. The phrase is echoed in Book 15, where Eriphyle's treachery is discussed in the same terms: *gunaiōn heneka dōrōn*. The myth of Eriphyle as a stereotypical bad woman seems to have had more currency than that of Astyoche.[14] At *Odyssey* 11.326–27, she is "hateful Eriphyle, who took precious gold in exchange for her dear husband['s life]" (*stugerēn t' Eriphulēn, / hē chruson philou andros edexato timēenta*).

The passive meaning here is dictated by the myths to which the Homeric passages allude, but we shall soon see equally problematic examples in which the woman is the giver. The inherent ambiguity of the phrase points in the end to the dangerous conjunction of gifts and woman, independent of the direction of the exchange. Not all exchanges with women are deadly, but there is danger particularly whenever the type and context of the gift deviate from that prescribed by custom.

A scene in Book 15 of the *Odyssey*, in which Helen and Menelaos select guest-gifts for Telemachos, neatly illustrates the complementarity of textiles and metals:

ἀλλ' ὅτε δή ῥ' ἵκανον ὅθι κειμήλια κεῖτο,
Ἀτρεΐδης μὲν ἔπειτα δέπας λάβεν ἀμφικύπελλον,
υἱὸν δὲ κρητῆρα φέρειν Μεγαπένθε' ἄνωγεν
ἀργύρεον· Ἑλένη δὲ παρίστατο φωριαμοῖσιν,
ἔνθ' ἔσαν οἱ πέπλοι παμποίκιλοι, οὓς κάμεν αὐτή.
τῶν ἕν' ἀειραμένη Ἑλένη φέρε, δῖα γυναικῶν,
ὃς κάλλιστος ἔην ποικίλμασιν ἠδὲ μέγιστος,
ἀστὴρ δ' ὣς ἀπέλαμπεν· ἔκειτο δὲ νείατος ἄλλων.

But when they came to the place where the treasure was stored,
the son of Atreus took a two-handled cup
and told his son Megapenthes to take a mixing bowl
of silver. Helen went to the chests, which held
beautifully adorned robes that she herself had made.
And choosing from among them, Helen, brightest of women,
picked the most beautifully adorned and largest.
It shone like a star from the bottom of the pile.
(*Od.* 15.101–8)

Helen's gift of a *peplos* is the parallel to the metal gifts given by her husband and stepson.[15] As Scheid-Tissinier (1994: 167) has noted, in telling Telemachos to entrust it to his mother until he marries, Helen foresees a future for the *peplos* as an object of transmission from woman to woman. It will be a treasure (*keimēlion*), lying (*keisthai*) in a chest until the day when it will once again serve as a gift (*dōron*), and what is more, a gift given in the context of marriage:

Ἑλένη δὲ παρίστατο καλλιπάρῃος
πέπλον ἔχους' ἐν χερσίν, ἔπος τ' ἔφατ' ἔκ τ' ὀνόμαζε·
"δῶρόν τοι καὶ ἐγώ, τέκνον φίλε, τοῦτο δίδωμι,
μνῆμ' Ἑλένης χειρῶν, πολυηράτου ἐς γάμου ὥρην,
σῇ ἀλόχῳ φορέειν· τῆος δὲ φίλῃ παρὰ μητρὶ
κεῖσθαι ἐνὶ μεγάρῳ. σὺ δέ μοι χαίρων ἀφίκοιο
οἶκον ἐϋκτίμενον καὶ σὴν ἐς πατρίδα γαῖαν."

Beautiful Helen approached with the robe
in her hands. She addressed him [Telemachos] with these words:

"I, too, give you this as a gift, dear child,
a remembrance of the hands of Helen, for your wife to wear
on your much-desired wedding day. Until then, let it lie
in the hall in the care of your mother. And I wish you
a happy return to your well-built house and native land.
(*Od.* 15.123–29)

There is an asymmetry here, however. In Chapter One, I discussed the relationship between what one makes and what one may give. Although Helen has made the *peplos* at home on her own loom, no one would imagine that Menelaos had taken up metalworking in his spare time. Objects like the two-handled cup, as we learn a few lines later, are the work of specialists—in this case, the most special of all specialists, the metalworking god Hephaistos. We also learn that it was a gift from the king of the Sidonians, which gives it a pedigree, and places it within an economy of guest-friendship rather than simple trade.

Moreover, in this poem in which reciprocity and exchange relations are a major concern, the exchange of and by women is much more complicated. Women are still exchanged—the family retainer Eurykleia was bought by Odysseus' father for twenty oxen (1.431), and the proposed remarriage of Penelope is clearly presented as an economic undertaking. Nonetheless, what is most striking is that this is a world in which women become economic actors. As Odysseus moves through a landscape peopled to a surprising degree by women and female divinities, he must enter into complicated relations of exchange with them. One might almost say that he must constantly exchange one guest-relationship for another, and the partners with whom he engages are mostly female: the nymph Kalypso; the sea-goddess Ino-Leukothea; the princess Nausikaa; her mother, Queen Arete; his patron goddess Athena; and finally, his redoubtable wife Penelope.

This preponderance of female figures encountered by Odysseus is one of the most commented-upon aspects of the poem. Here I wish to highlight the ways in which exchange structures these relationships. The pattern of exchange of clothing in the *Odyssey* has been recognized by Elizabeth Block (1985). I would like, building on her work, to stress the gendered aspects of this pattern. In Book 5, in danger of drowning, Odysseus must put off the cloak given him by Kalypso before he left her island. Although she offers him immortal life and eternal youth to stay, when the gods command her to release him, she gives him aid for the trip home, apparently in return for the companionship he has given her. But weighed down in the stormy sea by her heavy cloak, he must now throw it off and put on the protective veil (*krēdemnon*) given by the goddess Ino. He then discards this veil as well, as the goddess ordered him to do, before landing naked on the island of the Phaiakians, where he will receive clothing from the young princess Nausikaa and hospitality from her parents. The narrative emphasizes the importance of the hospitality of the queen Arete, who recognizes her own linens on the body of the hero. All of these relations are marked by gifts of clothing, the most characteristic of women's gifts. Since the poet of the *Odyssey* shows women actively engaging in "good" exchange relations, it is perhaps not surprising that textiles are most often the medium of exchange, since this seems to be the one commodity that women themselves produce, and therefore the one they can most safely and respectably give away.

If this is exchange, what does Odysseus offer in return? Although gifts of hospitality do not require immediate repayment, Odysseus most often reciprocates with a story—his own or some elaboration of his own—which is often welcomed as eagerly as a song by a famous bard. Indeed, Odysseus' enactment of the role of the poet has been noticed; his fondness for this particular kind of exchange is made into something of a joke in Book 14 (459ff.), where while in disguise he tells a tale in which "Odysseus" (i.e., not the speaker) comes up with a clever stratagem for getting himself (i.e., Odysseus taking on a fictive persona) a cloak. This tale has the desired effect of inspiring Eumaios to give up his own cloak.

In his dealings with the goddess Athena, Odysseus offers his wit, and she revels in their like-mindedness. She also offers clothing (16.173) and cleans up the hero in order to make him presentable (6.229ff.). In so doing, she turns him into a marriageable commodity, but also, explicitly in the first of these passages, into a work of art:

> ὡς δ᾽ ὅτε τις χρυσὸν περιχεύεται ἀργύρῳ ἀνὴρ
> ἴδρις, ὃν Ἥφαιστος δέδαεν καὶ Παλλὰς Ἀθήνη
> τέχνην παντοίην, χαρίεντα δὲ ἔργα τελείει,
> ὡς ἄρα τῷ κατέχευε χάριν κεφαλῇ τε καὶ ὤμοις.

> As when a clever craftsman pouring gold onto silver,
> a man to whom Hephaistos and Pallas Athena
> have given all manner of skill, completes his graceful work,
> just so did she pour grace over his head and shoulders.
> (*Od.* 6.232–35)

The constitution or representation of a human being, a mortal, as a work of art has its most striking parallel in the creation of the first woman (Pandora). The feminized world in which Odysseus moves leads perhaps finally to this, that Odysseus himself is fetishized, transformed into a desirable partner, like a woman, or more specifically, a bride.

The first sign of this fetishization occurs in the land of the Phaiakians, where both Athena and Odysseus exploit the ambiguity of Odysseus' encounter with the marriageable Nausikaa. Later, the same maneuvers are necessary to turn Odysseus back into a suitable bridegroom for Penelope. Penelope's care of the "stranger" also centers on care of the body and clothing. Of course, her own connection with clothing is established early on, with the story of the subterfuge of the loom.

Unlike the prototypical woman (Pandora) who lets the evils out of their jar, and implicitly squanders the household goods, Penelope is the paradigmatically faithful wife. Her role in the house is expressed in terms of keeping everything safe. At *Odyssey* 11.178–79, Odysseus in the Underworld asks his mother whether Penelope remains safe with their son and keeps his things safe, or whether she has already married "the best of the Achaians." Penelope herself repeats this formulation at 19.525–27, where she describes herself as "keeping everything (i.e., the household goods) safe" *(empeda panta phulassō)* and "honoring the marital bed" *(eunēn t' aidomenē posios)*. Fidelity to a husband implies keeping his possessions in order, neither giving them away, like Aerope, nor allowing them to be stolen, like Helen, nor accepting gifts from another, like Eriphyle. The good wife neither accepts gifts where she should not, nor gives away what must be kept. The good wife knows that she must not open the jar. Not for nothing is Penelope's frequent epithet *periphrōn* (wise, prudent).[16]

The narrative of the *Odyssey*, however, allows for the possibility that Penelope will not turn out to be a faithful wife, and it does so through a scene of gift-giving. In Book 18, Athena inspires Penelope to show herself to the suitors who are besieging her in her husband's absence (18.158–62). It is Athena's plan that this will increase her prestige with her son and husband, presumably by provoking competitive gift-giving among the suitors, a motive that is not, however, assigned to Penelope herself. Although Odysseus (18.281–83) interprets this action as a sign of his wife's cleverness, and rejoices to see his household's wealth replenished, there is something about it that has made critics uneasy, as Marilyn Katz has shown.[17] The gifts that Penelope receives from the suitors are precisely the wrong kind—gifts of metal, of jewelry, gifts of the kind that cause women to betray their men. There is a robe with golden clasps, and even worse, a chain with amber beads, earrings, and a necklace. Who could hear this and not think of Eriphyle? Katz as well as Zeitlin have shown how Penelope's actions play out different narrative possibilities, dramatizing the ambiguity presented by the figure of Helen back at home with Menelaos in Sparta.[18] A question is allowed to form in the minds of the audience: Is Penelope really going to turn out to be the good wife?

A similar sort of unease is aroused by Helen's gift of cloth to Telemachos in Book 4, but for the opposite reasons. There, a reformed "bad" wife gives a good womanly gift, whereas Penelope is a "good" wife receiving "bad" gifts. If the characterization in terms of good and bad sounds simplistic, that is precisely my point. The *Odyssey* repeatedly examines models of women and gift-exchange, playing out the anxieties apparent in misogynistic fears of womanly gifts (*gunaia dōra*), while at the same time allowing women an important role in networks of exchange.[19]

Throughout the *Odyssey*, there is the hint that with marriage to Penelope goes rule over Ithaka. This puzzling notion has given rise to a range of theories. Finkelberg (1991) argues that patterns of heroic succession in Greek myth reflect an earlier practice of at least partial matriliny. Atchity and Barber (1987) argue for an Aegean tradition of matriliny, displaced by the patriliny of the Greeks. For them, this explains the ambiguity of Penelope's situation, poised between the old and new patterns of succession. Westbrook (2005) argues instead that kingship on Ithaka was part of the dowry given Penelope by Ikarios, and could thus be expected to devolve upon any future husband of hers. Any of these theories would explain the care with which Odysseus approaches his homecoming.

The fragility of a man's grasp of his kingdom if his wife is unfaithful becomes even clearer from the Homeric passages describing the murder of Agamemnon (*Od.* 3.263–72). When he leaves for Troy, Agamemnon puts his wife in the care of a bard. At first she resists, for she is virtuous (*phresi gar kechrēt' agathēsi*), and Aigisthos is able to seduce her only after marooning the unfortunate poet on an island. The formerly virtuous wife is not able to hold out for long, and Aigisthos "willingly, led her willing home" (*tēn d' ethelōn ethelousan anēgagen onde domonde*, 3.272). Agamemnon's murder is then a logical conclusion, so much so that it is held up more than once as the paradigm for Odysseus, the reason for all his caution on his return to Ithaka. The Homeric account of Agamemnon's murder focuses on the transfer of a woman from one man to another, while Klytemnestra is barely implicated in the murder. The episode can be read, nonetheless, within the context of exchange. No less than Astyoche or Eriphyle, Klytemnestra engages in a fatal exchange: by bestowing her own person inappropriately, she is as responsible as they for the deaths of men close to them. Moreover, she, in re-enacting the deed of Atreus' wife Aerope in the next generation, effects a transfer of power from her husband to another man, even though in this case there is no magic talisman, no golden lamb, to signify the transmission of sovereignty.

As we will see in the next chapter, Aeschylus' version puts Klytemnestra at the center of these events, fully exploiting the codes of male and female wealth to highlight the overturning of proper gender roles in the house of Agamemnon.

CHAPTER FIVE

TRAGIC GIFTS

As I have shown, exchange between men and women in Homeric epic is harmless as long as the gendered protocol of exchange is respected. The exchanges represented in tragedy, however, are almost always destructive.[1] In this context, even gifts of cloth can be dangerous. In fact, horrific episodes from tragic stagings of the myths of Herakles and Medea suggest that when textiles are used destructively, they can be at least as deadly in women's hands as metal objects. Deianeira, realizing that her husband Herakles has fallen in love with another woman whom he brings into their house, sends him a cloak impregnated with what she believes to be a potion that will restore his love for her. The potion is in fact a burning poison, by means of which she unwittingly destroys him, and ultimately herself. Medea, on the other hand, knows exactly what she is doing when she brings death to her faithless husband Jason's new bride with wedding gifts of a poisoned robe and crown.[2] This gift combines textile and metal, thus making use of both male and female elements, as befits the character that Euripides gives his Medea. As I will show, not only an overturning of the gendered code of exchange, but a more generalized confusion of male and female roles pervades the tragic treatments of these mythic narratives.

Once again, moreover, in the examples to which we now turn, the context for the deadly exchange is a crisis in a marriage relationship. As Cynthia Patterson has put it, "In the work of the Athenian playwrights, we can witness the tragic paradigm of adultery represented as a complex crime of betrayal which corrupts the entire household and its relations of person to person and of person to property."[3] It is at such moments of crisis that the usual reciprocity between husband and wife fails, setting up the possibility of negative reciprocity—theft, violence, and other violations of expected norms.[4]

In tragedy, the pattern of destructive gift-giving can be directly connected with the overturning of the gendered codes of which I have been speaking. I now turn to a comparison of two such examples, from Aeschylus' *Agamemnon* and Sophocles' *Trachiniai*. I begin with the *Agamemnon*, in which textiles, both metaphoric and literalized on the stage, play a central role in a violent overturning of the traditional gendered division of labor.[5]

THE *AGAMEMNON*

In Aeschylus' *Agamemnon*, before he arrives, Klytemnestra proclaims her faithfulness to her husband by claiming to know as little about infidelity as she does about "the dipping (or dying) of bronze" (*chalkou baphas*, 612). This opaque phrase has confounded scholars' attempts to understand the exact technological process to which it refers. The most obvious interpretation, "tempering," is unlikely because bronze, unlike steel, is not tempered. The phrase is usually assumed to refer, if not to tempering, to some other technique associated with the making of weapons.[6] Having failed to clarify the exact nature of the process, critics have tended to content themselves with the observation that metalworking was far from the normal expertise of a woman, even one as formidable as Klytemnestra.[7]

The noun *baphē* and the related verb *baptō* refer both to the tempering of metal (usually for making weapons) and the dying of cloth. Thus the root contains within it a microcosm of male and female wealth, men's and women's pursuits. The exact nature of the metallurgical process described here is not the point. The vagueness of Klytemnestra's reference to a craft of which women have little knowledge is perhaps intended to back up her disclaimer. At the same time, the use of a word associated with textiles clearly invokes the idea of imbuing with color. This overdetermined use of *baphē* is framed by similar uses both earlier in the play and in the next play of the trilogy. The first of these is the phrase *krokou baphas* ("dyings of crocus or saffron yellow," *Ag.* 239), describing the saffron-dyed garments of Iphigeneia, while the context—a description of her sacrifice—reminds us that crocus is not the only substance with which her garments are to be stained.[8]

When the word *baptō* reappears in the *Choephoroi*, all its meanings are brought together explicitly.[9] There, Orestes holds up a garment, "dyed by the sword of Aigisthos" (1011), proclaiming it as a witness against his mother.[10] What is more, he uses the word *kēkis* ("gush," 1012), echoing the language of Klytemnestra at *Ag.* 960, and brackets it with another use of *baphē* in the next line.[11] His language suggests that the resources of the house—the "many dyings of cloth"—have been destroyed not, as Agamemnon feared, by his tread, but by the spilling of his blood.

ἔδρασεν ἢ οὐκ ἔδρασε; μαρτυρεῖ δέ μοι
φᾶρος τόδ᾽, ὡς ἔβαψεν Αἰγίσθου ξίφος.
φόνου δὲ κηκὶς ξὺν χρόνῳ ξυμβάλλεται,
πολλὰς βαφὰς φθείρουσα τοῦ ποικίλματος.

Did she do it or not? This garment is my
witness, how she dyed the sword of Aigisthos.
The gush of murder is brought together with time
to destroy many dyeings of cloth.
(Aesch. *Choe.* 1010-13)

In this way, the confusion of codes is worked into the very language of the drama itself. When Klytemnestra the man-minded (*androboulon, Ag.* 11) speaks of a male art, she simultaneously invokes its female counterpart. At the same time, her words hint at the darker meaning that will soon become apparent, when her weapon is dipped in Agamemnon's blood. The connection with textiles is reinforced later in the play, when Klytemnestra, in the context of the so-called carpet scene, again uses the word in the phrase *eimatōn baphas* (*Ag.* 960): "dyeings of clothing." Ultimately, the murder itself will further this conflation, when Klytemnestra reverses the gendered terms yet again by turning a garment, the robe without armholes, into a murder weapon.[12]

On his return from Troy, Klytemnestra insists that Agamemnon tread the crimson cloth.[13] In the end, her appeals to his vanity win out, but Agamemnon at first resists for fear of committing hubris and offending the gods.[14] He expresses the conflict between them in gendered terms, seeing the offer of the red cloth as an attempt to feminize him—"Do not spoil me according to the ways of women" (918ff.)— and accusing his wife of unwomanly behavior—"Surely this desire for conflict does not befit a woman" (940).[15] The implicit battle is over Klytemnestra's unwillingness to relinquish the control over the house that she has held during his ten-year absence. As Taplin has observed, Klytemnestra, as the "watchdog of the house" (607), controls the threshold, only allowing Agamemnon access under her conditions.[16] This struggle for command of the *oikos*, as will become clear, is a prelude to the struggle over the life of Agamemnon.

The cloth, originally within her purview as wife, could be said no longer to belong entirely to the category of female wealth.[17] By virtue of being dyed a royal crimson, it has become an *agalma*, in Gernet's terms, a royally, and even sacrally charged object.[18] As Morrell observes, Agamemnon's phrase "weavings bought with silver" (*argurōnētous th' huphas, Ag.* 949) "places the garments in the context of the extra-domestic economy."[19] But Klytemnestra counters, attempting to overcome Agamemnon's reluctance and to reassert her jurisdiction over the object by stressing the inexhaustible riches of the house and equating them with the riches of the sea, source of the purple murex-dye: "There is the sea, and who can drain it dry?" she asks (*estin thalassa, tis de nin katasbesei? Ag.* 958).[20] By invoking the treasures of the *oikos*, she reasserts her claim to the role of good housewife, which she has made unceasingly from the moment of Agamemnon's arrival, and stresses her faithfulness, as evidenced by the continued good order of the household. But her own reference to the purple dye as "worth its weight in silver" (*isarguron*, 959) gives the game away, as this external standard of value undermines her appeals to the self-sufficiency (*autarkeia*) of Agamemnon's *oikos*.[21] Klytemnestra speaks of the riches of the house in such a way as to obscure the distinction between those domestically produced and those acquired from abroad. She moves seamlessly from her evocation of the bounty of the sea ("Who can drain it dry?") to her defiant boast that "the house does not know how to be poor" (*penesthai d' ouk epistatai domos*, 962).

In fact, Klytemnestra's claims about the good order of the household are disingenuous. Despite her claim not to have broken the seal (*sēmantērion*, 609) during Agamemnon's absence, she has in fact allowed another man access to herself and by extension to the household wealth.[22] Her use of the metaphor of the seal is ironic, since a seal (*sphragis* is the usual word) was frequently used to guarantee the integrity of a locked storeroom. As an unfaithful wife, she is then not a good housewife, but is preparing to be as profligate with her husband's blood as she is with the crimson cloths.[23] Disposing of the cloths as she wishes is the sign of her infidelity, and even though she appears to be making a present of them to Agamemnon, she is not.

Ultimately, the murder of Agamemnon in the bath involves another ambiguous use of textiles, as Klytemnestra throws a robe over her husband that has no holes for arms or head. As he struggles to emerge from the impossible garment, the death blow is struck. These two pieces of textile link the dramatic actions of the plot with the leitmotif of binding and trapping metaphors that runs throughout the trilogy.[24] A gift that is no gift, a garment that is no garment, a bath in his own blood—by means of these perversions of the woman's role, the unfaithful wife destroys her husband.[25]

Klytemnestra's transgressions go yet a step further. Displaying the corpse of Agamemnon, she exults, "This is the work of my right hand, a just workman" (*tēsde dexias cheros / ergon, dikaias tektonos*, 1405–6). Here the *erga* of women take on their most sinister meaning yet.[26] Klytemnestra points to the body of her murdered husband as her *ergon*, and calls her own hand a *tektōn*, a worker in wood, but also by extension any craftsman. This word only rarely appears as feminine, and by applying it to her hand in this way, she attributes to herself masculine prowess in a masculine art.[27] By describing her action in terms that suggest a more mundane transgression of the norms of gender, she calls attention to her divergence from standards of female behavior. But her action has gone far beyond mere violation of the gendered division of labor, for this "making" is not the productive exercise of a craft, but the slaughter of her own husband. Killing is man's work, and Klytemnestra is the rare woman in Greek tragedy who wields an ax. This, however, does not begin to approach the horror of the spectacle of a husband-murdering wife. That this heinous deed should be described using the language of craft further emphasizes the perversion of the gendered protocols of labor and exchange. No longer simply the weavings with which women clothe their households, the *erga* of Klytemnestra are both the clothing used to ensnare Agamemnon and the corpse she has made of him.

It is a sign of Klytemnestra's alienation from her wifely role that the textiles with which she is associated are metaphorically or actually torn, stained, or otherwise unusable.

The purple cloths on which she encourages Agamemnon to walk are understood to be spoiled by his tread, and the garment in which she traps him for the kill is unwearable because it has no holes for arms or head and will later be exhibited, stained with his blood, as evidence of her guilt. Klytemnestra is associated with textiles that can no longer or never could fulfill their expected role of clothing and protecting the body, much less contribute to the wealth of the household. From productive contribution to vague sexual threat to complete destruction—here is a sinister devolution of the very idea of women's work.

THE *TRACHINIAI*

If the language cleverly manipulated by Klytemnestra in the *Agamemnon* bespeaks a deliberately perverted gift-economy, that of the *Trachiniai* presents destructive exchanges enacted unwittingly by characters in the grips of erotic desire and jealousy.[28] The central female figure, Herakles' wife Deianeira, presents an interesting foil to Klytemnestra, for her destructive act, also marked by the arrival of a new woman in the house, arises out of her love for her husband, and her own inability to recognize the fierceness of her jealousy and desire when faced with a rival. As Segal puts it, "It is an essential part of Deianeira's tragedy that she is by nature more a Penelope than a Clytaemnestra but is drawn into the destructive pattern against her will."[29] Although Deianeira recognizes that by bringing a concubine into the house, her husband offers a poor reward for her steadfastness, she is represented as too innocent, perhaps willfully so, to recognize the potentially destructive power of her own desires. Despite the very different motivations of Klytemnestra and Deianeira, their weapons remain much the same, as changes are rung on the usual gendered patterns of exchange.[30]

Deianeira, upon receiving her husband's new lover into her house, in a scene that is clearly modeled on Klytemnestra's reception of Kassandra in the *Agamemnon*, complains that this is a poor recompense for her years of devotion to him.[31] The word she uses for recompense, *oikouria*, short for the phrase *oikouria dōra*, indicates the "housewife's payment" or "gift in return for services" (542).[32] She has just described the situation in language that calls to mind the housewifely duty to clothe the members of the household. "We are," she says, "two women waiting under a single cloak for a single embrace."[33] The image, conventionally used of harmonious lovers, of two people under a single cloak or blanket is here used to show that something is very wrong in the domestic economy of Herakles' household.[34] It is he who imposes a perversion of the marriage arrangement, an inappropriate gift that Deianeira, for all her innocence, sees as a perversion also of the reciprocity expected between husband and wife. Her response to this situation is also couched in the language of gift-exchange.[35] She tells Lichas that she will give him gifts to take back to his master in exchange for what he has given her: *anti dōrōn dōra* (494). The metaphor of the cloak will now be transmuted to real textile, as Deianeira translates the usual domestic duties into an enactment of reciprocity. "It is not right for you to leave empty-handed, having come so well provided" (*sun pollōi stolōi*, 496). As Wohl has noted, Deianeira speaks as though Iole has been given to her as a present, and the use of *stolos* with its multiple meanings (equipment, fleet, army, etc.) is well suited to the elision of persons and things.[36] She introduces her plan to use the "love potion" by saying, "I have had now for a long time an old gift of an ancient beast, hidden in a bronze urn" (*ēn moi palaion dōron archaiou pote / thēros, lebēti chalkeōi kekrummenon*, 555–56). Whereas keeping things safe is a woman's proper role, the metal container is a signal that something is wrong. The dying centaur Nessos directed Deianeira to take some of his blood mixed with poison from the arrow that killed him, and to save it for use as a love potion should Herakles ever turn to another woman.[37] Merely accepting a gift from Nessos is a violation of the norm, that a woman should not accept gifts from a man to whom she is not married. The full implications of this transgression are played out explicitly in Apollodoros' version (2.7.6), in which the substance contains the centaur's semen.

"I dipped (or dyed) the cloak" (*chitōna tond' ebapsa*, 580), she reports to the chorus, using the same word, *baptō*, that played such a prominent role in the *Agamemnon* scene discussed above.[38] Although the centaur died at the hand of Herakles, who killed him for attempting to rape Deianeira, it does not occur to her until it is too late that the centaur's gift could in fact be a treacherous one. We, however, have been alerted to this possibility a few lines before, when she speaks of the black poison of the Lernaian hydra's offspring (*melangcholos . . . ios thremma Lernaias hudras*, 573–74). Mention of the Lernaian hydra, one of Herakles' victims, cannot but arouse the suspicions of the audience, if not the speaker.

Unlike Klytemnestra, whose claims to know nothing of dishonorable behavior are expressed in the indicative, Deianeira expresses a wish in the optative: "May I know nothing of evil daring nor may I ever learn, for I hate women who dare such things" (*kakas de tolmas mēt' epistaimēn egō / mēt' ekmathoimi, tas te tolmōsas stugō*, 582–83). Her fear of wrongdoing mingles with hope of resolving her difficulties, and the chorus reinforces her self-delusion. As she hands over the garment, she stresses both its status as a gift to her husband (*dōrēma*, 603) and its manufacture, calling the robe "finely woven by my own hand" (*tonde tanaüphē peplon, / dōrēm' ekeinōi tandri tēs emēs cheros*, 602–3).[39] Moreover, Deianeira says, this represents the discharge of a promise, that when she heard that Herakles had returned safely she would send him a new cloak in which he would appear properly arrayed for the thanksgiving sacrifice to the gods.[40] She tells Lichas that her husband will recognize the authenticity of the gift by the impress of her seal (*sēm' . . . sphragidos*, 614–15). The *sphragis*, as I have noted, recalls the role of the housewife in keeping safe the wealth of the household, while simultaneously operating as a metaphor for the wife's sexual fidelity, like the *sēmanterion* of which Klytemnestra speaks.[41]

Shortly, the doubts Deianeira had tried to shake off are to be confirmed, and the sacrifice will take on a different meaning. She returns to tell the chorus that she has discovered that the bits of wool she had used to anoint the cloak, exposed to the light of the sun, have all shrivelled up into nothing. Too late, she reviews the centaur's motives, and remembers how according to his instructions the potion has been kept hidden from the light in a bronze container, deep in the recesses of the house, like a *keimēlion*, a precious treasure. This potion and the circumstances of its discovery as a deadly poison bring together once again the elements of male and female wealth, as well as the categories of inside and outside discussed above in relation to the lamb with the golden fleece.

At the same time, the contents of the container and their location suggest female sexual secrets of a potentially threatening nature.[42] The poison is kept hidden in the inmost recesses of the house (*en muchois*, 686), a space that is unmistakably coded as female. A mixture of the centaur's blood and the hydra's bile, it contains both male and female elements.[43] Through the trickery of Nessos, the potion combines the destructive power of his long-suppressed and unlawful lust with Deianeira's own insufficiently recognized desire. The deadly object has been contained—but only for so long—in the bronze container, in the possession of a woman. When she releases it, as she must eventually do, like a kind of latter-day Pandora releasing the evils for men, it will destroy first the symbol of female domesticity, the tufts of wool, before going on to destroy both man and woman, and then the household, which was to have contained and regulated the wife's sexuality, if not that of the husband. Once again, as in Hesiod, the *erga gunaikōn*—in this case, the woven garment sent to Herakles—become *mermera erga*: the baneful and sexually threatening behavior of women.[44]

As is perhaps in keeping with the more retiring nature of Deianeira, this threat is never confronted head-on by Herakles, who, unlike Agamemnon, never meets his wife face-to-face within the drama. Nonetheless, the death that fells Herakles is almost a domestic one. He dies not in the manly way, by the sword, but rather by the use of a potion or poison, a feminine weapon, and by means of a feminine delivery system, the robe woven by his wife's own hand. After facing so many far-off dangers, he dies in sight of his own home. It is hard to imagine a greater violation of the code: the manliest of heroes is killed by a woman. His language emphasizes his incredulity at this development, ringing changes on this transgression of gender roles: "A woman, being female and unmanly in nature, a lone woman killed me without a sword" (*gunē de, thēlus ousa kanandros phusin, / monē me dē katheile phasganou dicha*, 1062–63). It does not, perhaps, require a Freudian sensibility to hear a phallic complaint in the climactic phrase *phasganon dicha* ("without a sword").[45] As he will soon make explicit, Herakles conceives of his death as an emasculation.[46] In the world of masculine competition he inhabits, it is hard for him to conceive suffering such an indignity at the hands of one who lacks the phallus.

Herakles' language also suggests an invocation of the *Agamemnon* model: Deianeira has fastened around him a woven snare, in which he will die (*kathēpsen ōmois tois emois Erinuōn / huphanton amphiblēstron, ōi diollu-*

mai, 1051–52). *Amphiblēstron* is precisely the term used for the garment that ensnares Agamemnon before the fatal blow (*Ag.* 1382). Not only is the garment fatal, however, but this feminine weapon also has the effect of turning Herakles into a woman: he describes himself as crying like a girl (*parthenos*) and says that his suffering makes him a woman (*nun d' ek toioutou thēlus eurēmai talas*, 1075).[47] Several scholars have noted in his uncovering of his body an obscene parody of the *anakalypteria*, the ritual in which the bride uncovers herself in the presence of her new husband's family.[48]

Deianeira's response to her horror at inadvertently killing her husband is suicide.[49] But once more the codes are violated. Just as Herakles' death is figured as a feminization of the hero, Deianeira's death also reverses the expected gender categories. She, the timid retiring wife, chooses a most unfeminine way of killing herself, by the sword (*amphiplēgi phasganōi*, 930). As Nicole Loraux has shown, the usual method of suicide for women in tragedy is hanging, an ignominious death.[50] At times, the noose is a veil or other article of women's clothing, as in Sophocles' *Antigone*, or when the *Suppliant Maidens* of Aeschylus threaten to make use of their own clothing—"a contrivance of sashes" (*mēchan suzōmatōn*, 462)—to hang themselves.[51] Loraux's analysis of tragic suicide suggests that the gendered code of textile and metal for which I have argued holds even in death, and that the few deviations from it that occur are significant. Wohl has used the phrase "transgendered death" to describe Deianeira's suicide: "In her mode of suicide—penetration by the Homeric sword—she showed herself both a failed man and a failed woman, constrained until the end by gender."[52]

Additional details both emphasize and complicate our reading of the code: in order to expose the place where she will strike with the sword, Deianeira must remove a golden pin (*chrusēlatos . . . peronis*) that holds her garments together (924–25).[53] In this way, not one but two metal objects mark the site of her suicide. Although one is coded as masculine, the other—the clasp or pin—is a traditional female adornment that can be used as a weapon.[54] Herodotos tells of an episode in which the women of Athens used their brooches to kill the sole survivor of a battle with the Aiginetans. This outrage led the Athenians to decree a change in female dress to eliminate the use of brooches:

πυθομένας δὲ τὰς γυναῖκας τῶν ἐπ' Αἴγιναν στρατευσαμένων ἀνδρῶν, δεινόν τι ποιησαμένας κεῖνον μοῦνον ἐξ ἁπάντων σωθῆναι, πέριξ τὸν ἄνθρωπον τοῦτον λαβούσας καὶ κεντεύσας τῇσι περόνῃσι τῶν ἱματίων εἰρωτᾶν ἑκάστην αὐτέων ὅκου εἴη ὁ ἑωυτῆς ἀνήρ. καὶ τοῦτον μὲν οὕτω διαφθαρῆναι, Ἀθηναίοισι

δὲ ἔτι τοῦ πάθεος δεινότερόν τι δόξαι εἶναι τὸ τῶν γυναικῶν
ἔργον. ἄλλῳ μὲν δὴ οὐκ ἔχειν ὅτεῳ ζημιώσωσι τὰς γυναῖκας,
τὴν δὲ ἐσθῆτα μετέβαλον αὐτέων ἐς τὴν Ἰάδα· ἐφόρεον γὰρ δὴ
πρὸ τοῦ αἱ τῶν Ἀθηναίων γυναῖκες ἐσθῆτα Δωρίδα, τῇ Κορινθίῃ
παραπλησιωτάτην· μετέβαλον ὦν ἐς τὸν λίνεον κιθῶνα, ἵνα δὴ
περόνῃσι μὴ χρέωνται.

When the wives of the men who had gone to attack Aegina heard this,
they were very angry that he alone should be safe. They gathered round
him and stabbed him with the brooch-pins of their garments, each asking him where her husband was. This is how this man met his end, and
the Athenians found the action of their women to be more dreadful than
their own misfortune. They could find, it is said, no other way to punish the women than changing their dress to the Ionian fashion. Until
then the Athenian women had worn Dorian dress, which is very like the
Corinthian. It was changed, therefore, to the linen tunic, so that they
might have no brooch-pins to use. (Hdt. 5.87.2–3, trans. Godley)

In Deianeira's death scene, the implement of female violence against
men is pushed aside to make way for a masculine form of violence visited by a woman on her own person.[55] Here is the sword that was missing in Herakles' outcry at lines 1062–63. Although the perverse exchanges
in this play continue, for Deianeira this is the end of the line. Trading the
peplos for the *phasganon*, she has effected an exchange between the textile-
entwined death of Herakles and her own death by the sword. Deianeira
overturns the code to the very end.

Sophocles' treatment of the character of Deianeira shows a complex alternate reality behind the hasty conclusions of her son Hyllos, the passion
of whose curses is answered only by his passionate regret when he learns
the truth. Some have seen in his precipitous denunciations a reflection of
his father's brutality, which will soon be visited upon him.[56] Although this
works very well structurally with the end of the play, there is no previous
hint of brutality in Hyllos' character, and unlike his father, he is shown to
be capable of second thoughts. Given this, why should it be so instantly
plausible to Hyllos that a wife should cruelly betray her husband? And not
just any wife, but his own mother, whom he knows to be his father's loving spouse? Here, Hyllos serves temporarily as a mouthpiece for traditional
male assumptions about women that transcend any individual experience
or prior relationship. Summed up in Agamemnon's diatribes in the Underworld (*Odyssey* 11.427–34 and 24.199–202), the common misogynist wis-
dom would keep all wives under suspicion of treachery.

The persistent anxiety about women and exchange observed in these tragic texts brings us back to Vernant's remarks about the paradoxical position of the daughter in the family.[57] Unlike Hestia, the perpetual daughter and keeper of the hearth, a woman must fulfull her destiny by leaving her natal family to enter a new one.[58] She can thus be imagined as a kind of double agent, part of two families, that of her birth and that which she enters by marriage, but belonging fully to neither. Ormand has described women as outsiders to both the *oikos* into which they marry and the *polis*.[59] Bound by most of the laws that govern the lives of citizens, they are nevertheless deprived of basic citizen rights and are never—at least in Athens—given the name that would mark them as full citizens.[60]

Recent writers on the *Agamemnon* and the *Trachiniai* have stressed both Klytemnestra's and Deianeira's awareness of themselves as alienated objects in marriage exchange.[61] Deianeira's speech about the battle between Herakles and Acheloos makes clear the character's alienated sense of being a prize in a marriage contest, while an alternate version of Klytemnestra's story makes her a prize that falls to Agamemnon after he has killed her first husband, Tantalos. According to Pausanias (2.22.3), this Tantalos may have been the son of Thyestes, which would add yet another enormity to the seemingly infinite cycle of revenge between the two branches of this ill-fated family. In this case, Klytemnestra would be doubly suspect, because of her allegiances not only to her natal family but also, through this first marriage, to an enemy branch of her own husband's house.

The flip side of the anxiety about admitting an alien into the household is expressed best in the lines Euripides wrote for Medea, who speaks eloquently from the woman's perspective about the difficulties of marriage (Eur. *Medea* 230-51). It is not enough that a woman must buy a husband and a master for her body (*posin priasthai, despotēn te sōmatos*, 234), but then she must learn to read his mind as she integrates herself into a foreign environment. If the husband is agreeable, all may be well, but if not, the wife—unlike the husband—has no recourse to outside companions. But Euripides gives with one hand while taking with the other: he puts this sensitive evocation of female alienation in the mouth of one of the most destructive women in Greek mythology. It is interesting that similar sentiments are expressed in a fragment of Sophocles' lost tragedy *Tereus* (frag. 583 Lloyd-Jones), apparently by Prokne, another wife who, like Medea, destroys her husband's line by killing their child.[62] These betrayed wives are well placed to speak of the uncertainties of marriage from the female perspective, but the legitimacy of their complaints is simultaneously undercut by the audience's knowledge of their own unspeakable deeds.

Medea is an alien in the truest sense of the word. Although she and Jason are living as *metoikoi* (resident aliens, metics) in Corinth, her origins are in barbarian Colchis. He, on the other hand, is Greek and about to become a member of the Corinthian royal family. Medea's murder of his bride and father-in-law leaves him in permanent exile, while she will go on to reside in Athens by invitation of the king. There she will enjoy the privileges of *metoikia* until discovered in her next misdeed, the attempted murder of Aigeus' son Theseus.

My use in this context of the words *metoikos* and *metoikia*, while not wholly inaccurate, does not reflect their appearance in tragedy, where they are applied not to wives, but instead to a series of unmarried women.[63] The Danaids in Aeschylus' *Suppliants* are offered *metoikia* in Argos, where they have fled to avoid unwelcome marriage with their cousins, the sons of Aigyptos. The Eumenides are called *metoikoi* to mark their acceptance into the city of Athens (Aesch., *Eumenides* 1018). Perhaps most poignantly, Antigone, when she has renounced marriage in favor of death, calls herself *metoikos*, in the sense that she is poised between life and death.[64]

Yet the status of a wife within the oikos seems to closely parallel the status of a foreigner within the polis. She has a legitimate place in the household, but it is not the place of one who was born there. This ambiguity gives meaning to a scene in Euripides' *Alkestis*. Toward the end of the play, Admetos contrives to hide from his guest Herakles the identity of the woman for whom the household is in mourning. Herakles asks if she is *othneios* (i.e., strange or foreign) or *sungenēs*, a relative. Her husband replies that she is a stranger:

—ὀθνεῖος ἢ σοὶ συγγενὴς γεγῶσά τις;
—ὀθνεῖος, ἄλλως δ' ἦν ἀναγκαία δόμοις.

Herakles. Was she an outsider or one of the family?
Admetos. An outsider, but still essential to the house.
(Eur. *Alkestis* 532–33)

He is technically correct that Alkestis is not *sungenēs*, since as his wife she is not related to him by blood. Euripides has Herakles use this word instead of the near-synonym *oikeios*, which would, as Just notes, include affines, those related by marriage.[65] In his reply, Admetos continues to skirt the issue by using the ambiguous word *anangkaios*, which has a double meaning of "necessary, essential" and "related by blood." In this context, however, the second meaning seems to be excluded by his prior use of *othneios*. The categorization of Alkestis as foreign to the household is used here as a dodge, to allow Admetos to offer Herakles his trademark hospitality. And yet, at the same time, it points to the curious position of a wife as in the household but not wholly of it. That she is in fact an essential part of the *oikos* seems to occur to her husband only after she is gone.

That the wife's presence is in any way *constitutive* of the *oikos* does not immediately occur to this husband, since she is conceived as fundamentally external, even extraneous, to it. The desolation he feels at her death suggests the gap that may exist between ideology and human experience. The notion of woman as "resident alien" calls to mind the flower-pot theory of human gestation proposed by Apollo in the *Eumenides*, according to which the mother is not the parent of the child she bears but "a stranger to a stranger" (*xenōi xenē*, 660). Here also, the alienated view of women's role is employed as a legal dodge, and should not be taken as the final word on social relations. Nonetheless, it exemplifies a tendency in Greek thought that goes back to the negative view of female fertility seen in Hesiod, according to which woman is external not only to the family, but in origin even to "mankind." At best she is a resident alien in the *oikos*; at worst, like Pandora, she is a sort of robot programmed to create havoc.

The nature of Greek marriages—at least in classical Athens, where they were usually contracted between a very young woman and an older man, who may have been unacquainted with each other until the wedding—can have done little to counter this alienation.[66] The like-mindedness of Penelope and Odysseus seems to have been an ideal not often realized, and perhaps it is no longer even an ideal by the fifth century. Men's and women's lives were lived rather separately from one another, in a way that may have been little conducive to the *homophrosunē* we see at the end of the *Odyssey*.[67] It is nearly impossible to recover the nature of affective relations in classical Athens, but the language of Lysias' oration is instructive. Marital happiness is expressed by the husband in these terms: "Until then, she had been the best of wives. She was a clever housekeeper and kept everything neat" (Lys. 1.7). The Greek husband married a virtual stranger who might in some ways always remain one, and yet he had to rely on her for the continuance of his *oikos*.

At the same time, women could have an economic impact on the *oikos* into which they married in several ways. Most obviously, the size of the dowry brought by the wife could make the family fortune, just as divorce, which brought with it an obligation to return the dowry, could break it. The story of Alkibiades physically preventing his wife Hipparete from leaving him has been cited to show how keenly this threat could be felt, although the very same episode suggests that divorce was not an option to which Athenian women had easy recourse.[68] Whatever power, economic or moral, was conferred on the wife by the institution of the dowry could last beyond the marriage itself. We have the evidence of Demosthenes about his widowed mother Kleoboule's efforts to regain the dowry appropriated by an unscrupulous guardian.[69]

In the myths and texts analyzed here, women are not portrayed as having ongoing economic power. They may occasionally enter into exchange relations, but something of the commodity seems to cling inescapably to them. At the same time, they do not predictably remain *merely* commodities. As they oscillate between commodity and actor, between object and agent of exchange, the anxiety about this unsteady state becomes evident. Women may be tokens of exchange among men to establish relations of kinship or alliance, but they also enter into their own relations with others, relations structured equally by the exchange of gifts.[70] They are not only gifts, but also givers.

Since women's social and economic roles find their definition in marriage, marriage becomes the site of greatest anxiety about women and exchange. Not coincidentally, it is within marriage that women exert what economic power they do have. Perhaps what is most troubling and ambiguous about women is not that they are capable of giving and receiving gifts, but that they can even give themselves away; that is, they can make erotic choices that put them temporarily beyond the reach of the patriarchal marriage economy. Thus the fear of female reciprocity is ultimately the fear of female agency. These anxieties reflect the concern about women as circulating objects, and as strangers to the household. The initial circulation of women makes marriage possible, but the association of women with circulation cannot easily be turned off once it has served its purpose. This is the ambiguity on which marriage is founded, and which turns women into potential Klytemnestras or Helens every one.

CHAPTER SIX

A FAMILY ROMANCE

The previous chapters have dealt with the kinds of relationships between men and women that in Greek myth tend to be characterized by risk, hostility, and danger. These include relationships between wives and husbands as well as between mothers and sons. As I have shown, the potential for harm in relationships between men and women is frequently activated by gifts of precious objects, or is marked by their circulation. In this chapter, I examine the one exception to this rule of hostile male-female dyads and fatal exchanges. When the male-female pair are brother and sister, the relationship is usually based on mutual support, and the outcome is usually positive.[1] In these relationships, too, the circulation of objects plays a significant role, but one quite different and far less sinister than in the examples seen so far.

Not surprisingly, in these pairings, the nature of both the exchange and the items exchanged is rather different. Most often the objects in circulation are textiles, although metals also play a role. Moreover, their uses are different—as tokens or ransom rather than as gifts or bribes. Although the examples considered in this chapter do not entirely free women from the association with dangerous exchange, they do show that women, when conceived of as sisters, are not the figures of dread that they often are in other contexts. The nature of the exchange is different in part because in these myths, women's allegiances lie by default with their brothers, and they use their textile wealth in ways that help and support brothers. In the myths of dangerous gifts I have discussed earlier, gifts are proffered in hopes of inducing women to change sides, to betray their allegiances. As with Eriphyle's necklace, the receipt of a gift may strengthen the tendency of a woman to ally herself with a brother against a husband.

This shift to a consideration of sibling relationships brings us back to the ambiguity of a woman's status as both gift and giver. In the context of the brother-sister relationship, as in the other relationships already explored, a woman may be conceptualized as an object of exchange. In ancient Greece, as in many other societies, brothers sometimes arrange their sisters' marriages. In many societies, in fact, marriage exchange is conceptualized in terms of brothers trading sisters for wives.

Since, in the absence of a father, the exchange of a woman may be in the hands of her brother, women are potentially circulating objects even within the context of sibling intimacy. I examine several examples in which this potentiality is realized, although not always with a expected results. As I argue below, in Euripides' *Elektra*, Orestes' contracting of a marriage for his sister with his best friend Pylades seems to be a way of keeping his sister, rather than giving her away.

In what follows, I explore the intricacies of the sibling relationship in ancient Greek myth, particularly in its tragic renditions, drawing on cross-cultural evidence and contemporary work in anthropology in an attempt to illuminate its ideological underpinnings. I start with a problematic text about male-female sibling relations from Sophocles' *Antigone*, which I attempt to place in the context of other relations between men and women in myth and tragedy. I then discuss several fantasies about siblings and gender relations found in Greek tragedy alongside recent anthropological work on siblings.

ANTIGONE'S CHOICE

According to Aristotle's *Poetics*, plots in which near relations kill or almost kill each other are the most tragic. Interestingly, many of the examples feature a woman attacking her own son or husband. Relations between women and their male kin are so often hostile and destructive that it is important to notice the one salient exception. Far from being universally hostile toward men, as I would argue, women in Greek myth are discriminating in both hostility and allegiance, often choosing the sibling bond over that between husbands and wives or even mothers and children. In fact, the one exception to the gender antagonism that so often causes instability and crisis in Greek myth is the relationship of affection and mutual aid that prevails between male-female pairs of siblings.[2]

In Sophocles' *Antigone*, the protagonist, faced with death for burying her brother Polyneikes, makes an admission that has profoundly shocked commentators:

οὐ γάρ ποτ' οὔτ' ἄν, εἰ τέκνων μήτηρ ἔφυν,
οὔτ' εἰ πόσις μοι κατθανὼν ἐτήκετο,

βίᾳ πολιτῶν τόνδ' ἂν ᾐρόμην πόνον.
τίνος νόμου δὴ ταῦτα πρὸς χάριν λέγω;
πόσις μὲν ἄν μοι κατθανόντος ἄλλος ἦν,
καὶ παῖς ἀπ' ἄλλου φωτός, εἰ τοῦδ' ἤμπλακον,
μητρὸς δ' ἐν Ἅιδου καὶ πατρὸς κεκευθότοιν
οὐκ ἔστ' ἀδελφὸς ὅστις ἂν βλάστοι ποτέ.

Had I been a mother
of children, and my husband been dead and rotten,
I would not have taken this weary task upon me
against the will of the city. What law backs me
when I say this? I will tell you:
If my husband were dead, I might have had another,
and child from another man, if I lost the first.
But when father and mother both were hidden in death
no brother's life would bloom for me again.
(Soph. *Antigone* 905–12, trans. Grene)

A surprising number of readers of these lines have been troubled by the sentiments Antigone expresses. All sorts of solutions to their supposed impossibility have been proposed, from pretending that Antigone doesn't really mean what she says, to that ultimate act of scholarly desperation, emending the text—even excising the offending lines altogether.[3] No less an authority than Goethe found these lines "ganz schlecht": "In the course of the piece, the heroine has given the most admirable reasons for her conduct, and has shown the noble courage of a stainless soul; but now, at the end, she puts forth a motive which is quite unworthy of her, and which almost borders on the comic." He ends with the hope that scholars will prove the passage to be spurious.[4]

Some have attributed the intrusive sentiments to a clumsy borrowing from an episode in Herodotos' histories, in which the wife of Intaphernes explains her reasons for deciding to save the life of her brother rather than that of her husband or son:[5]

ὦ βασιλεῦ, ἀνὴρ μέν μοι ἂν ἄλλος γένοιτο, εἰ δαίμων ἐθέλοι, καὶ τέκνα ἄλλα, εἰ ταῦτα ἀποβάλοιμι· πατρὸς δὲ καὶ μητρὸς οὐκέτι μευ ζωόντων ἀδελφεὸς ἂν ἄλλος οὐδενὶ τρόπῳ γένοιτο.

O King, I might have another husband, if the gods wish it, and other children, if I were to lose these; but with my father and mother no longer living, I could not possibly ever have another brother. (Hdt. 3.119.6, trans. de Selincourt)

A FAMILY ROMANCE

It is remarkable how many of the same critics who are shocked by Antigone's lines take the intimacy of the marriage relationship at face value, especially given the horrific counter-examples offered by the genre of tragedy itself.

A few critics have endeavored to defend the lines. Kamerbeek, in his 1978 commentary, notes that the lines, whatever their "absurd consequences," nonetheless convey the "complete and exclusive faithfulness to the dead brother."[6] Even Jebb, for all his skepticism, does make a half-hearted attempt at a culturally specific argument:

> Now, the "primitive sophism" employed by the wife of Intaphernes, and the tendency to exalt the fraternal tie, are things which we may recognise as characteristic of that age. And it is true that Aeschylus has some quaint subtleties of a similar kind: as when Apollo defends Orestes on the ground that a man's mother is not, properly speaking, his parent (*Eum.* 658); and when Athene votes for Orestes because she herself had had no mother at all (736).[7]

I do not propose to join the philological debate about the authenticity of these lines. Although I believe that the entire passage can be defended, I wish instead to broaden the context in which we read it. Several recent critics have taken the lines more nearly on their own terms and analyzed them in terms of near parallels, both Greek and non-Greek, or in terms of a discourse on marriage.[8] My own approach is to place them in the context of Greek mythic models for sibling interaction.

Two anthropological tropes in particular inform my analysis. The first is the idea, to which I have already referred, of the exchange of women in marriage as the originary or prototypical exchange, espoused by Claude Lévi-Strauss in *The Elementary Structures of Kinship*.[9] The second is the idea of the gendered nature of wealth, as elaborated in Chapter One, and discussed throughout.

I acknowledged in Chapter One the depth of my debt to Lévi-Strauss. Paradoxically, his contribution to the interpretions of the myth of Oidipous will not play a large role in my analysis. His ingenious (if not over-ingenious) analysis is structured around the categories of overvaluing and undervaluing kinship.[10] One is inclined to agree that sleeping with one's mother is an example of overvaluing kinship, and killing one's father an example of undervaluing it. But Lévi-Strauss wants to see Antigone's act in the same light, as overvaluation of kin relations, just as he wants to categorize Kadmos' search for his abducted sister Europe in the same light. The symmetry of his approach is appealing, and some recent critics have taken up the idea that Antigone's choice is natural for one born of an incestuous union. Although this is an attractive argument, it is ultimately insufficient, because it ignores the evidence of a large body of Greek myth about sibling relations. Examination of these myths allows us to refine our sense of the cultural specificity of sister-brother relations in Greece. But first, a look at some cross-cultural material may be helpful.

The Trobriand ethnography of Annette Weiner invites us to pay greater attention to sibling relations. Weiner's 1979 book *Women of Value, Men of Renown* hints at a theme made more explicit in her later *Inalienable Possessions: The Paradox of Keeping-While-Giving (1992)*, that of the importance of considering women's roles not only as daughters and wives, but also as sisters, in assessing their social, political, and economic contributions to the workings of society. Her material shows that women provide essential support to their brothers in large part through their production of textiles. (In the case of the Trobriands, this means fiber skirts and banana-leaf bundles.) These textiles must be on hand for distribution at mortuary rituals, if the brother is not to lose social standing. Weiner's insight into the importance of what anthropologists call "sibling intimacy" is fundamental to the present analysis.

Accounts of marriage systems such as that of Lévi-Strauss emphasize the exchange of women by their fathers or brothers in marriage relations, in an alchemy that transmutes daughters and sisters into wives. Wife becomes the primary role, subsuming all others. In the examples that Weiner discusses, however, sisters also always remain sisters, and derive their power precisely from this role. Among the Trobrianders, the brother-sister relationship derives its primacy from the need to ensure the continuance of the matrilineage.[11] Weiner has also analyzed the role of sibling relations in Samoa, where the relationship between sister and brother is paramount. Here, the institution of the so-called sacred sister throws women's power as siblings into high relief. The sacred sister is the eldest sister of a chief, who inherits powerful titles that give access to the ancestral *mana*, the source of his chiefly power. Where the powers of the sister are retained and recognized, as in Weiner's examples, women have higher status. From other ethnographic accounts, it can be seen that for the most part, in societies in which the exchange of women is regarded as absolute and complete, women have low status.[12] In this context, a woman will—to quote Congreve—"by degrees dwindle into a wife."[13]

To a lesser degree than in the matrilineal societies Weiner describes, Athenian inheritance laws and marriage customs also preserve the connection between women and their natal families. Athenian inheritance was bilateral, although it privileged paternal over maternal relations, and within that structure, it privileged males on the maternal side over females.[14] A woman's right to her dowry, protected by her male kin, guaranteed her continuing connection with her birth family. As I have argued in the previous chapters, this continuing connection seems to have been a source of anxiety about women, particularly in their roles as wives vis-à-vis their marital family, and more generally as exchange-partners.

To understand the significance of these relationships, it is important first to see how women's hostility toward their male relations is figured in myth. Not only are women shown to be dangerous to men, whether wittingly or unwittingly, but their allegiances are almost always constructed as a zero-sum game. Female affective choices are cast in an impossible either/or construction with fatal results for someone. A stark example of this dilemma can be seen in the myth of Hippodameia, whose father Oinomaos learned from an oracle that her marriage would mean his death. A psychological interpretation might suggest that the father's desire to keep his daughter for himself results in a series of projections, fostering a murderous impulse toward all prospective sons-in-law. For the successful suitor, winning Hippodameia means outwitting the father's murderous schemes and making the oracle come true, killing the father and taking his place, or at least the place that he occupies in fantasy. But this neat psychological reading does not adequately convey the degree to which in many cases the myths attribute the choice to the woman involved. In these cases, we must supplement with an awareness of the socially conditioned choices made by the mythic personae.

These choices, like those made by the actors in the marriage negotiations described by Lévi-Strauss, are also shown to be tied to a surprising degree to *economic* calculations. And these economic calculations are usually signaled by the presence of a talismanic object.[15] As discussed in Chapter One, the nature of the talismanic object can be interpreted according to the anthropological concept of gendered wealth. A hallmark of the generally co-operative relations between brothers and sisters is the benign use of textiles, deployed by sisters on behalf of their brothers. In these cases, the textiles are used as ransom or as tokens of recognition, and do not have a harmful effect on anyone. In other examples, however, in which textiles do not play a part, the allegiance of a sister to a brother means the death of a son or a husband.

This is very much in contrast to the deadly exchanges we have discussed in the previous chapters, which often arise from marital conflict and breakdown. Similarly, maternal relations can be disrupted, as in the case of Astyoche, mentioned briefly in the *Odyssey*, who engages in a similar transaction at the expense of her son. As we have seen, not only are women willing to murder their husbands, but this hostility often extends to their children by these husbands. Klytemnestra not only murders her husband, but in some versions seems ready to murder her son as well out of fear of his vengeance. Medea kills her sons to avenge her husband Jason's betrayal of her. Prokne and Philomela also kill a son to punish a husband. Here, the children do not seem to have a separate value, but are treated as part of the father or as his possessions. This is quite different from the contemporary Western assumption that under normal circumstances, a woman's main allegiance is to her husband and children, and that if the marriage breaks down, her allegiance to her children will trump everything else. This is, I believe, the root of the horror with which Antigone's words have been received through the last few centuries.

Women barter away the lives of their male relations, whether husbands, sons, or even fathers, in transactions that are notable for the inevitability of the misogynist logic with which they unfold. Gift-exchange with women is dangerous, because they are willing to make economic choices that are fatal to their men. In short, they are willing to trade affective for economic considerations—frequently figured (not to say trivialized) as a frivolous attraction to shiny objects.

The myths at times present marriage as a moment of choice for women between conflicting claims of affection, although this does not reflect the limited autonomy enjoyed by real Greek women in most periods. Hippodameia is not represented as actively seeking out either marriage to Pelops or the resulting death of her father. In an interesting if obscure mythic account, however, even Penelope has to make a choice between father and husband, but with a more benign outcome. Pausanias provides this version in the course of discussing an image of Aidos (modesty, reverence) in Lakonia. In his account, a woman uses her veil as a means of expressing her will, in a kind of reverse *anakalypteria*. In contrast to the usual ritual, in which the bride is uncovered at the moment of presentation to the husband's family, the situation here is anomalous. No relatives of the groom's family are present, and the father's inappropriate refusal to relinquish his daughter leads the bride to perform the exact opposite of the expected action. She covers her head to indicate her change of allegiance from father to husband. Here the usual ritual of incorporation into the husband's *oikos* is replaced with a gesture that emphasizes instead her separation from the *oikos* of her father:

ὅτ᾽ ἔδωκεν Ὀδυσσεῖ Πηνελόπην γυναῖκα Ἰκάριος, ἐπειρᾶτο μὲν κατοικίσαι καὶ αὐτὸν Ὀδυσσέα ἐν Λακεδαίμονι, διαμαρτάνων δὲ ἐκείνου δεύτερα τὴν θυγατέρα ἱκέτευε καταμεῖναι καὶ ἐξορμωμένης

A FAMILY ROMANCE

97

ἐς Ἰθάκην ἐπακολουθῶν τῷ ἅρματι ἐδεῖτο. Ὀδυσσεὺς δὲ τέως μὲν ἠνείχετο, τέλος δὲ ἐκέλευε Πηνελόπην συνακολουθεῖν ἑκοῦσαν ἢ τὸν πατέρα ἑλομένην ἀναχωρεῖν ἐς Λακεδαίμονα. καὶ τὴν ἀποκρίνασθαί φασιν οὐδέν· ἐγκαλυψαμένης δὲ πρὸς τὸ ἐρώτημα, Ἰκάριος τὴν μὲν ἅτε δὴ συνιεὶς ὡς βούλεται ἀπιέναι μετὰ Ὀδυσσέως ἀφίησιν, ἄγαλμα δὲ ἀνέθηκεν Αἰδοῦς· ἐνταῦθα γὰρ τῆς ὁδοῦ προήκουσαν ἤδη τὴν Πηνελόπην λέγουσιν ἐγκαλύψασθαι.

When Icarius gave Penelope in marriage to Odysseus, he tried to make Odysseus himself settle in Lacedaemon, but failing in the attempt, he next besought his daughter to remain behind, and when she was setting forth to Ithaca he followed the chariot, begging her to stay. Odysseus endured it for a time, but at last he bade Penelope either to accompany him willingly, or else, if she preferred her father, to go back to Lacedaemon. They say that she made no reply, but covered her face with a veil in reply to the question so that Icarius, realising that she wished to depart with Odysseus, let her go, and dedicated an image of Modesty; for Penelope, they say, had reached this point of the road when she veiled herself. (Paus. 3.20.10–11, trans. Jones and Ormerod)

Even when daughters choose to ally themselves with their fathers, that is not where mythic interest lies. Of the fifty Danaids, forty-nine obeyed their father's command to kill their husbands on their wedding night. Although Apollodoros (2.1.5) lists all their names, only Hypermnestra, the one in fifty who chose to disobey her father, is known to all. Pausanias tells us that she had to stand trial for disobedience to her father, although she was acquitted with the help of Aphrodite. In thanks for the goddess' defense against the charge of impiety, she dedicated an image of Aphrodite Nikephoros ("Bringer of Victory") as well as a temple to Artemis Peitho ("Persuasion").[16]

If we return now to myths in which the woman must choose between loyalty to her brother or to her other male relatives, the picture becomes clearer. Upon hearing that he has killed her brothers in a dispute over the Kalydonian boar, Althaia destroys her son Meleager by putting back in the fire the magic brand that will determine his life span.[17] According to Apollodoros (1.8.3), this choice is not without its price, and she thereafter commits suicide. He tells us that after Meleager's death, both Althaia and Meleager's wife Kleopatra hanged themselves, and the women mourning them were turned into birds.

Allegiance to brothers is also a motive for Alkmene, who refuses to allow her new husband Amphitryon to consummate their marriage until he has avenged the deaths of her brothers at the hands of the Teleboians. Apollodoros says that she agreed to marry him only after he had carried out the vengeance (2.4.6). The results of that delayed consummation are well known: while Amphitryon is off performing this service for his wife, Zeus steals a march on him and, appearing in the likeness of the husband, impregnates Alkmene with the hero Herakles.

This allegiance of sisters to their brothers is not unreciprocated. In Euripides' *Alkestis*, Pheres tells Admetos that Alkestis' brother will take revenge on him, since by allowing her to die for him he has as good as murdered her:

> θάψεις δ᾽ αὐτὸς ὢν αὐτῆς φονεύς,
> δίκας δὲ δώσεις σοῖσι κηδεσταῖς ἔτι·
> ἦ τἄρ᾽ Ἄκαστος οὐκέτ᾽ ἔστ᾽ ἐν ἀνδράσιν,
> εἰ μή σ᾽ ἀδελφῆς αἷμα τιμωρήσεται.

> You yourself, her murderer, will bury her,
> but yet you will pay the penalty to her kin,
> for Akastos is not to be numbered among men
> if he does not avenge his sister's blood.
> (*Alkestis* 730–33)

Elektra is represented by all three tragedians as counting on Orestes as the only one who can come to intervene in her miserable existence, as is Iphigeneia in *Iphigeneia among the Taurians*.[18]

We find the reverse of Kadmos' supposed overvaluing of kinship in searching for his sister in a more obscure example from Plutarch's *Greek Questions*. Here it is a sister, Hypera, who goes forth from her home in Anthedon to search for her missing brother, Anthos:

> ὁ σε Μνασιγείτων φησὶν Ὑπέρας ἀδελφὸν ὄντα τὸν Ἄνθον
> ἔτι νήπιον ἀπολέσθαι, καὶ τὴν Ὑπέραν κατὰ ζήτησιν αὐτοῦ
> πλανώμενον εἰς Φερὰς πρὸς Ἄκαστον ἐλθεῖν, ὅπου κατὰ τύχην
> ὁ Ἄνθος ἐδούλευεν οἰνοχοεῖν τεταγμένος. ὡς οὖν εἰστιῶντο, τὸν
> παῖδα προσφέροντα τῇ ἀδελφῇ τὸ ποτήριον ἐπιγνῶναι καὶ εἰπεῖν
> πρὸς αὐτὴν ἡσυχῇ
> πῖν᾽ οἶνον τρυγίαν, ἐπεὶ οὐκ Ἀνθηδόνα ναίεις.

Mnasigeiton says that Anthos, the brother of Hypera, disappeared from home while he was still a child, and that Hypera, while she was wandering about in search of him, came to Pherae to the house of Akastos, where it chanced that Anthos was the slave appointed to be cup-bearer. While they were feasting the boy recognized his sister, as he was bearing her cup to her, and said to her softly, "Drink wine turbid with lees, since thou dwellest not in Anthedon." (Plutarch, *Greek Questions* 19, 295f, trans. Babbitt, modified)

Despite the implausibility of a sister who goes abroad in the world, possibly alone, and attends feasts like a man, the story has all the poignance of a miniature novel, and all the romance that later ages associate not with siblings but with erotic liaisons and tales of thwarted love and miraculous reunion. As we will see, the plays of Euripides concerning the house of Atreus, particularly *Elektra* and *Iphigeneia among the Taurians*, recreate very much the same mood of passionate longing of brother for sister and sister for brother, and the romance of their reunion.

Of course, not every sibling relation in Greek myth is benign. Medea chops her little brother to pieces to create a diversion for her escape with Jason.[19] Sibling relations can be interrupted or subverted precisely by the intervention of erotic desire. Usually, as with Medea, that desire is for an outsider, a lover who will force the choice of loyalties, but it can also be incestuous desire. Rarely, however, do the myths address brother-sister incest. Only the gods are free to commit incest, and for Zeus, a brother-sister marriage is the clear solution to a troublesome dynastic problem, and an occasion for farce, not tragedy. (The divine regime ruled over by an incestuous pair of siblings has parallels in many traditional societies, including some of the Oceanic ones discussed by Weiner, that trace their lineage back to an originary incestous brother-sister pair.[20]) In the Greek material, I believe, the incestuous impulse reappears, most often in sublimated form, in wishes to avoid procreation, and regressive fantasies in which the children dream of reconstituting themselves as a family without parents or possibly even spouses. I return to these fantasies at the end of this chapter.

The degree to which allegiance to brother trumps allegiance to husband and children, as in the *Antigone*, may be missed because it is so uncomfortable for modern sensibilities. Certainly Jebb, in arguing against the relevance of the Herodotos passage for Antigone, misses the point when he says, "The sliding-scale-theory of the religious duty here involves a fallacy, from the Greek point of view. Greeks distinguished between the obligation in respect to *sungenes* and in respect to *thuraioi*. A husband and child are on the same side of that line as a brother."[21] In fact, the concern about a woman's foreign status in the family into which she has married is clear not only from the myths, but also from Athenian marriage laws.[22] In-marrying women are clearly not *sungenēs*.[23] Relationships between siblings seem to have been conceived of as more durable than those between husbands and wives, or even mothers and children.

As a final example of the theme of a sister's choice, let us turn to another telling, though less familiar, example, from Apollodoros (2.6.4), which has already been discussed in Chapter Three. After the first sack of Troy, King Laomedon's daughter Hesione is given to Telamon as a prize by Herakles, and is allowed to rescue one captive. She chooses her brother Podarkes, whom she ransoms with her veil (*kaluptra*), whence his new name, Priam ("the ransomed one"). As with Penelope in the Pausanias account, the veil, a textile, serves both as the instrument of choice and as the communication of that choice. By taking these examples together, it may be possible to make passages such as the one from *Antigone* more intelligible.

A SIBLING ROMANCE: THE ESCAPE FROM EXCHANGE

The problem of brothers and sisters is in part the problem of reconciling intimacy with distance, exchange with preservation of the family resources, the desire to stay together with the need to marry out. In this way, it echoes the tensions discussed earlier between inside and out, self-sufficiency and exchange, that govern the ideology of the *oikos*. Annette Weiner's idea of "keeping-while-giving" clearly was inspired in part by the end of *The Elementary Structures of Kinship*. Lévi-Strauss' epigraph for the concluding section of the book is a summary of a myth from the Andaman Islands that bears quoting: "The future life will be but a repetition of the present, but all will then remain in the prime of life, sickness and death will be unknown, and there will be no more marrying or giving in marriage."[24]

The close connection between marriage and exchange in general can be seen in Andrew Strathern's remarks about the Melpa people of Papua New Guinea, who recognize the existence of a spirit who "embodies the idea of sister as well as wife, the one to be given away as well as the one who comes to be married; she is the composite in this sense, and can stand for the overall flow of exchange."[25] For the Melpa, as for Lévi-Strauss, marriage is the prototype of all exchanges. The Melpa spirit blurs the usually enforced distinctions between sister and wife, while the Andaman Islanders dream of exiting altogether from the world of exchange. The nature of the fantasy becomes more explicit in Lévi-Strauss' concluding words:

To this very day, mankind has always dreamed of seizing and fixing that fleeting moment when it was permissible to believe that the law of exchange could be evaded, that one could gain without losing, enjoy without sharing. At either end of the earth and at both extremes of time, the Sumerian myth of the golden age and the Andaman myth of the future life correspond, the former placing the end of primitive happiness at a time when the confusion of languages made words into common property, the latter describing the bliss of the hereafter as a heaven where women will no longer be exchanged, i.e., removing to an equally unattainable past or future the joys, eternally denied to social man, of a world in which one might *keep to oneself.*

Weiner has built on this notion an entire critique of Marcel Mauss' concept of reciprocity, the idea that the obligation to return the gift comes from the gift itself. She argues instead that giving things of lesser value protects those possessions one most wants to keep. Constructing a continuum of exchange, she shows the correlation between matriliny, with its close alliances of brother and sister pairs, and high female status. At one end of her continuum are the Trobrianders, for whom the idea of keeping the sister is so powerful that they believe procreation comes about through impregnation by the spirits of the matrilineage. (The actual husband is thought to make only a modest contribution to the creation of offspring.) The woman's children inherit from her brother, and brother and sister give each other economic and political assistance throughout their lives. Although this approaches the dream of a world without exchange, the Trobrianders engage in elaborate rituals of gift-exchange (*kula*). At the other end of the continuum, Weiner places the patrilineal Melpa, among whom women are held in low esteem, who have no inalienable possessions, and who are more interested in giving than in keeping. Male dominance is strong, but Melpa men dream about and ritually enact the advantages of sibling intimacy, even as the actual contacts between sisters and brothers remain highly circumscribed.

So, what does all this have to do with the Greek case? The Greek society we know from Homer on shows no particular signs of having been matrilineal in origin (much less matriarchal, as some have claimed).[26] The figures of Greek myth seem to have more in common with the Melpa than with the Andaman Islanders, despite the prevalence of close sibling cooperation in the myths I have discussed. But our ancient texts are not field reports, and it would be foolhardy to expect to make a coherent system out of the mythic elements we have at our disposal. Nonetheless, the different types of social organization can be glimpsed in the heterogeneous mass of material of myth and epic. Among the societies Odysseus encounters is the incestuous one of the daughters and sons of Aiolos, married to each other on their island. These mythic and semi-divine beings seem to have a chance to enact the fantasy of a life without exchange. If we consider how the opposite pole might be represented in the Greek material, we return to what one scholar has called "The Dream of a World without Women," borrowing the title of an important article by Marylin Arthur [Katz] on the prooimium to Hesiod's *Theogony*. The particular fantasy I turn to now is not Hesiod's, but a related one from Euripides, who has been reviled as a misogynist and equally wrongheadedly cast as a feminist. These words do not represent the playwright's own views, but come from the mouth of his indubitably misogynist character Hippolytos, who says:

ὦ Ζεῦ, τί δὴ κίβδηλον ἀνθρώποις κακὸν
γυναῖκας ἐς φῶς ἡλίου κατῴκισας;
εἰ γὰρ βρότειον ἤθελες σπεῖραι γένος,
οὐκ ἐκ γυναικῶν χρῆν παρασχέσθαι τόδε,
ἀλλ᾿ ἀντιθέντας σοῖσιν ἐν ναοῖς βροτοὺς
ἢ χαλκὸν ἢ σίδηρον ἢ χρυσοῦ βάρος
παίδων πρίασθαι σπέρμα, του τιμήματος
τῆς ἀξίας ἕκαστον, ἐν δὲ δώμασιν
ναίειν ἐλευθέροισι θηλειῶν ἄτερ.

Oh Zeus, what evil counterfeit for men
have you brought into the light of the sun?
If you wished to propagate the mortal race,
why did it have to be from women?
Why not instead let the seed of children be sold
to men who placed bronze or iron or heavy gold
in your temples, each in accordance with his worth,
and let men live in their houses, free from women?
(Eur., *Hippolytos* 616–24)

Hippolytos has earlier expressed his own version of the Andaman fantasy that "the future life will be but a repetition of the present, but all will then remain in the prime of life" when he says, "So may I turn the post set at life's end even as I began the race."[27] Although the character's explicit meaning seems to be that he wishes to hold to his principles, the line identifies him as one of a class of mythic young men who fail to make the transition to adulthood, such as Hymenaios or Hyakinthos. In this way, among other unwelcome changes, he would avoid the social expectation that a mature man would engage in marriage and procreation.

A similar fantasy of alternate procreation methods is articulated by Jason in Euripides' *Medea*, but here it takes on a particularity suited to the character of Hippolytos, who is very concerned, like his father Theseus, with questions of worth, status, and legitimacy. The hierarchies of value suggested by Hippolytos' alternative model of human reproduction seem to go hand-in-hand with his fears about his standing in the city as the illegitimate noncitizen child of the Amazon.

Let us consider how this vision of procreative one-stop shopping fits into the continuum suggested by Weiner. Hippolytos' Dream of a World without Women is perhaps even further on the continuum than the Melpa. The patriarch takes women for granted, but the misogynist holds women beneath contempt, and imagines a world without them. As it turns out, in what may be either a perverse coincidence or a vindication of the notion that marriage is the prototype for exchange, Hippolytos' imagined world is one in which exchange would actually stand in for marriage.[28] The world Hippolytos desires would turn back the clock on the creation of woman and the institution of marriage. Instead of the usual methods, men would deposit metal offerings in the temple according to their worth, and receive children in return. The text is ambiguous, but it may suggest that the quality of the children is in relation to the value of the offerings.[29] At one pole, we find the "Dream of a World without Exchange," in which a man may keep his own sister, and at the other pole, no women at all, but only exchange, with payments in precious metals standing in for their indispensable biological contribution.

But, to return to our ethnographic examples, even a people like the Melpa are still very interested in sibling intimacy, despite their devaluation of women. The spirit who confounds the identities of sister and wife is evidence of this. And even Hippolytos, with his rejection of women, does not rule out a female presence in his life. That presence, which sadly becomes an absence at his moment of greatest need, is the virgin goddess Artemis, the sacred sister par excellence, whom one might almost call the divine embodiment of the incest taboo and of sibling cooperation. This cooperation is perhaps never so coldly demonstrated as when Artemis and her brother Apollo work together to destroy the children of Niobe. As shown on the Niobe Painter's name vase in Berlin, Artemis takes aim at the daughters of Niobe while Apollo brings down the sons. This can be seen as a macabre representation of the sexual division of labor, and, reflecting the general role of these two gods in bringing death, a job that also divides along gender lines. But Artemis the death-dealer may nonetheless not behold her faithful devotée Hippolytos in his last moments, and his dream ends with a death not attended by a divine sister who can never be touched.

The family romance of Hippolytos involves selecting divine and remote kinship over the messier relations of mortals, but the tragedies about the children of Agamemnon and Klytemnestra suggest another kind of family romance altogether, one in which brothers displace husbands as objects of desire, and reunited siblings indulge momentarily in a regressive dream of recapturing childhood, only this time without parents. (And with parents like these, who can blame them?)

I will give a few examples from Aeschylus' *Choephoroi*, Sophocles' *Elektra*, and Euripides' *Elektra*, as well as the *Iphigeneia among the Taurians*. In the three Elektra plays, the sister anxiously awaits Orestes, the only hope for her liberation and for revenge against her mother for the death of Agamemnon. For all three Elektras, Orestes is *philteros*, "dearer," or *philtatos*, "dearest."[30] In the *Choephoroi*, Elektra greets Orestes as *philtaton melēma dōmasin patros* ("best beloved darling of my father's house"). He is three times called *philtatos* by Elektra, which then makes the use of this endearment by Klytemnestra to refer to the dead Aigisthos even more shocking. Sophocles' Elektra (164–65) refers to herself as *ateknos*, without children, and *anumpheutos*, unmarried, but she waits not for a lover or husband, but for her brother, *philtatou brotōn pantōn Orestou* (903–4), most beloved of all men. When she thinks he is dead, she delivers a lengthy and passionate lament (1126–70). At the end of Euripides' play, the siblings, whose initial reunion is comparatively brief, when faced again with separation, engage in a passionate parting.

Ὀρέστης
ὦ σύγγονέ μοι, χρονίαν σ' ἐσιδὼν
τῶν σῶν εὐθὺς φίλτρων στέρομαι
καὶ σ' ἀπολείψω σοῦ λειπόμενος. . . .

Ἠλέκτρα
περί μοι στέρνοις στέρνα πρόσαψον,
σύγγονε φίλτατε·
διὰ γὰρ ζευγνῦσ' ἡμᾶς πατρίων
μελάθρων μητρὸς φόνιοι κατάραι.
Ὀρέστης
βάλε, πρόσπτυξον σῶμα· θανόντος δ'
ὡς ἐπὶ τύμβῳ καταθρήνησον. . . .
οὐκέτι σ' ὄψομαι.
Ἠλέκτρα
οὐδ' ἐγὼ ἐς σὸν βλέφαρον πελάσω.
Ὀρέστης
τάδε λοίσθιά μοι προσφθέγματά σου. . . .
ὦ πιστοτάτη, στείχεις ἤδη;

Orestes: O Sister, I found you so late, and so soon
    I lose you, robbed of your healing love, and leave you
    behind as you have left me. . . .

Elektra: Hold me now closely breast against breast,
    dear Brother, I love you. But the curses bred in a mother's blood
    dissolve our bonds and drive us from home.
Orestes: Come to me, clasp my body, lament
    as if at the tomb of a man now dead. . . .
    I shall not see you again.
Elektra: I shall never more walk in the light of your eye.
Orestes: Now is the last I can hear your voice. . . .
    O loyal love, do you go so soon?
    (Eur. *Elektra* 1308–36, trans. Vermeule)[31]

As this scene ends, Orestes' command to Pylades to be a good husband to his sister brings us up short. We already know that Orestes will give his sister in marriage to his dear friend Pylades, but this is information that belongs to the world of heroic genealogy. In Euripides' terms, this marriage has no affective power that can come near the emotionalism of the sister-brother bond.

The protagonist of Euripides' *Iphigeneia among the Taurians* has much in common with her sister Elektra in the Elektra plays. Iphigeneia laments her situation—"wife of no man and mother of no child"—as well as her lost brother, whom she last saw at her mother's breast, and one day expected to see as king of Argos (230–35). Orestes' reaction on discovering his sister is as strong as Elektra's in the other plays:

δέχομαι· παρεὶς δὲ γραμμάτων διαπτυχὰς
τὴν ἡδονὴν πρῶτ᾽ οὐ λόγοις αἱρήσομαι.
ὦ φιλτάτη μοι σύγγον᾽, ἐκπεπληγμένος
ὅμως σ᾽ ἀπίστῳ περιβαλὼν βραχίονι
ἐς τέρψιν εἶμι, πυθόμενος θαυμάστ᾽ ἐμοί.

I accept. I will not trouble to open the letter but will choose first a pleasure not of words but of deeds. Sister I love best, stunned though I am, with scarce believing arms, I yet come to the pleasure of your embrace. These are wonders I have heard. (*Iphigeneia among the Taurians* 793–97, trans. Kovacs)

Iphigeneia responds, once convinced,

⟨ὢ⟩ ψυχά, τί φῶ; θαυμάτων
πέρα καὶ λόγου πρόσω τάδ᾽ ἀπέβα.

O my soul, what am I to say? These events
surpass wonder and beggar speech!
(*Iphigeneia among the Taurians* 838–40)

Reunited against all expectation, Orestes and Iphigeneia, two siblings
who knew scarcely more than the myths about each other, rejoice in a fantasy of return to Argos. Until now, mythic chronologies and theatrical conventions have kept the siblings apart, especially the sisters, who seem to
have little recollection of one another, although each remembers vividly the
young Orestes, from whom they were separated when he was still a baby. It
is a shock even to think of Elektra, the daughter of an unmotherly mother
(*mētēr amētōr*, Soph. *El.* 1154), and Iphigeneia, the daughter who laments
her "fatherless fate" (*apator' apatora potmon*, Eur. *IT* 863), in the same play
or the same palace. In fact, they do not ever meet in tragedy, although Iphigeneia does inquire eagerly for news of her sister. For the first time, all the
siblings are incorporated into a notion of family. About their parents, however, they contrive to say as little as possible.

Despite her absence, Elektra plays an important part in her siblings' reunion. As Orestes tries to convince Iphigeneia of his identity, he reminds
her of stories about the family's past, about the quarrel between Atreus
and Thyestes, told to them by Elektra (811–12). Iphigeneia chimes in, re-
membering the golden lamb, and Orestes reminds her of the weaving she
did illustrating this piece of family history. Here, in a move of tragic self-
referentiality, the usual tokens of recognition— like the weaving produced
in the *Choephoroi* (231–32)—are transformed. Women's weaving retains its
importance, but here it is the characters' *memories* of the woven objects that
serve the traditional function of guaranteeing identity, rather than the objects themselves.[32]

The reunion scene, and the tokens in particular, provide a catalogue of
family treacheries, most of them between female and male family members. Here, unusually, the women are not always at fault. The very context of Iphigeneia's exile among the Taurians, and the separation from her
brother with which this scene will end, is Agamemnon's betrayal of her,
his young daughter, and of his wife. The tokens alternate between those
which recall the dismal family history, and those which pertain to Iphigeneia's own sorry tale. The recognition scene begins when Iphigeneia tells of
the planned sacrifice at Argos and the last-minute rescue, and Orestes re-
alizes who she is. The process of identification proceeds next to genealogy:

Iphigeneia asks, "Did the Spartan daughter of Tyndarios bear you?" (*all' hē Lakaina Tundaris s' egeinato*? Eur., IT 806).[33] Orestes answers with another genealogical reference: "I was born to the child of the child of Pelops" (*Pelopos ge paidi paidos, hou 'kpephuk' egō*, 807).

Soon, however, Iphigeneia wants proof (*tekmērion*, 808). This leads not to the production of actual tangible tokens, but to a question-and-answer session. The *tekmēria* are to be memories of stories, and of objects like those that serve as tokens in the earlier plays. Orestes asks Iphigeneia if she remembers the stories told by their sister Elektra, about the deadly rivalry between their grandfather Atreus and his brother Thyestes (811–12). In these two lines, two contrasting models of sibling relations are introduced. One model is of loving behavior between siblings, the other is of the most violent fraternal strife. For both Orestes and Iphigeneia, their sister Elektra becomes a kind of token, a shared memory of harmonious family relations, while the memory of her stories recalls the bitter enmity of two brothers, their ancestors, who are indirectly responsible for the bitterness of their own lives.

From memories of stories they were told, the siblings proceed to memories of the weavings depicting the high points of the stories—the quarrel between Atreus and Thyestes, the golden lamb and the reversal of the sun—two portents that signified the gods' involvement in the royal succession. The quarrel between the brothers was marked by the seduction of Atreus' wife Aerope by Thyestes, by means of which Thyestes got the golden lamb, leading to a gruesome revenge as Atreus fed Thyestes' children to him. But these details are not the stuff of children's pastimes, not even in the house of Agamemnon. Instead we find the storybook version, complete with harmless illustrations. All the same, these recalled images continue the process of establishing the common heredity of the two siblings.

Things start to take a more adult turn with the next set of remembrances, which pertain to Iphigeneia's own history again—the bath before the marriage and the lock of hair that Iphigeneia sent back as a memorial for her tomb. The final *tekmēria* (822) are Orestes' memories of Pelops' ancient spear that hung in Iphigeneia's bedroom when she was a young girl. Once again the token is the *memory* of the kind of tangible object, like Agamemnon's seal (*sphragis*) in Sophocles' *Elektra*, that elsewhere in tragedy serves as a token of recognition. In this shared memory, the past of the house of Atreus and the lived experience of the younger Iphigeneia come together. It is only now that Iphigeneia cries out for joy at having found her brother.

Even the marriage of Elektra is no obstacle to the fantasy of continuing sibling intimacy, since she has married Pylades, who is like a brother to

Orestes, and so by extension is like a brother to her. To quote Weiner, "Giving a sibling to a spouse is like giving an inalienable possession to an outsider. Some way must remain open to reclaim the sibling."[34] That way out in the case of Orestes and Elektra is through the fictive sibling relationship between brother and husband.

As the play ends, Orestes and Iphigeneia prepare to return to a land in which they can be sister and brother together without end, in apparent violation of the usual rule. It is the dream of a world without exchange, a world in which men do not have to give up their sisters; but this fantasy has been bought at great price. Not only that, it is fantasy that cannot be fulfilled. The prophecies of Athena make clear that they will return to Greece only to be separated again, as are the siblings at the end of Euripides' *Elektra*.

For the children of Agamemnon, the regressive fantasy is displaced by the social realities of the exchange system. In the end, Orestes must turn one sister over to a husband, and relinquish the other to the goddess to whom she owes her life, and to whom she has long been dedicated. Not so for the children of Oidipous, whose desire for sibling intimacy is no different, but whose incestuous origin calls for a harsher ending. For Antigone, in love with death, married to death, the only place where she can be reunited with her brother is the house of Hades. For the family of Oidipous, the family romance is a nightmare that can only be consummated in the Underworld. Antigone has chosen to reject Haimon, the world of marriage and child-bearing, has effectively chosen brother over husband or child. In the house of Oidipous, a kind of posthumous sibling intimacy rules, thoroughly displacing the exchange of women.

CHAPTER SEVEN

CONCLUSION:
The GENDER of RECIPROCITY

From women as gifts to women as givers, from benign to dangerous exchange, from treacherous marriages to the idealized bond between siblings, I have taken a sometimes circuitous path to end with a model of reciprocity between women and men that appears—in stark contrast to much of what came before—positive, even optimistic. My task in these final pages is to call that apparent optimism into question, and thus to bring my argument, like some endlessly circulating *agalma*, back to its beginning. The endpoint of these investigations is not, after all, that sibling relations are the solution to the problem of gender antagonism in ancient Greece. Instead, they are another manifestation of that problem.

In this book, I have used the theme of exchange so central to Greek thinking to untangle attitudes toward women in their dealings with husbands, sons, fathers, and brothers. Implicit in my explorations is an attempt to understand the misogyny so frequent in Greek texts, from its unadulterated form in Hesiod, to the casual male domination of the Homeric world, to the full-fledged fear of rule by women expressed so often in tragedy. I close with a consideration of *charis*, which one might call the animating force behind many of the transactions discussed in this book.

With the word *charis*, Greek expresses the charm Athena pours over Odysseus for his reunion with Penelope, the pleasure of song, and the enchantment of a beautifully wrought object. An object of admiration, whether a person or thing, is said to possess the property of *charis*, which may be inherent or bestowed by a god or a skilled craftsman. It is a quality that incites not only admiration, but also the desire for possession. In other words, *charis* objectifies the person or thing in which it is found. But this does not exhaust the possible meanings of the word.

Charis, sometimes translated as "grace," is also the closest word in Greek to the English "reciprocity." It renders both the favor given and the gratitude felt in return. *Charis* is central to the relationship of *xenia* ("guest-friendship," in the clumsy English approximation). *Xenia* is a relationship of generalized reciprocity, based on trust that hospitality will one day be repaid, if not in this generation, then in the next. The hereditary relationship of *xenoi* is nearly always a relationship between men, and consequently passes through the male line. The *xeneia*—"guest-gifts"—that solidify and commemorate these relationships are often *agalmata* that have their own genealogy, like the bowl Menelaos gives to Telemachos, a guest-gift to Menelaos from his guest-friend King Phaidimos of Sidon. These charismatic male objects commemorate and guarantee a sequence of relationships between men. Homer offers rare exceptions: Helen knows how to receive guests properly (and to give a guest-gift) in *Odyssey* 4, and Arete's reception is important in *Odyssey* 7. But for the most part, women's lack of mobility keeps them out of the *xenia* game.

I have argued that the ideal of *autarkeia*, self-sufficiency, in conflict with the principle of exogamy, is in part responsible for the disdain for women that we find full-strength in Hesiod, and to a milder degree in other ancient Greek texts. The concept of *charis* may also help to explain the ambivalence toward women as exchangers in Greek thinking. If *charis* on the one hand defines and objectifies the beautiful object, and on the other characterizes relationships of reciprocity between men, it is not hard to see that the objectification of women is over-determined by the ideology of *charis*, and that women's fitness for participation in exchange-relations is undermined by this ideology. Despite exceptions, especially in the *Odyssey*, the picture I have delineated generally places women on the wrong side of reciprocity.

By this reckoning, women only possess *charis* insofar as they are themselves charismatic objects, but this does not mean that they are immune to its allure. Objects themselves, their desire for *charis* expresses itself in the yearning for other objects in which it inheres. They are represented, apart from the rare exceptions like Penelope, as incapable of establishing relationships based on the *charis* of mutual regard and respect that we see among Homeric and tragic heroes. Women's desire for these charismatic objects, moreover, brings about the opposite of all that *charis* represents. It destroys relationships between men and women, as well as those between men. Female beauty and female desire for beauty are shown to be always at least potentially destructive to the *charis* of human relationships. If *autarkeia* represents safety, *charis* hints at disruption. This seems counterintuitive, and it is not a sentiment that is ever made explicit in Greek literature, but I think it is related to the consistent queasiness about women and exchange that I have detailed.

Why, then, are sibling relationships so different—as I have argued they are? Here, I think that the very different dynamic of family relations allows women as sisters to break out of the straitjacket of objectification that other male-female relationships enforce. The difference is marriage. Fathers give away their daughters, who are conventionally imbued with *charis*; husbands receive these charismatic objects; and sons are produced by these relationships. Only brothers (with some exceptions) do not take part in the marriage market of their sisters. The impassioned texts from tragedy that I quote in Chapter Six suggest a language of affective reciprocity between men and women—outside of the *charis* economy I have just sketched out—that is possible only in brother-sister relations in a gender-segregated society like that of ancient Greece.

It is only when a woman acts outside of her usual role as object in the economics of gender that true reciprocity between a man and a woman can flower. Otherwise, only the rarest of women and men, like Penelope and Odysseus, can find their own road of many turnings to a relationship of reciprocity conceived as simultaneously impossible and ideal. More often, women—once defined as commodities to be brought from the outside— remain always alienated and always alien, while men are forever thwarted from the ideal of self-sufficiency by the need to acquire these precious objects that cannot be made at home.

NOTES

INTRODUCTION

1. Not every gift given by a woman in Greek myth is destructive, nor is every gift given by a man benign. I have more to say about the role of women in benign exchanges below. On cross-cultural perceptions of the dangers of exchange, see Parry 1989.

2. Kurke 1991 and 1999; von Reden 1995; Seaford 1994; Gill et al. 1998; Wagner-Hasel 2000. Donlan (especially 1982 and 1989) specifically addresses Homeric reciprocity. Reciprocity is treated in a more purely historical context by Herman (1987) and Mitchell (2002).

3. Rabinowitz 1993; Wohl 1998; Ormand 1999. Foley (2001: 11–13) provides an excellent overview of previous work.

4. Scott (1986) makes the point that the word "gender" articulates a "relational notion."

5. For the distinction between optimism and pessimism in feminist approaches to classics, see Richlin 1993: 272–303. Just (1989: 106ff.) uses the same distinction in discussing the question of women's seclusion in ancient Athens.

6. For a more historical approach to some of the same issues, see Foley 2001.

7. This is not to say that endogamous marriage is unknown in Greek myth and in the historical record. See below, Chapter Two. For varying views on the conflict between reciprocity and autarky, see van Wees 1998: 38 n. 72.

8. In different contexts, *oikos* may mean family, household, estate, or "house" in the metaphorical sense. See Pomeroy 1997: 20, and the more extensive discussion in Cox 1998: 132–35. For the gendered coding of inside and outside, see the classic treatment of the Berber house by Bourdieu (1970). Cohen (1990 and 1991) builds on this and other ethnographies in his treatment of gendered space in classical Athens. On gendered domestic space, see Antonaccio 2000. See also Chapter One.

9. McInerney 2010: 6.

10. For the debate on "Homeric Society," see Snodgrass 1974; Finley 1978; Qviller 1981; Geddes 1984; Morris 1986b; and for an excellent overview, see Raaflaub 1997.

11. Especially by Snodgrass (1974). For a critique, see Morris (1986b: 105–15), who draws on the ideas of Goody and Tambiah 1973 and Goody 1976; and Donlan 1989: 4. I count myself among those who deny that Homeric epic provides evidence for the existence of the dowry. See Patterson 1998: 57–58, for a discussion of the opposing views of Finley ([1954] 1978) and Morris (1986b). Patterson also discusses (64) the absence of evidence for dowry in Hesiod. See also Chapter One, n. 18.

12. The work of David Cohen (1990, 1991) makes use of modern ethnographies to

suggest where there may be gaps between ideology and practice in the ancient world. See also Lyons 2007.

13. Seaford 1994: xvii; similarly (p. 6): "Although Homeric epic does not give us a photograph of an actual society, neither is it *merely* an ideological construction."

CHAPTER ONE

1. Gernet [1948] 1981: 253 n. 40. See von Reden 1995: 82, for a cursory treatment of dangerous gifts in Gernet, and von Reden 1999 for a more extended discussion of Gernet's article, which does not, however, address the question of dangerous gifts.

2. Mauss [1925] 1990.

3. "An ornament, a glory or delight," also used "of things offered to a god": Cunliffe [1924] 1963, s.v. ἄγαλμα.

4. See Goldhill 1984: 29, on the resonances of this usage. In time the word came to refer specifically to a dedication to the gods, and ultimately to a statue of a god. See Osborne 1994: 90–94, on the interconnection of these different meanings. See also Scodel 1996.

5. Gernet [1948] 1981: 114–15.

6. One of the most explicit statements of the different spheres encompassed by the Greek *oikos* is Xenophon's *Oikonomikos*, discussed in greater detail below. See also Vernant [1965] 1983.

7. For discussions of the uses classicists have made of anthropology and the attendant difficulties, see Humphreys 1978; Hunter 1981; Redfield 1991.

8. The reader will notice that most of the revisionist anthropology I cite was published in the 1980s and 1990s. This reflects a historical moment of reconsideration of these central themes of the discipline. As the field of anthropology has become more aware of its problematic relationship to colonialism, its focus has shifted to issues of reflexivity and transnationalism, while some of the more traditional issues with which I am concerned here have recently been somewhat eclipsed. On these issues, see Asad 1973; Marcus and Fischer 1986; Ahmed and Shore 1995; Herzfeld 2001.

9. Gayle Rubin's 1975 article, "The Traffic in Women," is a groundbreaking feminist critique of Lévi-Strauss. Weiner 1979 is a feminist restudy of a culture made famous by Malinowski. See Strathern (1981, 1987a, 1989) for a critique of what she regards as a problematic attempt to create a feminist anthropology.

10. Strathern 1981.

11. In Athens, marriage between uterine half-siblings was prohibited, whereas in Sparta, it was homopatric half-siblings who were forbidden to marry. See Pomeroy (1997: 34), who cites Demosthenes 57.20; Plutarch, *Them.* 32.2; and Philo, *De spec. leg.* 3.22.

12. Cox (1998: 31–37) covers the issues of endogamous marriage in some detail, including those less common contexts in which marriage within the matriline is advantageous. She puts the rate among documentable Athenian marriages in the orators at 19 percent, which, although not insignificant, is still relatively low for a society that practices in-marrying.

13. The term is usually translated as "heiress," which is somewhat misleading, but does suggest—probably accurately—the woman's greater than usual degree of economic autonomy.

14. Cox 1998: 94–99; Patterson 1998: 91–106.

15. Examples are cited in Foley 2001: 69–70.

16. Atchity and Barber 1987; Finkelberg 1991. Discussed further in Chapter Four.

17. Athenian bilateral inheritance is structured so as to privilege at every turn paternal over maternal relations, and within these groups, male over female, but it does not exclude maternal or female relations from inheriting. See Pomeroy 1997: 19. For the tension between bilateral elements of succession in Athens and patrilineality, see Patterson 1998: 98; Just 1989: 87–89, 94.

18. On Homeric marriage, see Vernant 1973; Redfield 1982; Morris 1986b; Finkelberg 1991; Foley 2001: 63–64; Westbrook 2005. As recently as van Reden 1995, some have continued to argue for the existence of dowry in Homer. Wagner-Hasel (1988) and Perysinakis (1991) between them have demolished all arguments in favor of the dowry, showing conclusively that the Homeric word *hedna* or *eedna* refers only to gifts given by the prospective bridegroom to the father of the bride. Wagner-Hasel ties *eedna* to the bride's change of residence from her father's to her husband's house. Both she and Finkelberg (1991) discuss the mythic pattern in which a suitor offers military service in lieu of bride-gifts.

19. Foley 2001: 84.

20. Most notably, Weiner 1992.

21. Cunningham 1996: 346.

22. An example from modern India (Patel 2007: 64–67) stresses the vulnerability of rural Hindu women, who are alienated from their natal family at marriage, and thus become entirely dependent on the goodwill of the marital family. Paradoxically, their only source of support if cast out by their husbands comes from their legal right to inherit land from their natal family, a right that by custom is never claimed. By not claiming their share, they maintain good relations with their brothers, to whom they may turn in case of need.

23. Fruzzetti (1982) describes the situation in Bengal, apparently more extreme than that discussed by Patel (previous note), where women are wholly incorporated into their husband's family, and remain there even when widowed. Their incorporation into the marital family makes remarriage all but impossible and divorce apparently unthinkable. See also Raheja 1996 for female reactions to this situation.

24. Cox 1998: 105; see 116–20 for size of dowry relative to inheritance.

25. Redfield 2003: 42. He argues (43) that the wife's continuing connection to her natal family is essential for her role in the family into which she marries. My emphasis on troublesome aspects of the connection with the natal family does not negate this point, but rather indicates one more instance in which social practice and anxieties expressed in myth do not mirror one another directly.

26. Sahlins 1972: 149–83; Weiner 1992; Godelier [1996] 1999: 10–107; Graeber 2001: 151–228. These respectful critiques are testament to the ongoing importance of Mauss' work, even when he has been shown to have misunderstood some of his material. See also van Wees 1998 for a valuable overview of theories of reciprocity.

27. As Mauss noted, the potlatch eventually evolved into the competitive destruction of wealth, a feature not found in Greek contexts.

28. The exchange of armor is discussed in Chapter Three. On Agamemnon's offer: see Beidelmann 1989.

29. See Rubin 1975 for a critique of the notion—fundamental to ancient Greek thinking—that the sexes are in opposition.

---

30. Friedl 1975.

31. For the Inuit, see Friedl 1975. For weavers of sails, see below, Chapter Two, note 16.

32. Peacock 1991: 342–47, on the history of the problem. See also Freidl 1967; Sanday 1981: 76–89. Some Marxist theorists cast women in the role of the proletariat, e.g., Coontz and Henderson 1986.

33. Peacock (1991) has observed and compared the activities of women with and without children to challenge some of these assumptions.

34. Gregory 1982: 47–51. His differences with Strathern are discussed in Graeber (2001: 41–43).

35. Gernet [1948] 1981; Kurke 1999; Seaford 2004.

36. Godelier [1996] 1999: 80. This brief example does not begin to do justice to the complexities of Melanesian gift terminology.

37. It will not come as a surprise that Freud attributed this achievement to the desire to conceal "genital deficiency." Here are his remarks on the subject in their entirety: "It seems that women have made few contributions to the discoveries and inventions in the history of civilization; there is, however, one technique which they may have invented—that of plaiting and weaving. If that is so, we should be tempted to guess the unconscious motive for the achievement. Nature herself would seem to have given the model which this achievement imitates by causing the growth at maturity of the pubic hair that conceals the genitals. The step that remained to be taken lay in making the threads adhere to one another, while on the body they stick into the skin and are only matted together. If you reject this idea as fantastic and regard my belief in the influence of lack of a penis on the configuration of femininity as an *idée fixe*, I am of course defenseless" (Freud [1933] 1965: 132).

38. The classic accounts of the *kula* are Malinowski 1920 and [1922] 1961.

39. Weiner 1979: 91–92.

40. As Weiner (1979) makes clear, the mortuary distributions emphasize women's allegiance to their natal families, particularly to their brothers, whose political fortunes are tied to the ability of their sisters to provide them with sufficient numbers of skirts and mats to make a good showing during funerary rites.

41. Weiner and Schneider 1989: 3, 21, with some counter-examples, mainly from Africa.

42. See Lombardi 1994 on the low prestige assigned to weaving, with citations from Plato and Aristotle.

43. Weiner 1979: 13, discussing M. Strathern's account of the Melpa.

44. The tripod provides an example from the ancient Greek material record of an object that changes its gender associations over time (Langdon 2008: 269-72). Found in women's graves in the Protogeometric through Middle Geometric periods, tripods take on male associations in the Early Iron Age. This gender transformation is accompanied by a change in size, material, and function: no longer small ceramic burial objects, they became monumental bronze dedications at Panhellenic sanctuaries.

45. Discussed in Chapter Three.

46. This scene is discussed in a different context by Scodel (2008: 42).

47. For example, among the Saramaka Maroons, Price (1984: 70) shows that because cloth is not domestically produced but imported, it becomes associated with men, who travel abroad for work and are the source of most imported commodities.

48. Hoskins 1998: 16. Her interest here is in the personal meanings of objects.

In this context, she observes, "they are involved in complex negotiations of sexual identity" (14).

49. Chowning 1987: 136.

50. See also Graeber 2001: 144–45: wampum is male or female depending on color. Nor is the gendering of objects completely divorced from their assignment of rank or sphere. As Graeber notes, in the work of Nancy Munn in Gawa (Papua New Guinea), we find an opposition between the heaviness of gardening (women's work) and the lightness of shells (men's path to fame) (82).

51. Strathern 1989: 202–3. In the Papuan ritual she cites from Schwimmer 1974, both methods of assigning gender are used. When the intention is to establish symbiosis, the gift and its recipient are identified, but later, when the separateness of the participants is emphasized, the gifts are chosen according to the gender of the giver, i.e., metonymically.

52. Schaps 1979: 10, see 9–12 for examples; also Hunter 1994: 27–28.

53. These alternate possibilities are explored in different ways by both Katz 1991 and Felson [1994] 1997. See below, Chapter Four.

54. See Delcourt [1957] 1982: 193–98, on the complementary roles of Athena and Hephaistos, and 48–55 for discussion of Hephaistos' creations, including Pandora.

55. Lévi-Strauss [1949] 1969: 496.

56. Irigaray (1985) suggests that women might remove themselves from the game altogether, but this is a costly option. Rare is the woman (or nymph) who makes this choice, involving loss of identity (Daphne) or eternal punishment (the Danaids). Even a resistant maiden like Atalanta proves to be susceptible to the gleam of golden apples.

57. Godelier ([1996] 1999: 41) tells of two types of marriage among the Baruya, "the exchange of women for women and the exchange of wealth for women."

58. Arete is the daughter of Alkinoos' brother, *Od.* 7.63–66; Aiolos' children: *Od.* 10.5–7.

59. Mauss [1925] 1990; Sahlins 1972; Parry 1989. The theme of "traffic in women" was memorably addressed by Rubin (1975) and later elaborated by Sedgwick (1985).

60. Redfield 1982.

61. The *Iliad* alone provides numerous examples, beside the obvious one of Helen. Agamemnon attempts to appease Achilles by offering him seven captive women (9.128, 130), and the choice of one of his own daughters in marriage (9.144–47). Briseis (1.275–76) and Chryseis (1.118–20) are awarded to Achilles and Agamemnon as prizes (*gera*). Among the prizes that Achilles offers at the funeral games of Patroklos are tripods, horses, cauldrons, and women (23.259–61). Most of these examples will be discussed further in Chapter Three.

62. De Ste. Croix 1970; Schaps 1979; Just 1989. For female landowners in the Hellenistic period, see Pomeroy 1997 and Schaps 1979.

63. Pol. 1269b12–1270a21. See Hodkinson 1989; Patterson 1998: 76–78; Pomeroy 1997: 42–43; Pomeroy 2002: 80–82.

64. Hunter 1989a, 1989b, and 1994; Foxhall 1989 and 1996; Cox 1998. Friedl (1967: 105–7) offers a parallel from twentieth-century Greek villages, where women's power derives from the dowry they bring to the marriage. Ormand (1999: 22) speaks of the economic power gained by women in marriage through the use of wealth they do not technically own.

65. Arthur [Katz] 1984.

66. Ormand 1999: 8.

67. See Todd 1990, and Hunter 1994: 192 n. 9, on the difficulties and benefits of orations as evidence. An excellent discussion of the social context of oratory in Athens can be found in Ober 1989: 43–46.

CHAPTER TWO

1. Although one might expect to find the passive voice used for women, the forms are mostly ambiguous, and, according to LSJ s.v. γαμέω, the use of the passive is rare. Foley (2001: 259) notes that Euripides' Medea tellingly speaks of marrying Jason in the active (γαμοῦσα, 606). By contrast, Anakreon (frag. 86 Bergk = 424 Campbell) uses the middle of a man dominated by his wife (κεῖνος οὐκ ἔγημεν ἀλλ' ἐγήματο). In English it is hard to avoid using the passive: "That man did not marry but was married," or perhaps "married himself off."

2. For a general discussion of these terms, see Goody and Tambiah 1973; Tambiah 1989.

3. Some other examples: *Od.* 4.7; *Iliad* 6.192. I have chosen Homeric examples, but the usage continues throughout the period under discussion. On Greek marriage, see Vernant 1973; Redfield 1982; Just 1989; and the excellent discussion in Foley 2001 of the "contradictions of tragic marriage."

4. See Westbrook 1994 for an overview of practices in the ancient Near East.

5. A similar notion is found in the Sumerian Courtship of Inanna and Dumuzi. The goddess Inanna says to her consort, "I will watch over your house of life, the storehouse. . . . I, the queen of this place, will watch over your house" (Wolkstein and Kramer 1983: 39). For Rome, with an overview of Greek parallels, see Pearce 1974.

6. See Zeitlin 1996: 29–31, for the theme of "keeping safe" and *empedos/-a* as they relate to Odysseus and Penelope.

7. Semonides 7.85–87, discussed further below. As Sussman (1984: 80–81) notes, this text contains an ambivalence about women similar to that found in the *Theogony*. Xenophon also uses the image of the bee, equating the wife to the queen: *Oik.* 7.32–35. Pomeroy 1994: 276–80; Just 1989: 240; Detienne [1972] 1994.

8. For the text, see Diggle 1998: 123; trans. Vellacott 1975: 97. Discussed by Cohen 1990: 151.

9. Xen. *Oik.* 8, etc. See Murnaghan 1988; Pomeroy 1994; Scaife 1995. For the continuity of metaphor between his precepts and the myth of Pandora, see Sissa 1990: 135–36, 156.

10. No more fortuitous, apparently, is the detail of the mother's funeral, since the mother-in-law would have served as a chaperone of the young wife. See Pomeroy 1997: 23. Just (1989: 120–21) notes that opportunities for seduction coincide with public events attended by women, such as weddings, funerals, and the like, as these are the few spaces not marked as belonging exclusively to either gender.

11. Goody 1976: 15; Peristiany 1965. See also Cohen 1991: 113 n. 45; Cox 1998: 73.

12. On the self-serving nature of the argument, see Cohen 1991: 178 n. 20; Sealey 1990: 28. On plausibility, see Lacey 1968: 10: "All those who spoke in Greek law-courts were prepared to be liars, and . . . habitual liars will be good liars, so that their lies must have sounded plausible to the audience to whom they were addressed." A similar position is taken by Davidson (1997: xxi): "Although the orators are unreliable witnesses of what went on in Athens, they are excellent witnesses of what was thought convincing."

13. The evidence for this law is Isaeus 10.10 and Aristophanes, *Ecclesiazusae* 1024–25, with scholia. The text of Isaeus is possibly corrupt, but the textual problems alone are not enough to challenge the standard interpretation. See Wyse 1979: 658–60. For further discussion, see Foxhall 1989 and 1996; Hunter 1994: 22; Hunter 1989b; Johnstone 2003.

14. Hunter 1989a, 1989b; Foxhall 1989.

15. I owe thanks to Lynette Mitchell for sharing with me a forthcoming article, "The Women of Ruling Families in Archaic and Classical Greece," in which she discusses this episode, noting that Euelthon's reply calls attention to Pheretime's gender deviance.

16. Elizabeth Barber (1992: 113) cites Aristotle and Plutarch to the effect that while the *peplos* dedicated to Athena at the Panathenaia was made by young women (the *ergastinai*), the *peplos* for the ship was made by professional male weavers (*Ath. Pol.* 60.1). Presumably this *peplos* was made of canvas, like a sail, and was therefore in the realm of male manufacture. Glotz ([1920] 1967: 225) gives names of male slaves engaged in the textile industry. See also Keuls 1985: 246–47; Thompson 1981–82.

17. A hydria attributed to the Leningrad Painter (Milan, Torno Coll. C 278; Beazley ARV² 571.73, c. 460 BCE, reproduced in Bron and Lissarrague 1989: fig. 1) shows a woman painting a vase. Petersen (1997: 37 n. 7) notes that this is the only known representation of a woman vase-painter and that she is decorating a volute, rather than painting the central image. Lewis (2002: 91) comments that the images on vases underrepresent women's engagement in production and trade. On women's work in Athens, see Brock 1994.

18. The robes from which Hekabe chooses her offering to Athena in *Iliad* 6.289–90 are the work of women of Sidon (*erga gunaikōn* / *Sidoniōn*). In *Odyssey* 7.96–97, the furniture in the palace of Alkinoos is adorned with beautiful robes woven by women (*erga gunaikōn*), and Arete recognizes her own handiwork in the clothing that Odysseus wears (7.234–35). Helen weaves: *Iliad* 3.125–28 (and spins: *Od.* 4.134–55), etc. Goddesses also, by implication, weave in epic: the Charites in *Iliad* 5.339; Athena in *Iliad* 5.734–35; Kalypso in *Od.* 10.222–23; Kirke in *Od.* 5.61–62. See Block 1985; Pomeroy 1994: 61–65; Barber 1991, 1994; Morrell 1997. Pantelia (1993) argues that spinning and weaving have quite different meanings, and that weaving is connected with uncertainty about the future. Or, as Buxton (1994: 127) puts it, "In Greek fantasy weaving seems to carry a more powerful ideological charge than spinning."

19. See Sutton 1981: 310: "Wreaths were made by women generally, which explains in good part the predominance of female wreath donors in our scenes." As discussed in Chapter One, in a number of cultures the plaiting or weaving of natural materials is, like weaving cloth, considered a female activity.

20. Scheid and Svenbro [1994] 1996; Papadopoulou-Belmehdi 1994a and 1994b.

21. Sometimes used in the singular: *anakalyterion*. The plural form also refers to gifts given to the bride at this time. See Oakley 1982; Oakley and Sinos 1993.

22. Langdon 2002: 151, "The donning and removing of belts thus punctuated female sexual life." See also her discussion of veiling at 148–50.

23. Scheid and Svenbro ([1994] 1996: 112–19) comment that although Homer equates weaving with speech, he never uses it as a metaphor for poetry, a trope first introduced by the choral poets Pindar and Bakchylides. For readings of Helen's first appearance in the *Iliad* as a scene of poetic performance, see Clader 1976; Kennedy 1986.

24. Block 1985; Pedrick 1988.

---

25. The story of Penelope's "loom trick" is told in three different versions in the *Odyssey*: 2.85–128, 19.137–61, 24.120–50. These are discussed in detail by Papadopoulou-Belmehdi (1994b: 30–41).

26. Loraux 1994: 16; Papadopoulou-Belmehdi 1994b.

27. McClure 1997: 128. Interestingly, Ovid in the *Metamorphoses* elaborates on two episodes, those of Prokne and of Arachne, in which the webs women weave are used to expose sexual crimes: in Prokne's case, a rape committed against her; and in the case of Arachne, crimes of the gods against mortal women.

28. Exchanges of precious-metal objects between men are not always benign. The exchange of armor between Glaukos and Diomedes has been read both positively and negatively. See Chapter Three.

29. Textiles are part of the ransom Priam pays to Achilles for Hektor (*Iliad* 24.229–31, discussed by Morrell 1997: 145); gifts of clothing (again together with gold) are given to Odysseus by the Phaiakians, on orders from their king (*Od.* 8.392–93).

30. A hydria attributed to the Leningrad Painter (Milan, Torno collection, C 278 = ARV2 571.73; published in Bérard et al. 1989: 10) shows Athena presenting a wreath to a potter, mentioned above, note 17.

31. For goddesses, see above, note 18. For other cultures in which metalworking is lower-caste or stigmatized, see Blakely 2003.

32. The speaker of Lysias, *On the Murder of Eratosthenes*, describes the manufacturing activities he oversees, but he does not himself engage in the work. The most obvious exception is Odysseus, who is frequently shown as a craftsman: Glotz [1920] 1967: 14–15.

33. Gernet [1948] 1981: 115.

34. Keuls (1985: 229) speaks of a separate work ethic for men and women, but does not qualify this in terms of class.

35. Humphreys 1995: 108.

36. The intersection of class and gender, although important for a full analysis of the economic system portrayed in epic, is beyond the scope of the present project. See Karydas 1998; Van Wees 1992: 70ff. On class in Homeric epic, see Rose 1992; Thalmann 1998.

37. On the unusually rich body of inscriptions documenting women's individual textile dedications to Artemis Brauronia, see Linders 1972. See also Euripides' *Iphigeneia among the Taurians* 1464–67, with discussion in Lyons 1997: 45.

38. The connection between adultery and theft is discussed by Cohen (1991: 111–13). His paraphrase of Dr. Johnson, to the effect that "the thief merely makes off with the sheep, but the adulterer gets the sheep and the farm as well," is surprisingly apt here (113 n. 45).

39. See Finley [1954] 1981: 88–90. This motif also occurs, in a non-Greek setting, in the tale of Gyges and Kandaules' wife (Hdt. 1.8–12). See Tourraix 1976 on women's role in the transmission of power in Herodotos. See also Finkelberg 1991; Westbrook (2005) argues that kingship on Ithaka was part of Penelope's dowry.

40. See Sergent 1990. The chorus in Sophocles' *Elektra* (837–38) mentions Amphiaraos, "destroyed by women's golden necklaces" (*chrusodetois herkesi gunaikōn*).

41. Here as elsewhere, allegiance to brother often trumps allegiance to husband. The privileging of natal family over that of the husband, and the special relationship between sisters and brothers, are taken up in Chapter Six.

42. See Brown 1997: 42.

43. Buxton (1994: 127–28) points to the selectivity that emphasizes the "*dangerousness* of golden necklaces and mirrors," when in fact "real women" (i.e., not murderous heroines) owned these objects without ill effects. Sutton (1981: 289) cites a number of texts to show the "unsavory reputation" of gifts of jewelry. As noted above in Chapter One, the technical term for the personal items that a woman brings with her to a marriage is *himatia kai chrysia*, robes and gold jewelry. For examples, see Schaps 1979: 10–12; Hunter 1994: 24–25.

44. See discussion in Chapter Four.

45. See in particular two oinochoai (Figs. 1 and 2) by the Schuwalow Painter in Ferrara (Mus. Naz. 2509 and 3914, fourth quarter of the fifth century, *ARV*² 1206, 4 and 12 = *LIMC* Eriphyle I.8 and 9), and an earlier kalpis most likely depicting the same scene by the Phiale Painter (Toronto, Royal Ontario Museum 919.5.27 [362], third quarter of the fifth century, *ARV*² 1020, 94; *LIMC* Eriphyle I.16). In a variant, an oinochoe by the Mannheim Painter has a standing Eriphyle, but again with hand outstretched toward the necklace that Polyneikes extracts from a chest or basket (third quarter of the fifth century, Louvre G442). The connection between these vases and genre scenes of erotic gift-giving is discussed in detail by Sutton (1981: 369–79). See also Lissarrague 1995: 93.

46. Several are reproduced in Reeder 1995: 181–83. See, e.g., cat. 36, a Nolan amphora by the Berlin Painter (San Antonio Museum of Art inv. no. 86.134.59; *Para.* 345, 184 ter), c. 490–480 BCE, in which the man holds a flower in one hand and a small bag in the other. Reeder cat. no. 37, another Nolan amphora by the Providence Painter (Harvard University, Sackler Museum, inv. no. 1972.45, *ARV*² 638, 43), c. 485–475 BCE, shows the woman holding and examining a gift of a wreath or garland.

47. On "Spinning Hetairai," see Rodenwaldt 1932; Crome 1966; Keuls 1985: 258–59; Sutton 1987; Bérard et al. 1989: 89–90. Davidson (1997: 86–89) argues that spinning and prostitution were complementary occupations, and that these images depict the transition from daytime to nighttime activities in the brothel. See Bundrick 2008 for the view that these are Athenian wives.

48. Meyer 1988. See also Sutton 1981: 283. Keuls refers to the purse as "an economic phallus" (1985: 262). See also Lewis 2002: 194–97. Ferrari (2002), on the other hand, claims that the purses hold knucklebones, intended as love-gifts; but this view has not attracted much support (see Bundrick 2008).

49. Lissarrague 1995: 91–101, esp. 93. Keuls (1985: 245) also notes that the frequently appearing walking stick suggests that the male intruder "is merely visiting from outside the world of men." Bundrick (2008) sees it rather as another attribute of the Athenian citizen.

50. Attic red figure pelike c. 460 BCE, attributed to the Chicago Painter, Museo Provinciale Castromediano Lecce (*ARV*² 629, 23). Discussed in Sutton 1981: 376.

51. Apollodoros (3.7.5) relates that the necklace continues to cause trouble until it is finally dedicated to Apollo at Delphi. See also Pausanias 8.24.8–10, 9.41.2.

52. Other accounts: Plut., *Solon* 4.1–4; Diodorus Siculus 9.3.3. For an overview of the tradition of the tripod, and some recent controversies, see Bollansée 1999.

53. In this version, after Helen threw it away, it was brought up along with a catch of fish and became the cause of a war between the Coans and the Milesians. The quarrel was resolved when an oracle instructed that it be given to the wisest man. All agreed upon Thales (Diogenes Laertius 1.32).

54. For an interesting ethnographic parallel, Hoskins 1998: 21: "Women are them-

selves 'objects exchanged in marriage,' so they identify with the domestic animals traded against them." Compare the Greek heroine name Alphesiboia, literally "she who fetches (much) cattle." (In the Hesiodic *Catalogue of Women* 139 = Apollodoros 3.14.4, she is the mother of Adonis.) Also, at *Iliad* 18.593, we find *parthenoi alphesiboiai*, "maidens who bring much cattle," a clear reference to bridewealth, discussed in Scheid-Tissinier 1994: 50–51. See now McInerney 2010: 86–87 and passim for the connections between cattle and women.

55. I have addressed this episode in a different context in Lyons 1997: 163.

56. Museum of Fine Arts, Boston, cat. no. 13.186 = *ARV*² 458, 1. See Ghali-Kahil 1955: cat. nos. 11 and 53, plates 4 and 48; *LIMC* Helene 166 = 243.

57. Ghali-Kahil's catalogue has only one other vase that pairs Helen on one side with Paris and on the other with Menelaos. This vase, a siphon in the Kerameikos Museum, gives no hint of the abduction, but shows a static Paris standing before a calmly seated Helen (Ghali-Kahil cat. nos. 22 and 47, plate 68.1–3; *LIMC* Helene 84 = 238).

58. Kunisch 1997: 155–56.

59. Kunisch 1997: 130: "The similarity of the events is reflected in the formal similarity of the composition of the two images" ("Die Vergleichbarkeit des Geschehens spiegelt sich in der Vergleichbarkeit des formalen Aufbaus beider Bilder").

60. Kunisch 1997: 95, on the scarcity of empty ground ("leeren Hintergrund") on this vase. He comments also on the negation of boundaries: "The image on the Boston Skyphos reveals an attempt—singular and also atypical of Makron—to dematerialize thoroughly the boundaries of the image (which cannot be concretized with reference to any objects), even to deny their existence" ("Das Bild des Bostoner Skyphos stellt den für Makron einzigartigen und auch untypischen Versuch dar, die hintere, gegenständlich nicht konkretisierbare Grenze des Bildes weitgehend zu entmaterialisieren, ihre Existenz geradezu zu leugnen").

61. I owe this suggestion to Robin Osborne.

62. My thanks to Karen Bassi for this suggestion.

63. See Padilla 2000.

64. Not all gifts of the gods are baneful: at *Odyssey* 4.615–19 = 15.115–19, the bowl Menelaos gives to Telemachos was made by Hephaistos.

65. "Les dons des dieux distinguent certains mortels; dans le même temps, ils peuvent, on l'a vu, jouer un rôle fatal dans leur destin" (Brillet-Dubois 1999–2000: 16). Brillet-Dubois notes (12–13) the gendered equivalence of the gods' nuptial gifts to Hektor and Andromache, a helmet and a veil (*krēdemnon*).

66. Scheid-Tissinier (1994: 54–56) lists the Homeric instances.

67. Scodel 2008: 34: "This account cleans up the nasty history of the Pelopidae."

68. Kirk (1985: 127) suggests that Homer knew this version but preferred to omit "distracting detail." Lowenstam (1993: 65 n. 13) elaborates slightly on Kirk.

69. Thyestes and his son Aigisthos are mentioned in *Od.* 4.517–18.

70. The golden lamb is further discussed in Chapters Five and Six.

71. The post-classical transition from jar to box is documented by Erwin and Dora Panofsky 1962.

72. See Redfield 1982: 192.

73. *Theogony* 507–616; *Works and Days* 42–105.

74. Vernant [1974] 1980: 183–201. Others who have focused on the theme of exchange in this episode and in Hesiod generally include Pucci 1977; Arthur [Katz] 1982; Saintillan 1996; Zeitlin 1996b; Nagy 1981.

---

75. The gods already practice marriage of a sort, but it is not for the most part the enduring institution known to mortals, e.g., *Iapetos . . . ēgageto Klymenē* (*Theog.* 507–8). "For the gods marriage, as both Homeric and Hesiodic man understand it, can have little or no meaning" (Brown 1997: 47).

76. Detienne 1963; Sussman 1984; Petropoulos 1994.

77. Neils (2005) argues that the *elpis* trapped in the jar must be a false hope.

78. Vernant [1974] 1980; Zeitlin 1995, 1996b. For the homology of Pandora and the jar, specifically through the association of the belly of the jar and the womb, see Sissa 1990: 154–55.

79. *kalon kakon, Theog.* 585; *pēm' andrasin, Works and Days* 82; *dolon aipun, Works and Days* 83. As Loraux notes, the poet hesitates even to call her *gynē* ([1981] 1993: 77).

80. *Theog.* 571–84. See duBois 1988: 46–47; Brown 1997: 29. Carson (1999: 160) discusses a cosmology related by Pherekydes (frag. 54 VS) in which Zeus throws a veil over the head of the goddess of the Underworld, thus transforming her into Gē, whom he takes as his wife. The veil has embroidered images of both earth and ocean.

81. Prier 1989: 95.

82. The figured headdress suggests, without replicating, known representations of the *potnia thērōn*, a similarity noted by Marquardt (1982: 287). (See Potnia 34, *LIMC* suppl., for a bronze *potnia* with animals sprouting from her head.) See Brown 1997 for similarities to Aphrodite. The texts used are those of West.

83. Lyons 2003; Zeitlin 1995 and 1996b.

84. On both the ambivalence and the artisanal nature of the creation of woman, see duBois 1988: 45–47. Also Pucci 1977; Loraux [1981] 1993; Zeitlin 1996b.

85. See Vernant [1974] 1980: 190; Marquardt 1982: 286; Zeitlin 1996b: 60. Vernant connects Pandora (also called Anesidora, "she who sends up gifts") with Demeter rather than Gē, that is to say, with fertility hard-won by (male) agricultural labor rather than by the spontaneous generosity of the (female) earth. See above, note 80, for other possible associations of Pandora and Gē.

86. *Pandoteiros/-a* has an agent ending that is common in Greek, making it unambiguously active. (The *–tor/-ter/-teiros* ending indicates one who performs an action.)

87. For *pandōra* as an epithet of the earth, *LSJ* cites Arist., *Birds* 971; Philo 1.32. The Homeric epigram 7 addresses "Lady Earth, all bounteous, giver of honey-sweet wealth" (*Potnia Gē, pandorōs, dōteira meliphronos olbou*). Physis and Demeter are *pandōteira* (Orph. H. 10.16, 40.3). For a summary of the connections between Pandora and Gē, see West 1978 at *Works and Days* 81. Hurwit (1995: 176 with n. 17) points to yet another etymology, promoted by Vernant: she whom the gods give as a gift. In the *Homeric Hymn to Gaia* (30.1), she is called *pammēteira*, "mother of all." Pandora, whose name begins with the same element, is—as the first woman—the "mother of all" mortals.

88. The phrase is from Arthur [Katz] 1982: 75; *contra*, Loraux [1981] 1993: 84. See also Zeitlin 1996b: 82 n. 61. For the iconography of Pandora, see Hurwit 1995: 176–77.

89. Hurwit (1995) concludes that the Athenian vase-painters have confused two different Pandoras, and does not know what to make of Pandora's chthonic associations. My own conclusions are similar to those of Arthur [Katz], Marquardt, and Zeitlin, that the double nature of Pandora reflects cultural ambivalence about women in general. See also West 1978.

90. Loraux [1981] 1993: 78–79.

91. See Lombardi 1994: 27–28, on the relationship between "femaleness" and divinity in Hesiod.

92. Detienne 1963; Sussman 1984; Petropoulos 1994.

93. West 1966: 333.

94. Sussman (1984) takes Hesiod's complaints about idle women more literally than I do. See Arthur [Katz] 1984; Petropoulos 1994; Brown 1997.

95. At *Works and Days* 779, however, Hesiod does give directions for the best time for a woman to set up her loom, on the twelfth day of the month: *Tē d' histon stēsaito gunē probaloito te ergon*.

96. Arthur [Katz] (1982: 75) notes the ambiguity of *erga*. Carson (1990: 149) surveys uses of *ergon/erga* to refer to procreative sex (e.g., *philotēsia erga*, *Od*. 11.246). See also Zeitlin [1995] 1996a: 32, on the phrase *ergon aeikes* ("an unseemly act") to refer to adultery in the *Odyssey*. None of these uses of *erga*, however, are qualified as *erga gunaikōn*, "the works of women."

97. On fear of women's reproductive powers, see Zeitlin 1996b: 59–60. In Aeschylus' *Eumenides*, women's reproductive powers will be completely elided.

98. For sources, see West 1978 on this passage. Detienne (1963: 22) ties this precept to a time of agrarian crisis, caused by partible inheritance.

99. Detienne (1963: 23) observes that this passage suggests that partibility is not an inevitable rule, even in Hesiod's world.

100. See note 78 above.

101. Vernant [1974] 1980: 191–92.

102. Zeitlin 1996b: 68.

103. Marquardt 1982. See below for further discussion of the wife as "keeper" of the household goods.

104. Patterson 1998: 63.

105. Ferrari's point (1988: 52) that Pandora "represents the indissoluble connection in our world of both good and bad exchange" speaks to the dilemma faced by the poet in his treatment of her.

106. The gift of technology is only implicit in Hesiod, but it becomes explicit in Plato's rewriting of the myth in *Protagoras* 321c-e: "Already the appointed day had come, when man too was to emerge from the earth into the daylight. Prometheus, being at a loss to provide any means of salvation for man, stole from Hephaistos and Athena the gift of skill in the arts, together with fire" (trans. Guthrie, in Hamilton and Cairns 1961).

107. This discussion reprises some parts of Lyons 2003, but with a significant change of emphasis.

108. Vernant [1965] 1983.

109. Discussed below.

110. Cox 1998; Foxhall 1989; Wolff 1944.

111. *Pol.* 1252a25ff.; see Cox 1998: 132.

112. Cox 1998: 131.

113. Glotz [1920] 1967: 8.

114. See van Wees 1998: 38 n. 72, on the tension between autarky and self-sufficiency.

115. Seaford 2004.

116. Redfield 2009: 278; see also McInerney (2010: 92), on the paucity of clear examples of trade in Homer.

117. The ideological nature of the gendered division between inside and out be-

comes clearer when one considers that it never applied to any but elite women. Poor women were known to sell vegetables in the markets and perform other outside work, and it was certainly the case that ancient Greek women (despite Xenophon) did work outside the *oikia*, if not always outside the *oikos*.

118. Discussed further in Chapter Five.

119. On the ancient Greek textile industry and trade, see Glotz [1920] 1967: 131–32. Aristophanes portrays women (e.g., in the *Lysistrata*) as very fond of imported fabrics and articles of clothing.

120. Seaford 2004: 261 n. 136. As Booth (1993: 37) makes clear, the locus of autarky has long since shifted from the *oikos* to the *polis*. It must also be mentioned that the Periklean citizenship reforms of the fifth century had ended the aristocratic practice of forming exogamous marriages with non-Athenian women.

CHAPTER THREE

1. Brown 1997: 26–27.

2. For structural similarities between the two, see Pucci 1977: 92. Helen is a "daughter of Zeus," the only mortal to whom this Homeric formula applies. Pucci (102) argues that an ambiguous phrase in Hesiod assigns the same parentage to Pandora. "Pandora is, in a peculiar way, the daughter of Zeus, and . . . the text of the Theogony, if it is sound, refers to woman in exactly that way (Διὸς . . . ὑπέδεκτο . . . παρθένον [*Theog.* 514 ff.])." Against this view, see Zeitlin 1996b: 82: "Zeus is Pandora's author, not her natural sire." If the parallel is not exact, it is nevertheless suggestive.

3. See Constantinidou 1990: 47 n. 1, for two other points of contact with Pandora: Helen is "regarded as a punishment for those who possess her"; and her return to Paris in *Iliad* 3 is figured as a marriage, and she as a bride.

4. According to the *Kypria* (schol. D, *Il.* 2.5), Zeus created Helen in order to start a war that would kill off many mortals, either to punish them or to lighten Earth's burden.

5. While Pucci (1977: 92) maintains that Pandora and Helen are both said to have the "mind of a bitch," it is significant that in the *Iliad*, the epithet *kunōpis* (literally, "dog-faced," i.e., shameless) is uttered only by Helen herself, calling into question the accuracy of the charge.

6. Brown 1997: 40, on the connections between Epimetheus and Paris.

7. Suzuki (1989: 16) credits the *Iliad* with endowing Helen with a subjectivity that all later accounts deny her, although I would add that Sappho fragment 16 does so as well.

8. The phrase *amumona erga iduias* occurs at *Iliad* 9.128; 19.245; etc. The Odyssean equivalent, *aglaa erga iduiēi*, is found at 13.289 and 16.158, referring to the sort of woman Athena is pretending to be, and at 15.418, of the servant who betrayed Eumaios to his kidnappers.

9. Pomeroy (1994: 59) accords Xenophon the honor of being "the first Greek author to give full recognition to the use-value of women's work, and to understand that domestic labour has economic value even if it lacks exchange value." In my view, the Homeric epics do show an (admittedly unsystematic) awareness of those forms of female labor that have a tangible result, primarily the making of textiles and the prepa-

ration of food. To this short list one might add—thinking of Eurykleia—the raising of children.

10. Seaford 2004: 27: "The only measure of value in Homer is provided by cattle." See also Macrakis 1984 and McInerney 2010.

11. Euripides seems to have invented an alternate version in which Agamemnon takes Klytemnestra as a wife after killing her first husband Tantalos and the infant at her breast (*Iphigeneia at Aulis* 1149–52), thus reducing her to the status of a spear-captive like Chryseis.

12. See Chapter Two.

13. Mauss [1925] 1990.

14. Van Wees (1992: 224–27) notes that these prize lists combine *keimēlia*, or treasure, with other kinds of less durable wealth, such as horses or slaves.

15. The pairing appears repeatedly in *Iliad* 3: *Helenēi kai ktēmasi pasi* (70), and again at 3.72, where *ktēmata . . . panta* is linked with *gunaika*. See also lines 90, 283, 285, 458, etc. Scheid-Tissinier (1994:48) also remarks on this collocation.

16. On this point, I want to acknowledge the provocative recent contribution of Gottschall (2008), who argues from evolutionary biology that access to women's sexuality or fertility was the primary impetus for war in the Homeric world. See van Wees (1992) for the contrary view that heroes fight for status, and that access to women is both a sign and a welcome benefit of that status.

17. My general approach here is influenced by Sedgwick 1985 on male homosociality.

18. Seaford 1994; 2004.

19. Seaford (1994) sees it as a resolution of the twin crises of reciprocity and ritual, and does not appear to notice who is left out.

20. On Briseis as *geras*, see Arthur [Katz] 1981: 24–25.

21. See Scully 1990: 33–34.

22. Lyons 1997: 155; Burkert [1972] 1983: 67.

23. Sahlins 1972, esp. 193–95.

24. Donlan 1989: 6.

25. In generalized and balanced reciprocity the time allotted for repayment, and the strictness of the demand for repayment, are correlated to the closeness or distance of the social relationship, allowing for trade between strangers or even enemies. Negative reciprocity, on the other hand, is structured quite differently. It can occur in any context, although it may tend to destroy existing relationships. See discussion in Chapter One.

26. A similar dynamic is at work in Book 18, when Thetis goes to Hephaistos to ask for armor for Achilles, but in this case, although she says that she is at his knees (457), there is no need for her to supplicate him. Nor is there any need for her to recall past favors, since Hephaistos himself spontaneously recounts how she saved him from the violence of his mother, and declares that he owes her the price (*zōiagria*, 407) for saving his life.

27. Seaford (2004: 34–35) comments on the surprising fact that Achilles has been engaged in trade, and notes that the lines are often mistranslated to turn the transaction into one of ransom. See also Scodel 2008: 79–80.

28. See Wilson 2002: 206 n. 55, for a list of expressions.

29. Lykaon and Polydoros (22.50). I omit uses that do not mean "ransom," as well

as the many imperatives directed at Achilles as various gods and mortals attempt to cajole him into behaving properly. Wilson (2002: 179ff.) lists "Compensation Themes" in the *Iliad*.

30. See Wilson 2002: 150.

31. Donlan (1989) argues rather that Glaukos, by giving a superior gift, acknowledges the greater status or strength of Diomedes. He compares this episode to others of unequal exchange in the *Iliad*. In all cases, Trojans get the short end of the stick. Other views: Craig 1967; Walcot 1969; Calder 1984; Martin 1989: 126–30; Alden 1996.

32. Frazer notes in his commentary on Apollodoros (*Epitome* 3.2) that the apple appears first in Lucian and Hyginus, so it is not clear how old a detail it is.

33. See Redfield 2003.

34. Pindar (*Pythian* 11.7) considers only two motives, her anger at Agamemnon's slaughter of their daughter Iphigeneia, and her adulterous passion for Aigisthos.

35. See Anderson 1997: 93 n. 1.

36. Anderson 1997: 93. Wilson (2002: 25–26) points out that ransom and sale are always distinguished by the use of different terms.

CHAPTER FOUR

1. Sussman 1984: 82.

2. One exception to the general silence on women's production in the *Iliad* is the scene of Helen at her weaving (3.125–28). On Helen, weaving, and poetry, see Clader 1976: 6–9; Bergren 1980 and 1983. These essays appear in revised form in Bergren 2008.

3. Finley [1954] 1981: 88–90. Finkelberg (1991) argues that in fact, there was no clear pattern of father-to-son inheritance of kingship, and that the pattern hinted at in the *Odyssey* is not unknown in Greek myth, although inheritance combined with marriage to the king's daughter, rather than his wife, is for obvious reasons by far the more common pattern.

4. Arete gives Odysseus a cloak and tunic (8.441). Helen gives Telemachos a *peplos* (15.125–29), on which see below. On women's gifts of cloth to Odysseus, see Block 1985 and Pedrick 1988.

5. The precise phrase is *gunaiōn heineka dōrōn*, *Od.* 11.521; 15.247. On the concept of para-narratives in Homer, see Alden 2000, which, although it deals with the *Iliad*, is equally applicable to the *Odyssey*. Alden in fact uses several examples from the *Odyssey* to introduce the concept (2000: 2ff.).

6. Lissarrague 1995: 100.

7. See Bergren 1981.

8. Faraone 1994; 1999. As Zerba (2009: 310) remarks upon surveying the wreckage of their marriage, "No wonder they need drugs!"

9. Faraone 1999.

10. See Bergren 1981, revised in Bergren 2008; Suzuki 1989: 66–67.

11. See Chapter Two for discussion of the ambiguous meaning of the name Pandora.

12. Schol. Eur. *Tro.* 822 = *Little Iliad* frag. 6 West 2003: "The vine that Zeus gave

in compensation for his son; it was of gold, luxuriant with splendid foliage and grape clusters, which Hephaistos fashioned and gave to father Zeus, and he gave it to Laomedon in lieu of Ganymede" (trans. West).

13. This is not the only present by means of which Zeus hoped to buy off the father of Ganymede: the *Homeric Hymn to Aphrodite* (210–12) tells of the immortal horses given to Tros (here considered the father of Ganymede rather than Laomedon) for the same purpose. As I have discussed above in Chapter Three, these horses were also the source of troubles for future owners, and caused further tainted exchanges after their initial deployment.

14. Fragments exist, probably from Sophocles' *Eurypalos*, in which Astyoche laments her son (Lloyd-Jones 1996: 83ff.), but her story is not treated widely in other sources. Eriphyle, on the other hand, is mentioned in Pindar, *Nem.* 9.16; Apollodoros 3.7.5; Diodorus Siculus 4.66.3; Pausanias 9.41.2–3, etc.

15. Morrell (1997: 145) describes this passage as linking the "extra-domestic and intra-domestic spheres of production."

16. *Od.* 1.329, 4.787, 5.216, etc. The same epithet is applied to Arete (11.345) and Eurykleia (20.134, etc.). Papadopoulou-Belmehdi (1994b: 185-88) calls into question the positive nature of this epithet.

17. Katz 1991: 78–93.

18. Katz 1991: 79–80.

19. Not all gifts of textiles are benign. The next chapter deals with examples of destructive textile gifts in tragedy, specifically in the context of marital crisis and breakdown.

CHAPTER FIVE

1. See the introduction for an overview of recent treatments of reciprocity in tragedy. Belfiore's 1998 article, "Harming Friends: Problematic Reciprocity in Greek Tragedy," despite its title, concerns relations of *philia* and *xenia*, rather than the tragic exchanges discussed here.

2. The earliest source for this version of the story is Euripides, but whether he drew on older versions or simply improvised using familiar mythic elements is impossible to determine.

3. Patterson 1998: 4.

4. Sahlins 1972: 195–96, discussed in Chapter One.

5. Two important treatments of the theme of exchange in this play are Goldhill 1984 and Wohl 1998. Seaford (1994: 369–75) touches on it as well. Foley (2001: 210, 228) discusses the ways in which Klytemnestra overturns gender expectations.

6. The *locus classicus* is Eduard Fraenkel, *Aeschylus. Agamemnon* (Oxford: Oxford University Press, 1950), 2:304–5, although after almost two pages, he does allow the possibility of a hint of the murder to come, a possibility rejected by Rosenmayer (1982: 238). See Lebeck 1971: 41–42, on an earlier reference to bronze at lines 390–93, and Fraenkel's "detailed metallurgical analysis" of that passage (2:202–5).

7. Fraenkel takes this as the main point.

8. See Lebeck 1971: 81–86; McClure 1997: 128; Morrell 1997: 160–62.

9. Macleod (1975) sketches the theme of clothing throughout the trilogy. See also Rosenmeyer 1982: 137.

10. In the *Agamemnon*, it is clear that she has done the deed herself (lines 1380, 1384–86), and although Aigisthos at 1608–9 tries to claim the deed, the chorus (1643–46) sees through this, accusing him of leaving the murder to a woman. The implication of Orestes' words is that Klytemnestra struck using her lover's sword.

11. *Ag.* 959–960: τρέφουσα πολλῆς πορφύρας ἰσάργυρον / κηκῖδα παγκαί-νιστον, εἱμάτων βαφάς. Seaford (2004: 168) comments on the repetition and the implications of the word *kēkis*.

12. Also *Eum.* 1028: φοινικοβάπτοις ἐνδυτοῖς ἐσθήμασι, for the Erinyes. See Lebeck 1971: 63–68, for a detailed working out of the textile-net imagery.

13. My remarks on this scene owe much to Jenkins 1985: 116–20. See also Crane (1993), much of whose argument is anticipated by Flintoff (1987). For a different interpretation, see Morrell 1997.

14. For a more psychologizing approach to Agamemnon's capitulation, see Dover 1987: 151–60. See also Lebeck (1971: 74–79) and Taplin (1977: 310–16), both of whom reject a largely psychological interpretation. Sailor and Stroup propose a political reading, according to which Agamemnon's willingness to participate in the destruction of household wealth reveals anti-democratic and tyrannical leanings (1999: 154, 174–78). Wohl (1998: 105) similarly sees Klytemnestra as violating both democratic and aristocratic principles in proposing the destruction of the cloth.

15. Morrell (1997) stresses the aspect of competition.

16. Taplin 1997: 299–300, 306–8.

17. Klytemnestra's relation to this form of female wealth is somewhat ambiguous. Unlike Helen and Penelope, and indeed most female figures in Homeric epic, she is never associated with weaving. This may be related to the fact that she is never represented directly in epic, but only appears in the reported speech of others. Nonetheless, she embodies a third paradigm for female behavior in marriage, a thoroughly negative one that significantly influences the actions of Odysseus, in response to Agamemnon's posthumous warnings. See Katz 1991.

18. Gernet [1948] 1981; Flintoff 1987: 123: "Something with a religious dimension." Morrell (1997: 157) is more explicit: "The garments are better suited as dedicatory offerings to the gods."

19. Morrell 1997: 149. Wohl 1998: 86–87; von Reden 1995: 163–64.

20. Her appeal to the sea as a bountiful force of nature is perhaps not unmixed with the idea of the sea as a medium of trade. See Seaford 2004: 167 n. 94.

21. See Jenkins 1985: 125–26, on the significance of the dye. Crane (1993: 129) argues that Agamemnon's hesitation about walking on the cloths represents a failure to embody *megaloprepeia* and a misunderstanding of the "ethics of generosity." Also, von Reden 1995: 163–64; Wohl 1998: 87, 105: "Clytemnestra herself speaks the play's most explicit disenchantments: it is she who transforms the tapestry into mere money in her 'sea of purple' speech." On *autarkeia*, see Chapter Two above.

22. See Brown 1997: 44, on her combining of these two aspects of the wife's role. See also Pearce 1974, esp. 31.

23. See Flintoff (1987) on Klytemnestra's "cavalier attitude towards the resources of her household" (121), although I believe that he exaggerates the expense involved. Goldhill (1984: 75) discusses this passage in the context of Penelope's decision to stay and guard her husband's possessions (*Odyssey* 19.525–29).

24. Flintoff (1987: 125) also notes the similarity. See Lebeck 1971: 63–68, for treatment of metaphors of trapping throughout the trilogy.

25. On the perversion of death ritual in this scene, see Seaford 1984; 1994: 62.

26. The word *erga* is picked up again in Orestes' lines at *Choe.* 1016, where it is clearly connected to Klytemnestra's murder of Agamemnon.

27. The word appears in the feminine only here and in Euripides' *Medea* 409, where Medea calls women *kakōn de pantōn tektones sophōtatai*, "the cleverest devisers of all evils."

28. Wohl 1998; Ormand 1999, on the theme of exchange in this play.

29. Segal 1995: 91. Elsewhere (1986: 58), Segal couches the same point in semiotic terms.

30. My discussion here owes much to Wohl 1998.

31. For this scene's deliberate echoes of the *Agamemnon*, see Segal 1995: 40.

32. See Wohl 1998: 26–28.

33. καὶ νῦν δύ' οὖσαι μίμνομεν μιᾶς ὑπὸ / χλαίνης ὑπαγκάλισμα, *Trach.* 539–40. See Wohl 1998: 34.

34. In visual art, this image is reserved for the portrayal of homosexual lovers, an observation I owe to Alan Shapiro.

35. Segal 1995: 82–83; Wohl 1998: 23–29.

36. See Wohl (1998: 23–24), from whom I borrow the phrase "so well provided" as a translation for this difficult phrase. The chorus that follows, 497–530, presents the episode from Deianeira's own history in which she herself was treated like a prize. See Wohl 1998: 52–54.

37. The poison, the blood of the female hydra, represents yet another deadly female gift. Wohl 1998: 28.

38. Segal notes that Herakles' language at lines 1051–52 and 1057 recalls that of Aeschylus about Klytemnestra (1995: 65).

39. The text implies, but does not make explicit, that Deianeira herself was the weaver.

40. The robe, which alternates between being called a *chiton* (580, 769) and a *peplos* (602, 674, 758: *thanasimon peplon*; 774), is here once again a *chiton* but also a *peplōma* (612–13). At 662, it is a *pharos* (if we accept Haupt's reading); and at 764, a *stolē*. Interestingly, Flintoff (1987: 121) notes that in the *Agamemnon*, Klytemnestra and Agamemnon even disagree about the nature of the cloth—whether it is clothing, and how it is decorated. On the ambiguity of Herakles' garment, see Loraux 1995: 125–31, esp. 130. Seaford (1994: 390–91) discusses the gift of the cloak in the context of perversions of "ritual attire."

41. See above on *Ag.* 609.

42. See Segal 1995: 45, on the "explosive sexuality" within the house. See Faraone 1994 and 1999 for a rather different reading than my own, of the nature of "Deianeira's mistake."

43. See above for the alternate tradition that the potion contains the centaur's semen.

44. See discussion in Chapter Two.

45. Loraux 1995: 42; Wohl 1998: 9, with n. 21.

46. Pozzi 1994: 584.

47. See Loraux 1995: 121; Winnington-Ingram 1980: 85; Wohl 1998: 9.

48. Segal 1995: 83; see 75 n. 21 for bibliography.

49. It is "a highly sexual suicide," to quote Foley (2001: 97).

50. Loraux [1985] 1987.

51. See Soph. *Ant.* 1222: *brochōi mitōdei sindonos* (with a noose of linen threads). Loraux takes this as unambiguously referring to an item of Antigone's own dress. This seems reasonable enough, since she would not have had anything else available. Loraux ([1985] 1987: 10, with n. 10) cites Aesch. *Suppl.* 462 as a parallel.

52. Wohl 1998: 36, 49.

53. Segal (1995: 85) sees "loosing the *peplos*" as an evocation of the consummation of the wedding night. Wohl (1998: 49), on the other hand, emphasizes sexual violation: Deianeira's body is "eroticized at the moment of death" and "penetrated by the Homeric sword."

54. As when the female attendants of Hekabe use *porphas* (brooches) to blind Polymnestor in Euripides' *Hekabe* 1169–71.

55. Oidipous' attack on his eyes using Iocasta's golden brooches (*chrusēlatous / peronas*; Soph. *OT* 1268–69) can be seen as analogous to Deianeira's turning of her husband's sword upon herself. Both choose weapons that belong to, and represent, the loved one who has been inadvertently harmed, and consequently, implements belonging to and identified with the opposite gender. Although Herakles' sword serves no other purpose, the function of weapon is only latent in Iocasta's brooch-pins.

56. Wohl (1998:11–13) discusses the trade-off of mother for father offered to Hyllos.

57. Discussed at greater length in Chapter Two. See also Foley 2001.

58. Alkestis, when preparing to die, prays to Hestia at the hearth and all the altars in the house (Eur., *Alkestis* 161–74). Women's relationship to this goddess is not exclusively tied to her role as daughter.

59. Ormand 1999: 10, 13, 19–21.

60. The women of Athens are never called "Athenaiai," but only "Attikai." See Patterson 1986.

61. *Agamemnon*: Goldhill 1984: 17. *Trachiniai*: Wohl 1998: 17–22, etc.; Ormand 1999: 41–45.

62. Tereus has raped and mutilated her sister Philomela. The sisters retaliate by killing Tereus' and Prokne's son Itys and serving him up to his father.

63. I am grateful to Sarah Morris for calling my attention to this phenomenon.

64. Soph., *Antigone* 853, 867, discussed by Ormand (1999: 94–95), who observes that for her, as for Deianeira, the experience of marriage is alienating and deepens her sense of foreignness.

65. Just 1989: 84, 93. On the wife as a foreigner, see Visser 1986.

66. On the differences in age, see Just 1989: 151–52; Cox 1998: 70, 121.

67. On the Homeric ideal of *homophrosunē*, see Winkler 1990: 160-61; Wohl 1993; Zerba 2009: 306.

68. [And.] 4.14; Plut., *Alkibiades* 8.3–4. See Cox 1998: 115, 118, 186, on Alkibiades' forcible reclamation of his wife.

69. Our source is Demosthenes 27-29 (*Against Aphobos* 1–3). See Hunter 1989a and 1989b.

70. Rubin 1975; Sedgwick 1985.

CHAPTER SIX

1. The obvious exception—Medea's murder of her brother Absyrtos—is discussed below.

2. Some examples from Just 1989: 128–29: Isaeus 7.15; Dem. 50.60–63. Unless otherwise specified, in this chapter the word "siblings" refers to a sister-brother pair. On brother-sister relationships, see Visser 1986; Bremmer 1997.

3. Although Jebb (1892) is content to athetize lines 904–20, he notes that Dindorf had proposed eliminating the entire passage from line 900 to 928.

4. Quoted by Eckermann, quoted by Jebb (1892). As recently as 1987, Andrew Brown wrote, "In the end I cannot believe that Soph[ocles] wrote this rubbish" (200).

5. See Hardy 1996. Though Sophocles apparently knew Herodotos personally, this is not enough to explain why he would have borrowed an idea from him if it were irrevelant to his tragedy.

6. Kamerbeek 1978: 159.

7. Jebb 1892: 258.

8. See Beekes 1986: 225–39, for parallels, rather sketchily treated. Murnaghan (1986b) also offers some parallels, but her main point is the abstract nature of Antigone's thinking about marriage compared to the passionate nature of her attachment to her brother.

9. Lévi-Strauss [1949] 1969.

10. Lévi-Strauss [1958] 1963: 213–17.

11. Weiner 1992: 74. See also the discussion in Chapter One.

12. For the general principle, see also Sacks 1979: passim, discussed in Chapter One.

13. William Congreve, *The Way of the World*, act IV, scene 5.

14. Cox 1998; Just 1989.

15. See Gernet [1948] 1981: 253 n. 40.

16. Paus. 2.19.6, 2.21.1. Allegiance to the father is not even particularly well rewarded: a later tradition, which may in fact be Roman, has it that the Danaids were condemned to carry water in leaky sieves in the Underworld. What seems like a coincidence—that these two moments of separation of father and daughter are commemorated and thus leave their marks on the landscape of Greece—is perhaps attributable to the nature of Pausanias' interests and principles of selection.

17. When her brother or brothers were accidently killed by her son, in her anger she cursed him (ἐξ ἀρέων μητρὸς κεχολωμένος, ἥ ῥα θεοῖσι / πόλλ᾽ ἀχέους᾽ ἠρᾶτο κασιγνήτοιο φόνοιο, *Iliad* 9.566–67) or burned the fire-brand to which his survival was linked (Hes., *Catalogue of Women* 25; Bakchyl. 5.142; Aesch., *Choe.* 602ff.; Apollod. 1.8.2–3). Apollodoros is clear that there is more than one brother: Ἀλθαία δὲ λυπηθεῖσα ἐπὶ τῇ τῶν ἀδελφῶν ἀπωλείᾳ τὸν δαλὸν ἧψε, καὶ ὁ Μελέαγρος ἐξαίφνης ἀπέθανεν (1.8.3).

18. Aesch. *Choe.* 138, although the chorus thinks she requires some prompting, at lines 115. Cf. Soph. *El.* 117.

19. See Bremmer 1997; Visser 1986.

20. Weiner 1992; 1979.

21. Jebb 1892: 258.

22. Vernant [1965] 1983.

23. This fact is essential for the evasion practiced by Admetos in *Alkestis* 530–32, discussed in Chapter Five.

24. Lévi-Strauss [1949] 1969: 457, adopted from E. H. Man, *On the Aboriginal Inhabitants of the Andaman Islands* (London, n.d.), 94–95.

25. Cited by Weiner 1992: 121.

26. Eller 2000.

27. τέλος δὲ κάμψαιμ᾽ ὥσπερ ἠρξάμην βίου, *Hipp.* 87, trans. Grene.

28. Zeitlin (1985: 71) has discussed this passage in connection with the myth of Pandora: "One might say that Hippolytus' replication of the Hesiodic discourse at the heart of the drama defines him as the nostalgic standard-bearer of the Golden Age."

29. Barrett 1964: ad loc.

30. Aesch. *Choe.* 235: ὦ φίλτατον μέλημα δώμασιν πατρός; Soph. *El.* 1126–28: ὦ φιλτάτου μνημεῖον ἀνθρώπων ἐμοὶ / ψυχῆς Ὀρέστου λοιπόν, ὥς σ᾽ ἀπ᾽ ἐλπίδων / οὐχ ὧνπερ ἐξέπεμπον εἰσεδεξάμην; Soph. *El.* 1163. Eur. *El.* 243: οἴμοι, τί γάρ μοι τῶνδέ γ᾽ ἐστὶ φίλτερον.

31. I have omitted lines 1311–20, 1327–30, and 1334–35, as they do not have direct bearing on the relationship between the siblings.

32. Compare to the *tekmēria* of Elektra in the *Choephoroi*: first is the lock of hair, second the footprint. In Soph. *El.* 1221–22, it is the *sphragis* (seal) of Agamemnon.

33. Here *Lakaina* must mean Klytemnestra; elsewhere used alone, it almost always means her sister Helen. This question oddly reflects an alternate version about Iphigeneia's own birth, that Helen was her actual mother, and that she gave her to her married sister to raise.

34. Weiner 1992: 73.

BIBLIOGRAPHY

Ahmed, Akbar, and Chris Shore, eds. 1995. *The Future of Anthropology: Its Relevance to the Contemporary World*. London: Athlone.

Alden, M. J. 1996. "Genealogy as Paradigm: The Example of Bellerophon." *Hermes* 124: 257–63.

———. 2000. *Homer Beside Himself: Para-narratives in the Iliad*. Oxford: Oxford University Press.

Anderson, Michael. 1997. *The Fall of Troy in Early Greek Poetry and Art*. Oxford: Clarendon Press.

Antonaccio, Carla. 2000. "Building Gender into Greek Houses." *Classical World* 93: 517–33.

Appadurai, Arjun, ed. 1986. *The Social Life of Things: Commodities in Cultural Perspective*. Cambridge: Cambridge University Press.

Arthur, Marylin B. [Marilyn Katz]. 1981. "The Divided World of *Iliad* VI." In Foley: 19–44.

———. 1982. "Cultural Strategies in Hesiod's *Theogony*: Law, Family, Society." *Arethusa* 15: 63–82.

———. 1983. "The Dream of a World without Women: Poetics and the Circles of Order in the *Theogony* Prooemium." *Arethusa* 16: 97–116.

———. 1984. "Early Greece: The Origins of the Western Attitude toward Women." In Peradotto and Sullivan: 7–58.

Asad, Talal, ed. 1973. *Anthropology and the Colonial Encounter*. Atlantic Highlands, NJ: Humanities Press.

Atchity, Kenneth, and Elizabeth Wayland Barber. 1987. "Greek Princes and Aegean Princesses: The Role of Women in the Homeric Poems." In K. Atchity, R. Hogart, and D. Price, eds., *Critical Essays on Homer*, 15–36. Boston: G. K. Hall.

Atkinson, Jane Monnig, and Shelly Errington. 1990. *Power and Difference: Gender in Island Southeast Asia*. Stanford, CA: Stanford University Press.

Austin, M., and P. Vidal-Nacquet. [1972] 1977. *The Economic and Social History of Ancient Greece*. Berkeley: University of California Press.

Austin, Norman. 1994. *Helen of Troy and Her Shameless Phantom*. Ithaca, NY: Cornell University Press.

Bakewell, Geoffrey. 1997. "Μετοικία in the 'Supplices' of Aeschylus." *Classical Antiquity* 16: 209–28.

Bamberger, Joan. 1974. "The Myth of Matriarchy: Why Men Rule in Primitive Society." In Rosaldo and Lamphere: 263–80.

Barber, Elizabeth Wayland. 1991. *Prehistoric Textiles: The Development of Cloth in the Neolithic and Bronze Ages with Special Reference to the Aegean.* Princeton, NJ: Princeton University Press.

———. 1992. "The Peplos of Athena." In J. Neils, ed., *Goddess and Polis: The Panathenaic Festival in Ancient Athens*, 103–17. Princeton, NJ: Princeton University Press.

———. 1994. *Women's Work: The First 20,000 Years: Women, Cloth, and Society in Early Times.* New York: Norton.

Barrett, W. S. 1964. *Euripides* Hippolytos. Oxford: Clarendon Press.

Bassi, Karen. 1993. "Helen and the Discourse of Denial in Stesichorus' Palinode." *Arethusa* 26: 51–75.

Battaglia, Debbora. 1994. "Retaining Reality: Some Practical Problems with Objects as Property." *Man*, n.s. 29: 1–15.

Beekes, R.S.P. 1986. "'You Can Get New Children.'" *Mnemosyne* 39: 225–39.

Beidelmann, T. O. 1989. "Agonistic Exchange: Homeric Reciprocity and the Heritage of Simmel and Mauss." *Cultural Anthropology* 4.3: 227–79.

Belfiore, Elizabeth. 1998. "Harming Friends: Problematic Reciprocity in Greek Tragedy." In Gill et al.: 139–58.

Benveniste, Emile. 1969. *Le Vocabulaire des institutions indo-européennes.* Paris: Minuit.

Bérard, Claude. 1989. "The Order of Women" In Bérard et al.: 88–107.

Bérard, Claude, et al. 1989. *The City of Images: Iconography and Society in Ancient Greece.* Translated by D. Lyons. Princeton, NJ: Princeton University Press.

Bergren, Ann. 1980. "Helen's Web: Time and Tableau in the *Iliad*." *Helios* 7.1: 19–34.

———. 1981. "Helen's 'Good Drug': *Odyssey* IV 1–305." In S. Kresic, ed., *Contemporary Literary Hermeneutics and the Interpretation of Classical Texts*, 201–14. Ottawa: Ottawa University Press.

———. 1983. "Language and the Female in Early Greek Thought." *Arethusa* 16: 69–95.

———. 2008. *Weaving Truth: Essays on Language and the Female in Greek Thought.* Washington, DC: Center for Hellenic Studies.

Beye, Charles Rowan. 1974. "Male and Female in the *Odyssey*." *Ramus* 3: 87–101.

Bickerman, E. J. 1975. "La conception du mariage à Athènes." *Bullettino dell' Istituto di Diritto Romano* 78: 1–28.

Blakely, Sandra. 2003. *Myth, Ritual, and Metallurgy in Ancient Greece and Recent Africa.* Cambridge: Cambridge University Press.

Block, Elizabeth. 1985. "Clothing Makes the Man: A Pattern in the *Odyssey*." *Transactions of the American Philological Association* 115: 1–11.

Blok, Josine, and Peter Mason, eds. 1987. *Sexual Asymmetry: Studies in Ancient Society.* Amsterdam: Gieben.

Boegehold, Alan L., ed. 1984. *Studies Presented to Sterling Dow on His Eightieth Birthday.* Durham, NC: Duke University Press.

Bollansée, J. 1999. "Fact and Fiction, Falsehood and Truth: D. Fehling and Ancient Legendry about the Seven Sages." *Museum Helveticum* 56.2: 65–75.

Booth, William James. 1993. *Households: On the Moral Architecture of the Economy.* Ithaca, NY: Cornell University Press.

Bourdieu, Pierre. 1970. "The Berber House, or the World Reversed." *Social Science Information* 9: 151–70.

Bowra, C. M. 1963. "The Two Palinodes of Stesichorus." *Classical Review* 77: 245–52.

Bremmer, Jan N. 1981. "Plutarch and the Naming of Greek Women." *American Journal of Philology* 102: 425–26.

———. 1997. "Why Did Medea Kill Her Brother?" In James J. Clauss and Sarah Iles Johnston, eds., *Medea: Essays on Medea in Myth Literature, Philosophy and Art*, 83–100. Princeton, NJ: Princeton University Press.

Brillet-Dubois, Pascale. 1999–2000. "Les Dons divins faits aux Troyens." *Gaia* 4: 9–16.

Brock, Roger. 1994. "The Labours of Women in Classical Athens." *Classical Quarterly* 44: 336–46.

Bron, Christiane, and François Lissarrague. 1989. "Looking at the Vase." In Bérard et al.: 11–21.

Brown, A. S. 1997. "Aphrodite and the Pandora Complex." *Classical Quarterly* 47: 26–47.

Brown, Andrew. 1987. *Sophocles:* Antigone. Warminster: Aris and Phillips.

Brulé, Pierre. 1987. *La Fille d'Athènes: La Religion des filles à Athènes à l'époque classique*. Centre de Recherches d'Histoire Ancienne. Paris: Les Belles Lettres.

Bundrick, Sheramy D. 2008. "The Fabric of the City: Imaging Textile Production in Classical Athens." *Hesperia* 77: 284–334.

Burkert, Walter. 1966. "Kekropidensage und Arrhephoria: Vom Initiationsritus zum Panathenäenfest." *Hermes* 94: 1–25.

———. [1972] 1983. *Homo Necans: The Anthropology of Ancient Greek Sacrificial Ritual and Myth*. Translated by P. Bing. Berkeley: University of California Press.

Buxton, Richard. 1994. *Imaginary Greece: The Contexts of Mythology*. Cambridge: Cambridge University Press.

Cahill, Nicholas. 2005. "Household Industry in Greece and Anatolia." In Bradley A. Ault and Lisa C. Nevett, eds., *Ancient Greek Houses and Households*, 54–66. Philadelphia: University of Pennsylvania Press.

Calame, Claude. 1977. *Les Choeurs de jeunes filles en Grèce archaïque*. Rome: Ateneo e Bizzari.

Calder, W. M., III. 1984. "Gold for Bronze: *Iliad* 6.232–36." In Boegehold et al.: 31–35.

Cameron, Averil, and Amélie Kuhrt, eds. 1983. *Images of Women in Antiquity*. Detroit, MI: Wayne State University Press.

Carson, Anne. 1990. "Putting Her in Her Place: Women, Dirt, and Desire." In Halperin et al.: 135–69.

Chowning, Ann. 1987. "'Women Are Our Business': Women, Exchange and Prestige in Kove." In Strathern 1987b: 130–49.

Clader, Linda Lee. 1976. *Helen: The Evolution from Divine to Heroic in Greek Epic Tradition*. Leiden: Brill.

Cohen, David. 1990. "The Social Context of Adultery in Classical Athens." In P. Cartledge, P. Millett, and S. C. Todd, eds., *NOMOS: Essays in Athenian Law, Politics and Society*, 147–65. Cambridge: Cambridge University Press.

———. 1991. *Law, Sexuality, and Society: The Enforcement of Morals in Classical Athens*. Cambridge: Cambridge University Press.

Constantinidou, Soteroula. 1990. "Evidence for Marriage Ritual in Iliad 3." ΔΩΔΩΝΗ 19.2: 47–59.

Coontz, S., and P. Henderson, eds. 1986. *Women's Work, Men's Property: The Origins of Gender and Class*. London: Verso.

Cox, Cheryl Ann. 1998. *Household Interests: Property, Marriage Strategies, and Family Dynamics in Ancient Athens.* Princeton, NJ: Princeton University Press.

Craig, J. D. 1967. "ΧΡΥΣΕΑ ΧΑΛΚΕΙΟΝ." *Classical Review* 17: 243–45.

Crane, Gregory. 1993. "Politics of Consumption and Generosity in the Carpet Scene of the Agamemnon." *Classical Philology* 88: 117–36.

Crome, Johann Friedrich. 1966. "Spinnende Hetairen?" *Gymnasium* 73: 245–47.

Cunliffe, Richard John. [1924] 1963. *A Lexicon of the Homeric Dialect.* Norman: University of Oklahoma Press.

Cunningham, Kiran. 1996. "Let's Go to My Place: Residence, Gender and Power in a Mende Community." In Maynes et al.: 335–49.

Dacher, Michele, and Suzanne Lallemand. 1992. *Prix des épouses, valeur des soeurs.* Paris: L'Harmattan.

Damm, Charlotte Brysting. 2000. "Time, Gender and Production." In Donald and Hurcome, eds.: 110–22.

Davidson, James. 1997. *Courtesans and Fishcakes: The Consuming Passions of Classical Athens.* London: Harper Collins.

Davis, Mark I. 1977. "The Reclamation of Helen." *Antike Kunst* 20: 73–85.

Davison, J. A. 1966. "De Helena Stesichori." *Quaderni urbinati di cultura classica* 2: 80–90.

Delcourt, Marie. [1957] 1982. *Héphaistos ou la légende du magicien.* Paris: Les Belle lettres.

Dellner, Jennifer J. 2000. "Alcestis' Double Life." *Classical Journal* 96: 1–25.

Detienne, Marcel. 1963. *Crise agraire et attitude religieuse chez Hésiode.* Brussels: Latomus.

———. [1972] 1994. *The Gardens of Adonis: Spices in Greek Mythology.* Translated by J. Lloyd. Princeton, NJ: Princeton University Press.

Diggle, James, ed. 1998. *Tragicorum Graecorum fragmenta selecta.* Oxford: Oxford University Press.

Donald, Moira, and Linda Hurcombe, eds. 2000. *Gender and Material Culture in Archaeological Perspective.* New York: St. Martin's Press.

Donlan, Walter. [1980] 1999. *The Aristocratic Ideal and Selected Papers.* Wauconda, IL: Bolchazy-Carducci.

———. 1981. "Scale, Value and Function in the Homeric Economy." *American Journal of Ancient History* 6: 101–17.

———. 1982. "Reciprocities in Homer." *Classical World* 75: 137–75.

———. 1989. "The Unequal Exchange between Glaucus and Diomedes in the Light of the Homeric Gift-Economy." *Phoinix* 43: 1–15.

Dover, K. J. 1987. "The Red Fabric in the Agamemnon." In *Greek and the Greeks: Collected Papers.* Vol. 1: *Language, Poetry, Drama,* 151–60. Oxford: Blackwell.

duBois, Page. 1988. *Sowing the Body: Psychoanalysis and Ancient Representations of Women.* Chicago: University of Chicago Press.

Eller, Cynthia. 2000. *The Myth of Matriarchal Prehistory: Why an Invented Past Won't Give Women a Future.* Boston: Beacon.

Errington, Frederick, and Deborah Gewertz. 1987. *Cultural Alternatives and a Feminist Anthropology.* Cambridge: Cambridge University Press.

Etienne, Mona. 1980. "Women and Men, Cloth and Colonization: The Transformation of Production-Distribution Relations among the Baule." In Etienne and Leacock: 214–38.

Etienne, Mona, and Elinor Leacock, eds. 1980. *Women and Colonization*. New York: Praeger.

Evelyn-White, H. G., ed. and trans. 1964. *Hesiod, the Homeric Hymns, and Homerica.* Cambridge, MA.: Harvard University Press.

Faraone, Christopher A. 1990. "Aphrodite's ΚΕΣΤΟΣ and Apples for Atalanta: Aphrodisiacs in Early Greek Myth and Ritual." *Phoinix* 44: 219–43.

———. 1992. *Talismans and Trojan Horses: Guardian Statues in Ancient Greek Myth and Ritual.* Oxford: Oxford University Press.

———. 1994. "Deianira's Mistake and the Demise of Heracles: Erotic Magic in Sophocles' *Trachiniae.*" *Helios* 21: 115–35.

———. 1999. *Ancient Greek Love Magic.* Cambridge, MA: Harvard University Press.

Felson, Nancy. [1994] 1997. *Regarding Penelope: From Character to Poetics.* Norman: University of Oklahoma Press.

Ferrari, Giovanni. 1988. "Hesiod's Mimetic Muses and the Strategies of Deconstruction." In A. Benjamin, ed., *Post-Structuralist Classics*, 45–78. London: Routledge.

Ferrari, Gloria. 2002. *Figures of Speech: Men and Maidens in Ancient Greece.* Chicago: University of Chicago Press.

Finkelberg, Margalit. 1991. "Royal Succession in Heroic Greece." *Classical Quarterly* 41: 303–16.

Finley, M. I. [1954] 1978. *The World of Odysseus.* New York: Viking Press.

———. [1955] 1981. "Marriage, Sale and Gift in the Homeric World." In *Economy and Society in Ancient Greece*, 233–45. Harmondsworth: Penguin.

———. [1975] 1987. *The Use and Abuse of History.* London: Penguin.

Fisher, N.E.R. 1992. *Hybris: A Study in the Values of Honour and Shame in Ancient Greece.* Warminster: Aris and Phillips.

Fitzgerald, Robert, trans. 1990. *Homer, The Odyssey.* New York: Vintage.

Flintoff, Everard. 1987. "The Treading of the Cloth." *Quaderni urbinati di cultura classica,* n.s. 25: 119–30.

Foley, Helene P., ed. 1981. *Reflections of Women in Antiquity.* New York: Gordon and Breach.

———. 2001. *Female Acts in Greek Tragedy.* Princeton, NJ: Princeton University Press.

Forge, Anthony. 1972. "The Golden Fleece." *Man* 7: 527–40.

Foxhall, Lin. 1989. "Household, Gender and Property in Classical Athens." *Classical Quarterly* 39: 22–44.

———. 1996. "The Law and the Lady: Women and Legal Proceedings in Classical Athens." In L. Foxhall and A.D.E. Lewis, eds., *Greek Law in Its Political Setting: Justifications Not Justice*, 133–52. Oxford: Oxford University Press.

Fraenkel, Eduard. 1950. *Aeschylus. Agamemnon.* Oxford: Clarendon Press.

Freud, Sigmund. [1933] 1965. *New Introductory Lectures on Psychoanalysis.* Edited and translated by J. Strachey. New York: Norton.

Friedl, Ernestine. 1967. "The Position of Women: Appearance and Reality." *Anthropological Quarterly* 40: 97–108.

———. 1975. *Women and Men: An Anthropologist's View.* New York: Holt, Rinehart and Winston.

Frontisi-Ducroux, Françoise. 1975. *Dédale: Mythologie de l'artisan en Grèce ancienne.* Paris: La Découverte.

Fruzzetti, Lina M. 1982. *The Gift of a Virgin: Women, Marriage, and Ritual in Bengali Society.* New Brunswick, NJ: Rutgers University Press.

Fuller, C. J. 1992. "Review of Marcel Mauss, *The Gift: The Form and Reason for Exchange in Archaic Societies.*" *Man*, n.s. 27: 431–33.

Gailey, Christine. 1980. "Putting Down Sisters and Wives: Tongan Women and Colonization." In Etienne and Leacock: 294–322.

Geddes, A. G. 1984. "Who's Who in Homeric Society." *Classical Quarterly* 34: 17–36.

Gernet, Louis. [1948] 1981. "'Value' in Greece." In R. L. Gordon and R.G.A. Buxton, eds., *Myth, Religion and Society*, 111–46. Cambridge: Cambridge University Press.

———. 1983. *Les Grecs sans miracles: Textes 1903–1960.* Paris: Maspero.

Gero, J. M., and M. W. Conkey, eds. 1991. *Engendering Archaeology: Women and Prehistory.* Oxford: Oxford University Press.

Gewertz, Deborah. 1985. "The Golden Age Revisited: A History of the Chambri between 1905 and 1927." In E. Schieffelin and D. Gewertz, eds., *History and Ethnohistory in Papua New Guinea*, 58–76. Sydney: Oceania Publications.

Ghali-Kahil, Lilly. 1955. *Les Enlevements et le retour d'Hélène dans les textes et les documents figurés.* Paris: École Françaises d'Athènes.

Gill, Christopher, Norman Postlethwaite, and Richard Seaford, eds. 1998. *Reciprocity in Ancient Greece.* Oxford: Oxford University Press.

Glotz, Gustave. [1920] 1967. *Ancient Greece at Work: An Economic History of Greece.* New York: Norton.

Godelier, Maurice. [1996] 1999. *The Enigma of the Gift.* Translated by N. Scott. Chicago: University of Chicago Press.

Golden, Mark. 1986. "Names and Naming at Athens: Three Studies." *Echoes du monde classique/Classical Views* 30, n.s. 5: 245–69.

———. 1990. *Children and Childhood in Classical Athens.* Baltimore, MD: The Johns Hopkins University Press.

Goldhill, Simon. 1984. *Language, Sexuality, Narrative: The Oresteia.* Cambridge: Cambridge University Press.

Goody, Jack. 1976. *Production and Reproduction.* Cambridge: Cambridge University Press.

———. 1990. *The Oriental, the Ancient and the Primitive: Systems of Marriage and the Family in the Pre-Industrial Societies of Eurasia.* Cambridge: Cambridge University Press.

Goody, Jack, and S. J. Tambiah. 1973. *Bridewealth and Dowry.* Cambridge: Cambridge University Press.

Gottschall, Jonathan. 2008. *The Rape of Troy: Evolution, Violence, and the World of Homer.* Cambridge: Cambridge University Press.

Gould, J. 1980. "Law, Custom and Myth: Aspects of the Social Position of Women in Classical Athens." *Journal of Hellenic Studies* 100: 38–59.

Graeber, David. 2001. *Toward an Anthropological Theory of Value: The False Coin of Our Own Dreams.* New York: Palgrave.

Gregor, Thomas A., and Donald Tuzin, eds. 2001. *Gender in Amazonia and Melanesia: An Exploration of the Comparative Method.* Berkeley: University of California Press.

Gregory, C. A. 1980. "Gifts to Men and Gifts to God: Gift Exchange and Capital Accumulation in Contemporary Papua." *Man*, n.s. 15: 626–52.

———. 1982. *Gifts and Commodities.* London: Academic Press.

Gregory, Elizabeth. 1996. "Unravelling Penelope: The Construction of the Faithful Wife in Homer's Heroines." *Helios* 23: 3–20.

Hallett, Judith P. 1984. *Fathers and Daughters in Roman Society: Women in the Elite Family.* Princeton, NJ: Princeton University Press.

Halperin, David, John J. Winkler, and Froma Zeitlin, eds. 1990. *Before Sexuality: The Construction of Erotic Experience in the Ancient World.* Princeton, NJ: Princeton University Press.

Hamilton, Edith, and Huntington Cairns, eds. 1961. *The Collected Dialogues of Plato.* Bollingen Series 71. Princeton, NJ: Princeton University Press.

Hamilton, Richard. 1989. "Alkman and the Athenian *Arkteia*." *Hesperia* 58: 449–72 (pl. 83–86).

Hardy, Clara Shaw. 1996. "Nomos and Replaceability in the Story of Intaphernes and His Wife." *Transactions of the American Philological Association* 126: 101–9.

Herman, Gabriel. 1987. *Ritualized Friendship and the Greek City.* Cambridge: Cambridge University Press.

Herzfeld, Michael. 1980. "The Dowry in Greece: Terminological Usage and Historical Reconstruction." *Ethnohistory* 27: 225–41.

———. 1986. "Within and Without: The Category of 'Female' in the Ethnography of Modern Greece." In J. Dubisch, ed., *Gender and Power in Rural Greece*, 215–33. Princeton, NJ: Princeton University Press.

———. 2001. *Anthropology: Theoretical Practice in Culture and Society.* Oxford: Blackwell.

Hirschon, Renée, ed. 1984. *Women and Property, Women as Property.* New York: St. Martin's Press.

Hodkinson, Stephen. 1989. "Inheritance, Marriage, and Demography: Perspectives upon the Success and Decline of Classical Sparta." In A. Powell, ed., *Classical Sparta: Techniques behind Her Success*, 79–121. London: Routledge.

———. 2005. "Female Property Ownership and Status in Classical and Hellenistic Sparta." In Lyons and Westbrook.

Hooker, J. T. 1989. "Gifts in Homer." *Bulletin of the Institute for Classical Studies* 36: 79–90.

Hoskins, Janet. 1987. "Complementarity in This World and the Next: Gender and Agency in Kodi Mortuary Ceremonies." In Strathern 1987b: 174–206.

———. 1998. *Biographical Objects: How Things Tell the Stories of People's Lives.* New York: Routledge.

Hugh-Jones, Stephen. 2001. "The Gender of Some Amazonian Gifts: An Experiment with an Experiment." In Gregor and Tuzin: 245–78.

Humphreys, S. C. 1978. *Anthropology and the Greeks.* London.

———. 1986. "Kinship Patterns in the Athenian Courts." *Greek, Roman, and Byzantine Studies* 37: 57–91.

———. 1987. "Law, Custom, and Culture in Herodotus." *Arethusa* 20: 212–14.

———. 1993. *The Family, Women and Death.* 2d ed. Ann Arbor: University of Michigan Press.

———. 1995. "Women's Stories." In Reeder: 102–10.

Hunter, Virginia. 1981. "Classics and Anthropology." *Phoenix* 35: 145–55.

———. 1989a. "The Athenian Widow and Her Kin." *Journal of Family History* 14: 291–311.

———. 1989b. "Women's Authority in Classical Athens: The Example of Kleoboule and Her Son (Dem. 27–29)." *Echoes du monde classique/Classical Views* 33, n.s. 8: 39–48.

———. 1994. *Policing Athens: Social Control in the Attic Lawsuits, 420–320 B.C.* Princeton, NJ: Princeton University Press.

Hurcombe, Linda. 2000. "Time, Skill and Craft Specialization as Gender Relations." In Donald and Hurcombe: 88–109.

Hurwit, Jeffrey M. 1995. "Beautiful Evil: Pandora and the Athena Parthenos." *American Journal of Archaeology* 99: 171–86.

Irigaray, Luce. 1985. *This Sex Which Is Not One.* Ithaca, NY: Cornell University Press.

Irwin, M. Eleanor. 1990. "Odysseus' 'Hyacinthine Hair' in *Odyssey* 6.231." *Phoinix* 44: 205–18.

Jebb, Richard. 1892. *Sophocles: The Plays and Fragments.* Part III: *The Antigone.* Cambridge: Cambridge University Press.

Jenkins, I. D. 1985. "The Ambiguity of Greek Textiles." *Arethusa* 18: 109–32.

Johnstone, Steven. 2003. "Women, Property, and Surveillance in Classical Athens." *Classical Antiquity* 22: 247–74.

Joshel, Sandra R. 1997. "Female Desire and the Discourse of Empire: Tacitus' Messalina." In Judith Hallett and Marilyn Skinner, eds., *Roman Sexualities*, 221–54. Princeton, NJ: Princeton University Press.

Just, Roger. 1989. *Women in Athenian Law and Life.* London: Routledge.

Kamerbeek, J. C. 1978. *The Plays of Sophocles: Antigone.* Leiden: Brill.

Kardulias, Dianna Rhyan. 2001. "Odysseus in Ino's Veil: Feminine Headdress and the Hero in *Odyssey* 5." *Transactions of the American Philological Association* 31: 23–51.

Karydas, Helen Pournara. 1998. *Eurykleia and Her Successors: Female Figures of Authority in Greek Poetics.* Lanham, MD: Rowman and Littlefield.

Katz, Marilyn. 1991. *Penelope's Renown: Meaning and Indeterminacy in the* Odyssey. Princeton, NJ: Princeton University Press.

Kennedy, George. 1986. "Helen's Web Unraveled." *Arethusa* 19: 5–14.

Keuls, Eva. 1982. "The Conjugal Side of Dionysiac Ritual and Symbolism in the Fifth Century B.C." *Mededelingen Van Het Nederlands Historisch Instituut Te Rome*, n.s. 11, 46: 25–34.

———. 1983. "Attic Vase Painting and the Home Textile Industry." In W. G. Moon, ed., *Ancient Greek Painting and Iconography*, 209–30. Madison: University of Wisconsin Press.

———. 1985. *The Reign of the Phallus: Sexual Politics in Ancient Athens.* Berkeley: University of California Press.

Kirk, G. S., ed. 1985. *The* Iliad: *A Commentary.* Vol. 1: *Books 1–4.* Cambridge: Cambridge University Press.

Knox, B. M. W. 1977. "The *Medea* of Euripides." *Yale Classical Studies* 25: 193–25.

Koch-Harnack, Gundel. 1989. *Erotiche Symbole: Lotosbluite und gemeinsamer Mantel auf antiken Vasen.* Berlin: Gebr. Mann.

Konstan, David. 1983. "The Stories in Herodotus' *Histories*: Book I." *Helios* 10: 1–22.

Kovacs, David, ed. and trans. 1999. *Euripides: Trojan Women, Iphigeneia among the Taurians, Ion.* Cambridge, MA: Harvard University Press.

Krappe, A. H. 1939. "La Robe de Déjanire." *Revue des études grecques* 52: 565–72.

Kunisch, Norbert. 1997. *Makron.* Mainz: Zabern.

Kurke, Leslie. 1991. *The Traffic in Praise: Pindar and the Poetics of Social Economy.* Ithaca, NY: Cornell University Press.

———. 1999. *Coins, Bodies, Games, and Gold: The Politics of Meaning in Archaic Greece.* Princeton, NJ: Princeton University Press.

Lacey, W. C. 1966. "Homeric ΕΔΝΑ and Penelope's ΚΥΡΙΟΣ." *Journal of Hellenic Studies* 86: 55–68.

———. 1968. *The Family in Classical Athens.* Ithaca, NY: Cornell University Press.

Lamb, W. R. M., trans. [1930] 1976. *Lysias.* Cambridge, MA: Harvard University Press.

Lamberton, Robert. 1988. *Hesiod.* New Haven, CT: Yale University Press.

Langdon, Susan. 2008. *Art and Identity in Dark Age Greece, 1100–700 BC.* Cambridge: Cambridge University Press.

Lebeck, Ann. 1971. *The Oresteia: A Study in Language and Structure.* Washington, DC: Center for Hellenic Studies.

Lévi-Strauss, Claude. [1949] 1969. *The Elementary Structures of Kinship.* Translated by J. H. Bell, R. von Sturmer, and R. Needham. Rev. ed. Boston: Beacon.

———. [1958] 1963. *Structural Anthropology.* New York: Basic Books.

Lewis, Sian. 2002. *The Athenian Woman: An Iconographic Handbook.* London: Routledge.

Linders, Tullia. 1972. *Studies in the Treasure Records of Artemis Brauronia Found in Athens. Skrifter Ulgivna av Svenska institutet: Athen* 4.19. Stockholm: Swedish Institute.

Linders, Tullia, and G. Nordquist, eds. 1987. *Gifts to the Gods. Proceedings of the Uppsala Symposium 1985.* Uppsala: Boreas.

Link, Stefan. 2005. "'. . . But Not More!': Female Inheritance in Cretan Gortyn." In Lyons and Westbrook.

Lissarrague, François. 1995. "Women, Boxes, Containers: Some Signs and Metaphors." In Reeder: 91–101.

———. 2001. "La Fabrique de Pandora: Naissance d'images." In Jean-Claude Schmitt, ed., *Eve et Pandora: La Création de la première femme,* 39–67. Paris: Gallimard.

Llewellen-Jones, Lloyd. 2002. *Aphrodite's Tortoise: The Veiled Women of Ancient Greece.* Swansea: Classical Press of Wales.

Lloyd-Jones, Hugh, ed. and trans. 1996. *Sophocles: Fragments.* Cambridge, MA: Harvard University Press.

Lombardi, Tiziana. 1994. "Alcune considerazioni sul mito di Pandora." *Quaderni urbinati di cultura classica,* n.s. 46: 23–34.

Loraux, Nicole. 1978. "Sur la race des femmes et quelques-unes de ses tribus." *Arethusa* 11: 43–87.

———. [1981] 1993. *The Children of Athena.* Translated by C. Levine. Princeton, NJ: Princeton University Press.

———. [1985] 1987. *Tragic Ways of Killing a Woman.* Translated by A. Foster. Cambridge, MA: Harvard University Press.

———. 1992. "What Is a Goddess?" In P. Schmitt Pantel, ed., *A History of Women.* Vol. 1: *From Ancient Goddesses to Christian Saints,* 11–44. Translated by A. Goldhammer. Cambridge, MA: Harvard University Press.

———. 1994. "Pénélope-analyse." Preface to Papadopoulou-Belmehdi 1994b: 7–17.

———. 1995. *The Experiences of Tiresias: The Feminine and the Greek Man.* Translated by P. Wissing. Princeton, NJ: Princeton University Press.

Lowenstam, Steven. 1993. *The Scepter and the Spear: Studies on the Forms of Repetition in the Homeric Poems.* Lanham, MD: Rowman and Littlefield.

Lyons, Deborah. 1997. *Gender and Immortality: Heroines in Greek Myth and Cult.* Princeton, NJ: Princeton University Press.

———. 2003. "Dangerous Gifts." *Classical Antiquity* 22.1: 93–134. Reprinted in Lyons and Westbrook 2005.

———. 2007. "The Scandal of Women's Ritual." In A. Tzanetou and M. Parca, eds., *Finding Persephone: Women's Rituals in the Ancient Mediterranean*, 29–51. Bloomington: Indiana University Press.

———. Forthcoming. "Pandora and the Ambiguous Works of Women: All-Taking or All-Giving?" In Morny Joy, ed., *Beyond the All-Given and the All-Giving: Women and the Gift.* Bloomington: Indiana University Press.

Lyons, Deborah, and Raymond Westbrook, eds. 2005. *Women and Property in Ancient Near Eastern and Mediterranean Societies.* Washington, DC: Center for Hellenic Studies. (http://chs.harvard.edu/chs/women_and_property)

MacCormick, C., and M. Strathern, eds. 1980. *Nature, Culture, and Gender.* Cambridge: Cambridge University Press.

MacDowell, Douglas M. 1989. "The *Oikos* in Athenian Law." *Classical Quarterly* 39: 10–21.

Macleod, C. W. 1975. "Clothing in the *Oresteia*." *Maia* 27: 201–203. Reprinted in *Collected Essays* (Oxford, 1983), 41–43.

Macrakis, A. Lily. 1984. "Comparative Economic Values in the *Iliad*: The Oxen-Worth." In Boegehold et al.: 211–15.

Malinowski, Bronislaw. 1920. "Kula: The Circulating Exchange of Valuables in the Archipelagoes of Eastern New Guinea." *Man* 20: 97–105.

———. [1922] 1961. *Argonauts of the Western Pacific.* New York: E. P. Dutton.

Marcus, George E., and Michael M. J. Fischer. 1986. *Anthropology as Cultural Critique: An Experimental Moment in the Human Sciences.* Chicago: University of Chicago Press.

Marquardt, Patricia. 1982. "Hesiod's Ambiguous View of Women." *Classical Philology* 77: 283–91.

———. 1992. "Clytemnestra: A Felicitous Spelling in the *Odyssey*." *Arethusa* 25: 241–54.

Martin, Richard P. 1989. *The Language of Heroes: Speech and Performance in the Iliad.* Ithaca, NY: Cornell University Press.

Mauss, Marcel. 1925. *Essai sur le don: Forme et raison de l'échange dans les sociétés archaïques. L'Année sociologique*, n.s. 1: 30–186.

———. [1925] 1990. *The Gift: The Form and Reason for Exchange in Archaic Societies.* Translated by W. C. Halls. New York: Norton.

———. 1969. "L'âme, le nom et la personne." In *Oeuvres 2: Représentations collectives et diversité des civilisations*, 131–35. Paris: Les Editions de minuit.

Maynes, Mary Jo, Ann Waltner, Birgitte Soland, and Ulrike Strasser, eds. 1996. *Gender, Kinship, Power: A Comparative and Interdisciplinary History.* New York: Routledge.

McClure, Laura. 1997. "Clytemnestra's Binding Spell (*Ag.* 958–974)." *Classical Journal* 92: 123–40.

McInerney, Jeremy. 2010. *The Cattle of the Sun: Cows and Culture in the World of the Ancient Greeks.* Princeton, NJ: Princeton University Press.

Meillassoux, Claude. [1975] 1981. *Maidens, Meal and Money.* Cambridge: Cambridge University Press.

Merkelbach, R., and M. L. West. 1967. *Fragmenta Hesiodea.* Oxford: Clarendon Press.

Meyer, Marion. 1988. "Manner mit Geld: Zu einer rotfigurigen Vase mit 'Alltagsszene.'" *Jahrbuch des Deutschen Archaeologischen Instituts* 103: 87–125.

Mezzadri, Bernard. 1989. "La Toison de Thyeste et le soleil d'Atree: Images refractées de la guerre des Ases et des Vanes." *L'Homme* 109: 129–38.

———. 1990. "Autour de Béliers d'or: L'Investiture de Jason et d'Atrée." *L'Homme* 113: 43–52.

Mills, S. P. 1980. "The Sorrows of Medea." *Classical Philology* 75: 289–96.

Milne, M. J. 1945. "A Prize for Wool Working." *American Journal of Archaeology* 49: 528–33.

Minadeo, Richard W. 1985. "Characterization and Theme in the *Antigone*." *Arethusa* 18: 133–54.

Mitchell, Lynette. 2002. *Greeks Bearing Gifts: The Public Use of Private Relationships in the Greek World, 435–323 BC*. Cambridge: Cambridge University Press.

———. Forthcoming. "The Women of Ruling Families in Archaic and Classical Greece." *Classical Quarterly*.

Mizera, Suzanne. 1984. "Unions Holy and Unholy: Fundamental Structures of Myths of Marriage in Early Greek Poetry and Tragedy." Ph.D. dissertation, Princeton University.

Moore, Henrietta L. 1983. *Feminism and Anthropology*. Minneapolis: University of Minnesota Press.

Morgan, Gareth. 1982. "Euphiletos' House: Lysias I." *Transactions of the American Philological Association* 112: 115–23.

Morrell, Kenneth Scott. 1997. "The Fabric of Persuasion: Clytaemnestra, Agamemnon, and the Sea of Garments." *Classical Journal* 92: 141–65.

Morris, Ian. 1986a. "Gift and Commodity in Archaic Greece." *Man*, n.s. 21: 1–17.

———. 1986b. "The Use and Abuse of Homer." *Classical Antiquity* 5: 81–138.

Most, Glenn W. 1989. "The Stranger's Stratagem: Self-Disclosure and Self-Sufficiency in Greek Culture." *Journal of Hellenic Studies* 109: 114–33.

Murnaghan, Sheila. 1986a. "Penelope's *Agnoia*: Knowledge, Power, and Gender in the *Odyssey*." In Skinner: 103–15.

———. 1986b. "Sophocles' *Antigone* 904–920 and the Institution of Marriage." *American Journal of Philology* 107: 192–207.

———. 1988. "How a Woman Can Be More Like a Man: The Dialogue between Ischomachus and His Wife in Xenophon's *Oeconomicus*." *Helios* 15: 9–22.

Nagy, Joseph Falaky. 1981. "The Deceptive Gift in Greek Mythology." *Arethusa* 14: 191–204.

Neils, Jenifer. 2005. "The Girl in the Pithos: Hesiod's Elpis." In J. M. Barringer and J. M. Herwit, eds., *Periklean Athens and Its Legacy*, 37–45. Austin: University of Texas Press.

Neuberg, M. 1990. "How Like a Woman: Antigone's 'Inconsistency.'" *Classical Quarterly* 40: 54–76.

Newton, R. M. 1984. "The Rebirth of Odysseus." *Greek, Roman, and Byzantine Studies* 25: 5–20.

O'Higgins, Delores. 1993. "Above Rubies: Admetus' Perfect Wife." *Arethusa* 26: 77–97.

Oakley, J. H. 1982. "The Anakalypteria." *Archäologischer Anzeiger* 97: 113–18.

Oakley, J. H., and R. H. Sinos. 1993. *The Wedding in Ancient Athens*. Madison: University of Wisconsin Press.

Ober, Joshua. 1989. *Mass and Elite in Democratic Athens*. Princeton, NJ: Princeton University Press.

Ormand, Kirk. 1996. "Silent by Convention? Sophocles' Tekmessa." *American Journal of Philology* 117: 37–64.

———. 1999. *Exchange and the Maiden: Marriage in Sophoclean Tragedy*. Austin: University of Texas Press.

Ortner, Sherry B. 1974. "Is Female to Male as Nature Is to Culture?" In Rosaldo and Lamphere: 67–87.

Osborne, Robin. 1994. "Looking on—Greek Style. Does the Sculpted Girl Speak to Women Too?" In I. Morris, ed., *Classical Greece: Ancient Histories and Modern Archaeologies*, 81–96. Cambridge: Cambridge University Press.

Padilla, Mark. 2000. "Gifts of Humiliation: *Charis* and Tragic Experience in *Alcestis*." *American Journal of Philology* 121: 179–211.

Panofsky, Dora, and Erwin Panofsky. 1962. *Pandora's Box: The Changing Aspects of a Mythical Symbol*. New York: Bollingen Foundation.

Pantelia, Maria C. 1993. "Spinning and Weaving: Ideas of Domestic Order in Homer." *American Journal of Philology* 114: 493–501.

Papadopoulou-Belmehdi, Ionna. 1994a. "Greek Weaving or the Feminine in Antithesis." *Diogenes* 167: 39–56.

———. 1994b. *Le Chant de Pénélope: Poétique du tissage feminine dans l'Odyssée*. Paris: Belin.

Papalexandrou, Nassos. 2005. *The Visual Poetics of Power: Warriors, Youths, and Tripods in Early Greece*. Lanham, MD: Lexington.

Parry, Jonathan. 1989. "On the Moral Perils of Exchange." In Jonathan Parry and Maurice Bloch, eds., *Money and the Morality of Exchange*, 64–93. Cambridge: Cambridge University Press.

Patel, Reena. 2007. *Hindu Women's Property Rights in Rural India: Law, Labour and Culture in Action*. London: Ashgate.

Patterson, Cynthia B. 1986. "Hai Attikai: The Other Athenians." In Skinner: 49–67.

———. 1991. "Marriage and the Married Woman in Athenian Law." In Sarah Pomeroy, ed., *Women's History and Ancient History*, 48–72. Chapel Hill: University of North Carolina Press.

———. 1998. *The Family in Greek History*. Cambridge, MA: Harvard University Press.

Peacock, Nadine R. 1991. "Rethinking the Sexual Division of Labor: Reproduction and Women's Work among the Efe." In Micaela di Leonardo, ed., *Gender at the Crossroads of Knowledge*, 339–60. Berkeley: University of California Press.

Pearce, T.E.V. 1974. "The Role of the Wife as CUSTOS in Ancient Rome." *Eranos* 72: 16–33.

Pedrick, Victoria. 1988. "The Hospitality of Noble Women in the *Odyssey*." *Helios* 15: 85–101.

Pembroke, S. 1967. "Women in Charge: The Functions of Alternatives in Early Greek Tradition and the Ancient Idea of Matriarchy." *Journal of the Warburg and Courtauld Institutes* 30: 1–35.

Peradotto, John, and J. P. Sullivan, eds. 1984. *Women in the Ancient World: The Arethusa Papers*. Albany: SUNY Press.

Peristiany, J. G., ed. 1966. *Honour and Shame: The Values of Mediterranean Society*. Chicago: University of Chicago Press.

Perysinakis, I. N. 1991. "Penelope's EEDNA Again." *Classical Quarterly* 41: 297–302.

Petersen, Lauren Hackworth. 1997. "Divided Consciousness and Female Companionship: Reconstructing Female Subjectivity on Greek Vases." *Arethusa* 30: 35–74.

Petropoulos, J.C.B. 1994. *Heat and Lust: Hesiod's Midsummer Festival Scene Revisited.* Lanham, MD: Rowman and Littlefield.

Pinney, Gloria Ferrari. 1986. "Money-bags?" *American Journal of Archaeology* 90: 218.

Pitt-Rivers, Julian. 1977. *The Fate of Sechem or the Politics of Sex: Essays in the Anthropology of the Mediterranean.* Cambridge: Cambridge University Press.

Platnauer, M. 1967. *Euripides. Helen.* Edition and commentary. Oxford: Clarendon Press.

Polanyi, K. 1968. *Primitive, Archaic and Modern Economies.* Edited by George Dalton. Garden City, NY: Doubleday.

Pomeroy, Sarah B. 1994. *Xenophon. Oeconomicus: A Social and Historical Commentary.* Oxford: Clarendon Press.

———. 1997. *Families in Hellenistic and Classical Greece.* Oxford: Oxford University Press.

———. 2002. *Spartan Women.* New York: Oxford University Press.

Pozzi, Dora. 1994. "Deianeira's Robe: Diction in Sophocles' *Trachiniae.*" *Mnemosyne* 47: 577–85.

———. 1996. "Deianira Vere Oenei Filia." *Hermes* 124: 104–8.

Price, Sally. 1984. *Co-Wives and Calabashes.* Ann Arbor: University of Michigan Press.

Prier, Raymond Adolph. 1989. Thauma idesthai: *The Phenomenology of Sight and Appearance in Archaic Greek.* Tallahassee: Florida State University Press.

Pucci, Pietro. 1977. *Hesiod and the Language of Poetry.* Baltimore, MD: The Johns Hopkins University Press.

Qviller, B. 1981. "The Dynamics of the Homeric Society." *Symbolae Osloenses* 56: 109–55.

Raaflaub, Kurt. 1997. "Homeric Society." In I. Morris and B. Powell, eds., *A New Companion to Homer,* 624–48. Leiden: Brill.

Rabinowitz, Nancy Sorkin. 1992. "Tragedy and the Politics of Containment." In Amy Richlin, ed., *Pornography and Representation in Greece and Rome,* 36–52. New York: Oxford University Press.

———. 1993. *Anxiety Veiled: Euripides and the Traffic in Women.* Ithaca, NY: Cornell University Press.

Raheja, Gloria Goodwin. 1996. "The Limits of Patriliny: Kinship, Gender and Women's Speech Practices in Rural Northern India." In Maynes et al.: 149–74.

Redfield, James M. 1982. "Notes on the Greek Wedding." *Arethusa* 15: 181–201.

———. [1983] 2009. "Economic Man." In Lillian E. Doherty, ed., *Homer's* Odyssey, 265–87. Oxford Readings in Classical Studies. Oxford: Oxford University Press.

———. 1990. "From Sex to Politics: The Rites of Artemis Triklaria and Dionysos Aisymnetes at Patras." In Halperin et al.: 114–34.

———. 1991. "Anthropology and the Classics." *Arion,* 3d ser., 1.2: 5–23.

———. 1994. *Nature and Culture in the* Iliad: *The Tragedy of Hector.* 2d ed. Durham, NC: Duke University Press.

———. 2003. *The Locrian Maidens: Love and Death in Greek Italy.* Princeton, NJ: Princeton University Press.

Reece, S. 1993. *The Stranger's Welcome: Oral Theory and the Aesthetics of the Homeric Hospitality Scene.* Ann Arbor: University of Michigan Press.

Reeder, Ellen D., ed. 1995. *Pandora: Women in Classical Greece.* Princeton, NJ: Princeton University Press.

Richlin, Amy. 1993. "The Ethnographer's Dilemma and the Dream of a Lost Golden Age." In N. S. Rabinowitz and A. Richlin, eds., *Feminist Theory and the Classics,* 272–303. New York: Routledge.

Ridgway, Brunilde Sismondo. 1987. "Ancient Greek Women and Art: The Material Evidence." *American Journal of Archaeology* 91: 399–409.

———. 1992. "Images of Athena on the Akropolis." In J. Neils, ed., *Goddess and Polis,* 119–42. Princeton, NJ: Princeton University Press.

Rodenwaldt, G. 1932. "Spinnende Hetären." *Archäologischer Anzeiger* 47: 7–22.

Roller, Duane W., and Letitia K. Roller. 1994. "Penelope's Thick Hand (*Odyssey* 21.6)." *Classical Journal* 90: 9–19.

Rosaldo, M., and L. Lamphere, eds. 1974. *Woman, Culture, and Society.* Stanford, CA: Stanford University Press.

Rose, Peter W. 1992. *Sons of the Gods, Children of Earth: Ideology and Literary Form in Ancient Greece.* Ithaca, NY: Cornell University Press.

Rosenmeyer, Thomas. 1982. *The Art of Aeschylus.* Berkeley: University of California Press.

Rubin, Gayle. 1975. "The Traffic in Women: Notes on the 'Political Economy' of Sex." In R. Reiter, ed., *Toward an Anthropology of Women,* 157–210. New York: Monthly Review Press.

Sacks, Karen. 1979. *Sisters and Wives: The Past and Future of Sexual Equality.* Westport, CT: Greenwood Press.

Sahlins, M. D. 1963. "Poor Man, Rich Man, Big-Man, Chief: Political Types in Melanesia and Polynesia." *Comparative Studies in History and Society* 5: 285–303.

———. 1965. "On the Sociology of Primitive Exchange." In M. Banton, ed., *The Relevance of Models for Social Anthropology,* 139–236. ASA Monographs I. London: Tavistock.

———. 1972. *Stone Age Economics.* New York: Aldine de Gruyter.

Sailor, Dylan, and Sarah Culpepper Stroup. 1999. "ΦΘΟΝΟΣ Δ'ΑΠΕΣΤΩ: The Translation of Transgression in Aiskhylos' *Agamemnon.*" *Classical Antiquity* 18: 153–82.

Saintillan, David. 1996. "Du festin à l'échange: Les Grâces de Pandore." In F. Blaise, P. Judet de la Combe, and P. Rousseau, eds., *Le Métier du mythe: Lectures d'Hésiode,* 315–48. [Villeneuve d'Ascq]: Presses universitaires du Septentrion.

Saller, Richard. 1994. *Patriarchy, Property and Death in the Roman Family.* Cambridge: Cambridge University Press.

Sanday, Peggy Reeves. 1981. *Female Power and Male Domination: On the Origins of Sexual Inequality.* Cambridge: Cambridge University Press.

Scaife, Ross. 1995. "Ritual and Persuasion in the House of Ischomachus." *Classical Journal* 90: 225–32.

Schaps, David. 1979. *Economic Rights of Women in Ancient Greece.* Edinburgh: Edinburgh University Press.

Scheid, John, and Jesper Svenbro. [1994] 1996. *The Craft of Zeus: Myths of Weaving and Fabric.* Translated by C. Volk. Princeton, NJ: Princeton University Press.

Scheid-Tissinier, Évelyne. 1994. *Les Usages du don chez Homère: Vocabulaire et pratiques.* Nancy: Presses Universitaires de Nancy.

Schnapp, Alain. 1984. "Seduction and Gesture in Ancient Imagery." *History and Anthropology* 1: 49–55.

Schneider, Jane. 1971. "Of Vigilance and Virgins: Honor, Shame and Access to Resources in Mediterranean Societies." *Ethnology* 10: 1–24.

Schwimmer, Erik. 1974. "Objects of Mediation: Myth and Praxis." In I. Rossi, ed., *The Unconscious in Culture: The Structuralism of Claude Lévi-Strauss in Perspective*, 209–55. New York: E.P. Dutton.

Scodel, Ruth. 1996. "Δόμων ἄγαλμα: Virgin Sacrifice and Aesthetic Object." *Transactions of the American Philological Association* 126: 111–28.

———. 2008. *Epic Facework: Self-Presentation and Social Interaction in Homer.* Swansea: Classical Press of Wales.

Scott, Joan W. 1986. "Gender: A Useful Category of Historical Analysis." *American Historical Review* 91: 1053–75.

Scully, Stephen. 1990. *Homer and the Sacred City.* Ithaca, NY: Cornell University Press.

Seaford, Richard. 1984. "The Last Bath of Agamemnon." *Classical Quarterly* 34: 247–54.

———. 1987. "The Tragic Wedding." *Journal of Hellenic Studies* 107: 106–30.

———. 1994. *Reciprocity and Ritual: Homer and Tragedy in the Developing City-State.* Oxford: Clarendon Press.

———. 1998. "Tragic Money." *Journal of Hellenic Studies* 118: 119–39.

———. 2004. *Money and the Early Greek Mind.* Cambridge: Cambridge University Press.

Sealey, Raphael. 1990. *Women and Law in Classical Greece.* Chapel Hill: University of North Carolina Press.

Sedgwick, Eve Kosofsky. 1985. *Between Men: English Literature and Male Homosocial Desire.* New York: Columbia University Press.

Segal, Charles. 1981. *Tragedy and Civilization: An Interpretation of Sophocles.* Cambridge, MA: Harvard University Press.

———. 1986. *Interpreting Greek Tragedy: Myth, Poetry, Text.* Ithaca, NY: Cornell University Press.

———. 1995. *Sophocles' Tragic World: Divinity, Nature, Society.* Cambridge, MA: Harvard University Press.

Sen, Amartya. 1990. "More Than 100 Million Women Are Missing." *New York Review of Books* 37, no. 20 (Dec. 20): 61–66.

Senior, Louise M. 2000. "Gender and Craft Innovation: Proposal of a Model." In Donald and Hurcombe: 71–87.

Sergent, Bernard. 1990. *"L'Or et la mauvaise femme." L'Homme* 113: 13–42.

Shaw, Brent. 1992. "Explaining Incest: Brother-Sister Marriage in Greco-Roman Egypt." *Man* 27: 267–99.

Sissa, Giulia. 1990. *Greek Virginity.* Translated by A. Goldhammer. Cambridge, MA: Harvard University Press.

Skinner, M., ed. 1986. *Rescuing Creusa: New Methodological Approaches to Women in Antiquity. Helios*, Special Issue 13.

Slatkin, Laura M. 1991. *The Power of Thetis: Allusion and Interpretation in the* Iliad. Berkeley: University of California Press.

Snodgrass, A. 1974. "An Historical Homeric Society?" *Journal of Hellenic Studies* 94: 114–25.

———

BIBLIOGRAPHY

Sommerstein, A. 1980. "The Naming of Women in Greek and Roman Comedy." *Quaderni di storia* 11: 395–418.

Ste. Croix, G.E.M. de. 1970. "Some Observations on the Property Rights of Women." *Classical Review* 20: 273–78.

Stehle, Eva. 1990. "Sappho's Gaze: Fantasies of a Goddess and Young Man." *Differences* 2: 88–125.

Strathern, Marilyn. 1981."Culture in a Net Bag: The Manufacture of a Subdiscipline in Anthropology." *Man*, n.s. 16: 665–88.

———. 1987a. "An Awkward Relationship: The Case of Feminism and Anthropology." *Signs* 12: 276–92.

———, ed. 1987b. *Dealing with Inequality: Analysing Gender Relations in Melanesia and Beyond*. Cambridge: Cambridge University Press.

———. 1989. *The Gender of the Gift*. Berkeley: University of California Press.

Sussman, Linda S. 1984. "Workers and Drones: Labor, Idleness and Gender Definition in Hesiod's Beehive." In Peradotto and Sullivan: 79–93.

Sutton, Robert F., Jr. 1981. "The Interaction between Men and Women Portrayed on Attic Red-Figure Pottery." Ph.D. dissertation, University of North Carolina.

Suzuki, Mihoko. 1989. *Metamorphoses of Helen: Authority, Difference, and the Epic*. Ithaca, NY: Cornell University Press.

Tambiah, Stanley J. 1989. "Bridewealth and Dowry Revisited: The Position of Women in Sub-Saharan Africa and North India." *Current Anthropology* 30: 413–35.

Taplin, Oliver. 1977. *The Stagecraft of Aeschylus: The Dramatic Use of Exits and Entrances in Greek Tragedy*. Oxford: Clarendon Press.

Tcherkezoff, Serge. 1993. "The Illusion of Dualism in Samoa: 'Brothers-and-Sisters' Are Not 'Men-and-Women.'" Translated by S. M. Tenison. In Teresa del Valle, ed., *Gendered Anthropology*, 54–87. London: Routledge.

Thalmann, William G. 1998. *The Swineherd and the Bow: Representations of Class in the Odyssey*. Ithaca, NY: Cornell University Press.

Thomas, Nicholas. 1991. *Entangled Objects: Exchange, Material Culture, and Colonialism in the Pacific*. Cambridge, MA: Harvard University Press.

Thompson, W. E. 1981–82. "Weaving: A Man's Work." *Classical World* 75: 217–22.

Tilley, C. 1990. "Claude Lévi-Strauss: Structuralism and Beyond." In C. Tilley, ed., *Reading Material Culture*, 3–81. Oxford: Oxford University Press.

Todd, Stephen. 1990. "The Use and Abuse of the Attic Orators." *Greece & Rome* 37: 159–78.

Tourraix, A. 1976. "La Femme et le pouvoir chez Hérodote." *Dialogues d'histoire ancienne* 2: 369–90.

Trautman, Thomas R. 1987. *Lewis Henry Morgan and the Invention of Kinship*. Berkeley: University of California Press.

Valeri, Valerio. 1994. "Buying Women but Not Selling Them: Gift and Commodity Exchange in Huaulu Alliance." *Man* 29.1: 1–26.

Van Baal, J. 1976. "Offering, Sacrifice, and Gift." *Numen* 23: 161–78.

van Wees, Hans. 1992. *Status Warriors: War, Violence, and Society in Homer and History*. Amsterdam: Gieben.

———. 1998. "The Law of Gratitude: Reciprocity in Anthropological Theory." In Gill et al.: 13–49.

———. 2002. "Greed, Generosity and Gift-Exchange in Early Greece and the Western Pacific." In W. Jongman and M. Kleijwegt, eds., *After the Past*, 341–78. Leiden: Brill.

Vellacott, Philip. 1975. *Ironic Drama: A Study of Euripides' Method and Meaning*. London and New York: Cambridge University Press.

Vernant, J.-P. [1965] 1983. "Hestia-Hermes: The Religious Expression of Space and Movement in Ancient Greece." In *Myth and Thought among the Greeks*, 127–75. London: Routledge and Kegan Paul.

———. 1973. "Le Mariage en Grèce Antique." *Parola del passato* 28: 51–74.

———. [1974] 1980. *Myth and Society in Ancient Greece*. Translated by J. Lloyd. London: Methuen.

———. [1979] 1989. "At Man's Table: Hesiod's Foundation Myth of Sacrifice." In M. Detienne and J.-P. Vernant, *The Cuisine of Sacrifice among the Greeks*, 21–86. Translated by P. Wissing. Chicago: University of Chicago Press.

———. 2000. *Pandora, la première femme*. Paris: Bayard.

Vidal-Naquet, Pierre. 1981. "Slavery and the Rule of Women in Tradition, Myth and Utopia." In R. L. Gordon, ed., *Myth, Religion and Society*, 187–200. Cambridge: Cambridge University Press.

Visser, Margaret. 1986. "Medea: Daughter, Sister, Wife, and Mother: Natal Family Versus Conjugal Family in Greek and Roman Myths about Women." In Martin Cropp, Elaine Fantham, and S. E. Scully, eds., *Greek Tragedy and Its Legacy: Essays Presented to D. J. Conacher*, 149–65. Calgary: University of Calgary Press.

von Reden, Sitta. 1995. *Exchange in Ancient Greece*. London: Duckworth.

———. 1999. "Re-evaluating Gernet: Value and Greek Myth." In R. Buxton, ed., *From Myth to Reason*, 51–70. Oxford: Oxford University Press.

Wagner-Hasel, Beate. 1988. "Geschlecht und Gabe: Zum Brautgütersystem bei Homer." *Zeitschrift der Savigny-Stiftung für Rechtsgeschichte* 105: 41–49.

———. 2000. *Der Stoff der Gaben. Kultur und Politik des Schenkens und Tausches im archaischen Griechenland*. Frankfurt: Campus.

Walcot, Peter. 1969. "ΧΡΥΣΕΑ ΧΑΛΚΕΙΟΝ: A Further Comment." *Classical Review* 19: 12–13.

Waldo, D., and N. D. Willows, eds. 1991. *Archaeology of Gender*. Calgary: University of Calgary Press.

Weiner, Annette B. 1979. *Women of Value, Men of Renown*. Austin: University of Texas Press.

———. 1992. *Inalienable Possessions: The Paradox of Keeping-While-Giving*. Berkeley: University of California Press.

Weiner, Annette B., and Jane Schneider, eds. 1989. *Cloth and Human Experience*. Washington, DC: Smithsonian.

West, M. L. 1966. *Hesiod's* Theogony. Oxford: Clarendon Press.

———. 1978. *Hesiod's* Works and Days. Oxford: Clarendon Press.

———, ed. 2003. *Greek Epic Fragments from the Seventh to the Fifth Centuries BC*. Cambridge, MA: Harvard University Press.

Westbrook, Raymond. 1994. "Mitgift." *Reallexikon der Assyrologie*, 273–83. Berlin: de Gruyter.

———. 2005. "Penelope's Dowry and Odysseus' Kingship." *Symposion* 2001, 3–23. Vienna: Osterreichischen Akademie der Wissenschaften. Reprinted in Lyons and Westbrook.

Willetts, Ronald. 1967. *The Law Code of Gortyn. Kadmos* suppl. 1. Berlin.

Wilson, Donna. 2002. *Ransom, Revenge, and Heroic Identity in the* Iliad. Cambridge: Cambridge University Press.

Winkler, John J. 1990. *The Constraints of Desire*. New York: Routledge.

Winnington-Ingram, R. P. 1980. *Sophocles: An Interpretation*. Cambridge: Cambridge University Press.

Wohl, Victoria J. 1993. "Standing by the Stathmos: The Creation of Sexual Ideology in the *Odyssey*." *Arethusa* 26: 19–50.

———. 1998. *Intimate Commerce: Exchange, Gender, and Subjectivity in Greek Tragedy*. Austin: University of Texas Press.

Wolff, H. J. 1944. "Marriage Law and Family Organization in Ancient Athens." *Traditio* 2: 43–95.

Wolkstein, Diane, and Samuel Noah Kramer, eds. 1983. *Inanna: Queen of Heaven and Earth: Songs and Hymns from Sumer*. New York: Harper and Row.

Wyse, William. [1904] 1979. *The Speeches of Isaeus*. New York: Arno Press.

Zeitlin, Froma. 1981. "Travesties of Gender and Genre in Aristophanes' *Thesmophoriazusae*." In Foley: 169–217.

———. 1985. "The Power of Aphrodite: Eros and the Boundaries of the Self in the *Hippolytus*." In Peter Burian, ed., *Directions in Euripidean Criticism*, 52–111 with nn. 189–209. Durham, NC: Duke University Press.

———. 1995. "The Economics of Hesiod's Pandora." In Reeder: 49–56.

———. [1995] 1996a. "Figuring Fidelity in Homer's *Odyssey*." In *Playing the Other: Gender and Society in Classical Greek Literature*, 19–52. Chicago: University of Chicago Press. Reprinted from Beth Cohen, ed., *The Distaff Side: Representing the Female in Homer's* Odyssey, 117–52. Oxford: Oxford University Press.

———. 1996b. "Signifying the Difference: The Case of Hesiod's Pandora." In *Playing the Other: Gender and Society in Classical Greek Literature*, 53–86. Chicago: University of Chicago Press.

Zerba, Michelle. 2009. "What Penelope Knew: Doubt and Scepticism in the *Odyssey*." *Classical Quarterly* 59: 295–316.

INDEX

Page numbers in italics denote illustrations.

Alkibiades, 89–90

Alkinoos, 17, 65–66, 119n.18

Alkmene, 98–99

Alphesiboia, 122n.54

Althaia, 98, 132n.17

Amphiaraos, 1, 30, 120n.41

Amphitryon, 98–99

anaklypteria, 26

—reverse, Penelope's, 97–98

Anakreon, 118n.1

anangkaios, 88–89

Anchises, 54, 64

Andaman Islanders, dream of marriage avoidance, 101–102

Anderson, Michael, 64

androboulon, 79

Andromache, 26, 57, 122n.65

Anesidora, 42, 123n.85. *See also* Pandora

Anthos, 99–100

anthropology, and colonialism, 114n.8

Antigone, 88, 92–95, 109, 131n.51, 131n.64, 132n.16

Antimachos of Teos, 1

anxiety

—about children's legitimacy, 24

—about reproduction, 39

—about women and exchange, 20, 90

—about women in marriage, 21

—over women's sexual secrets, 84

Aphrodite, 34–35, 38, 41, 54, 63, 98

apoina, 59, 60

Apollo, 63, 104, 121n.51

—human gestation theory, 89, 94, 124n.97

Apollodoros, 63, 98, 99, 101, 121n.51, 132n.17

Arachne, 120n.27

Arete, Queen, 66, 72, 73, 111, 117n.56, 119n.18, 127n.4, 128n.16

Aristophanes, 125n.117

Aristotle

—on female land ownership in Sparta, 21

—on the *oikos*, 47

—*Poetics*, 92

—*Politics*, on self-sufficiency, 51–52

Arkesilaos of Cyrene, 25

arm-bands, shell, 9. *See also* shell valuables

armor

—of Achilles, 37, 126n.26

—of Glaukos and Diomedes, exchanged, 14, 61–62, 127n.31

Artemis

—Brauronia, textile offerings to, 29, 120n.37

—Peitho, temple of, 98

—as sacred sister, 104

Arthur, Marylin, 103

artisanal vs. domestic production, 50

Astyoche, 69, 70, 75, 96, 127–128n.12, 128n.14

Atalanta, 117n.56

Atchity, Kenneth, 75

Athena, 40, 41, 68, 109, 110, 119n.18, 120n.30, 124n.106, 125n.8

—and the creation of Pandora, 18, 28, 40, 44, 46

—motherless, 94

—patronage of Odysseus, 72, 73

Atreus, 37, 107, 108

autarkeia, 3, 5, 8, 46, 48, 50, 51, 80, 111, 125n.120

balanced reciprocity, 14, 58–59, 62

—and social distance, 126n.25

baptōl/baphē, 78–79, 83

Barber, Elizabeth, 75, 119n.16

Baruya (New Guinea)

—marriage exchange among, 117n.57

basket, for wool, 32

basketmaking, as women's work, 14

bee-women, 23, 45, 118n.7

belts, women's, 26, 119n.19

betrayal

—by Astyoche, of her son, 69

—by Eriphyle, of her husband, 10, 31–33, 69

—of men in exchange for gifts, 5

"Big Man" societies, 9

bilateral descent, Athenian, 11

bilateral inheritance, Athenian, 11, 95

binary thinking, in Greek thought, 49–50

birth family. *See* natal family

Block, Elizabeth, 72

bone, objects in, as men's work, 14

division of labor, gendered, 4, 8, 14–15, 16, 25, 29, 44, 50, 81

dolos, 27

domestic economy, vs. trade and artisanal production, 8

Donlan, Walter, 1

dowry, 4, 12, 18, 21, 89, 113n.11
—and connection with birth family, 96
—in Homer, 11, 115n.18
—inalienability of, 22, 25
—Penelope's, and Ithaka's kingship, 75, 120n.39
—and women's power, in 20th-c. Greece, 117n.64

"The Dream of a World without Women" (Arthur), 103

drugs, gift of, 67–68

earth-women, 45–46

"economic phallus," man's purse as, 121n.43

economics, 47–48
—of gender, 2, 5, 22, 111

economies, domestic vs. trade/artisanal, 8

eedna/hedna, 115n.18. *See also* dowry

Elektra, 105
—and reunion of her siblings, 107
—as token between Orestes and Iphigeneia, 108

elpis, 39. *See also* Hope

endogamy, 114n.12
—Alkinoos and Arete, 20
—Athenian, 9–10
—vs. exogamy, 8–9

enslavement of women, 56

epiklerate, 9–10

epiklēros, 10, 25, 114n.13

Epimetheus, 53

Eratosthenes. *See* Lysias

erga gunaikōn, 41, 44, 81, 84, 119n.18, 124n.96. *See also* women's work
—become *mermera erga*, 41, 84

Eriphyle, bribed with necklace, 1, 7, 10, 31, *31, 32*, 69, 74, 91
—currency of myth, 70, 128n.14
—in vase paintings, 30–34, *31, 32*, 121n.45

Eris (Strife/Discord), 38, 63

Essai sur le don (Mauss), 12

Euelthon, 25, 119n.15

Eumaios, 49, 73, 125n.8

Eumenides, 88

Euphiletos, in Lysias oration, 23–24

Euripides, 87, 118n.1
—*Alkestis*, 36, 88–89, 99
—*Elektra*, 92, 100, 105, 109
—*Hekabe*, 131n.54
—*Hippolytos*, 68, 103–104
—*Iphigeneia among the Taurians*, 99, 100, 106–109
—on Klytemnestra as spear captive, 126n.11
—*Medea*, 87–88, 103, 128n.2, 130n.37
—*Melanippê Desmotês*, 23

Europe, sister of Kadmos, 94

Eurykleia, 65, 72, 126n.9, 128n.16

Eurymedousa, 65–66

Eurypalos, 70

Eurypalos (Sophocles), 128n.14

exchange
—of armor, by Glaukos and Diomedes, 14, 61–62, 120n.28, 127n.31
—avoidance of, and sibling relations, 5
—corrupted, throughout Trojan War myths, 56
—dangerous, 5
—deadly, 20
—and gender difference, 2, 81
—good and bad, in Pandora, 44, 124n.105
—"good" female, textiles as medium of, 73
—marriage as site of, 19–20, 22
—in Odysseus' relations with women, 72–73
—perversion of, 5
—standing in for marriage, 104
—women as both objects and agents of, 1
—of women at hands of brother, 92
—with world outside the *oikos*, 49

exogamy
—Athenian, 9
—with non-Athenian women, 125n.120
—and suspicion, 2
—vs. endogamy, 8–9

extradomestic distribution, 17

family, solidarity of, 5
female wealth, 8, 16, 25, 67
—Klytemnestra's dyed cloth, 129n.14, 129n.17, 129n.23
"Femininity" (Freud), 16
Ferrari, Giovanni, 44, 124n.105
Ferrari, Gloria, 121n.48
fertility, female
—Hesiod on, 89
—wars over access to, 126n.16
fetishizing of Odysseus, 73–74
fidelity, female, 8, 83. *See also* adultery; infidelity
Finkelberg, Margalit, 75, 115n.18, 127n.3
fire, Prometheus' gift of, 38, 44, 124n.106
Fitzgerald, Robert, 70
flower-pot gestation theory, Apollo's, 89, 94, 124n.97
Foley, Helene P., 11
food, gathering and preparation of, 14, 126n.9
Foxhall, Lin, 25
Freud, Sigmund, 16, 116n.37
Friedl, Ernestine, 14, 17, 29, 117n.64
Fruzzetti, Lina F., 115n.23
funerals
—mother's, in Lysias, 118n.10
—Patroklos's, prizes at games, 55, 117n.61

Gaia, 42
Ganymede, 64, 128n.12
Gawa (Papua New Guinea), 117n.50
Gē, 123n.80, 123n.85
gender
—economics of, 2, 5, 22, 111
—of exchange valuables, 17–18 (*see also* female wealth; male wealth)
genealogies, of objects, 36–37
generalized reciprocity, 111
Gernet, Louis, 7–8, 12, 20, 29–30, 34, 80
gifts, *See also didōmi/dōron*
—ability to give, 29
—betrayal of men in exchange for, 5
—to brother, 10
—of clothing, 64, 72–73
—coercive power of, 30
—competitive giving of, among Penelope's suitors, 74–75

—Deianeira's, from Nessos, 82–83
—divine, 63, 70
—with erotic associations, 31–34, *35*, 121n.43, 121nn.45–46, 121n.48
—of fatal clothing, 84–85
—fire, 38, 44, 124n.106
—gendered, 117n.51
—of gods, ambiguity of, 36–38
—to Helen, gendered, 66–67
—high-rank, 55
—of jewelry, 121n.43
—nuptial, to Hektor and Andromache, from gods, 122n.65
—outside familial context, 30
—Pandora, 123n.87
—pedigreed, 72
—poisonous (*see* poisonous gifts)
—and reciprocity, 12–13
—of self in marriage, as agency, 19
—textile-related, 67
—"womanly," power and danger of, 66, 69–76 (*see also gunaia dōra*)
—and women, as deadly combination, 1
—*xeneia*, 111
—Zeus's, in compensation for Ganymede, 128nn.12–13
gimwali (Trobriand barter objects), 16
girdle. *See zonē*
Glaukos and Diomedes, armor exchange by, 14, 61–62, 120n.28, 127n.31
Glotz, Gustave, 119n.23
goddesses, women compared to, 54
Godelier, Maurice, 12, 18
Goethe, Johann Wolfgang von, 93
gold
—as funeral-games prize, 55
—in Kodi exchange, 20
gold cup, given by Alkinoos, 17
golden apples
—Atalanta's, 117n.56
—and the Judgment of Paris, 63, 127n.32
golden-fleeced lamb, 1, 7, 30, 37, 108
golden necklaces, 121n.43
—of Eriphyle, 1, 7, 10, 30, 32, 36, 69, 91, 120n.41, 121n.43, 121n.51
—of Pandora, 41

golden pin, Deianeira's, 85
golden vine, Astyoche's, 69, 70, 127–128n.12
gold jewelry, as male wealth, 18
Gottschall, Jonathan, 126n.16
Graeber, David, 12
Gregory, C. A., 12
guarding of household possessions, by wife, 23–24, 118n.5
guest-friendship, 58, 62–63, 110–111
guest-gifts, 111
gunaia dōra, 66, 69–70, 75
gunē, 21
Gyges and Kandaules, 120n.39

Haimon, 109
hanging, female suicide by, 85
Harmonia, 30, 36
headdress, figured, 123n.82
heirs, legitimacy of, 24
—attendants use brooches as weapons, 131n.1
Hekabe (Euripides), 131n.54
Hektor
—on Andromache's future, 57
—and Andromache's veil, 26
—body ransomed by Priam, 61, 120n.29
—gods' nuptial gifts to, 122n.65
—requests ransom of his body, 60, 62
Helen, 59–60, 74, 122n.57
—abducted by Paris, 33, *34*, 53
—circulation of, 34–35, 47
—compromised union with Menelaos, 20
—as "daughter of Zeus," 125n.2
—as echo of Pandora, 38
—as gift to Paris, 63
—gives guest-gift to Telemachos, 17, 71–72, 75
—and *ktēmata*, 55, 126n.15
—linked with property, 55
—at the loom, 26
—as mother of Iphigeneia, 133n.33
—as *perimachētos*, 34
—as a punishment, 125nn.3–4
—reclaimed by Menelaos, *32*, 34–35
—returns to Paris, 125n.3

—and the tripod of the Seven Sages, 33–34, 121n.53
—and *xenia*, 111
helmet, Hektor's, 122n.57
Hephaistos, 28–29
—and Achilles' armor, 126n.26
—and Agamemnon's scepter, 37
—artisanry of, in Homer, 49
—and the golden vine, 70, 128n.12
—maker of Menelaos' bowl, 72, 122n.64
—as maker of Pandora, 18, 41, 44, 46
—Prometheus steals fire from, 124n.106
Herakles, 1, 101
—conception of, 99
—and the first sack of Troy, 64
—and the poisoned cloak, 77
—sees death as emasculation, 84
Hermes, 37, 40, 41, 61
Herodotos, 25, 85–86, 132n.5
Hesiod, 3, 5, 110
—*Catalogue of Women*, 58
—*Elpis* (Hope) in, 39
—on female fertility, 89
—gift of technology, 124n.106
—on marriage, 37–39, 43
—misogyny of, 44, 110
—*oikos* self-sufficient in, 46–81
—Pandora story in, 37, 40–42
—seafaring, distrust of, 48
—self-sufficiency of the *oikos* in, 49, 51
—*Theogony*: Pandora story, 42–43, 46
—on women, 39–41, 43
—*Works and Days*, 37
Hesione, 64, 101
Hestia, 87, 131n.58
hetaira with customer scenes, 31
himatia kai chrysia, 18, 121n.43
Hipparete, 89–90
Hippodameia, 96, 97
Hippolytos, 133n.28
Hippolytos (Euripides), 68, 103–104
Homer, 3, 4, 11, 36, 119n.23, 126n.10. *See also Iliad*; *Odyssey*
Homeric Hymn V, to Aphrodite, 54, 128n.13
homophrosunē, 89
homosexual lovers, under single cloak, 130n.34

periphrōn, 74, 128n.16
Persuasion. *See* Peitho
Perysinakis, I. N., 115n.18
Phaidra, 68
pharmaka, 67–68
Pherekydes, 123n.80
Pheretime of Cyrene, 25, 119n.15
Phiale Painter, gift scene by, 121n.45
Philomela, 97, 131n.62
philteros/philtatos, 105
pig-women, 45
Pindar, 119n.23, 127n.34
pirates, and traders, 49
pithos, Pandora's. *See* jar
Plato, and Prometheus' gift of fire,
    124n.106
—*Charmides*, 51
—*Republic*, 34, 51
Plutarch
—*Greek Questions*, 99–100
Podarkes, 64, 101. *See also* Priam
poisonous gifts, 1, 77, 82–83, 130n.37,
    130nn.39–40
polis, *autarkeia* of, 125n.120
Polydamna, 67
Polymnestor, 131n.54
Polyneikes, gift of necklace to Eriphyle,
    30–34, *31*, *32*, 121n.45
—burial of, 92
Polyxene, 58
Pomeroy, Sarah, 118n.10, 125n.9
Poseidon, 63–64
potlatch, 14, 115n.27
potnia thērōn, 123n.82
pottery, women's role in making, 14, 25,
    119n.17. *See also* ceramics
precious objects. *See also* agalmata
—circulation of, 7–8, 91
—metal, as male wealth, 50
prestige, 16, 29
Priam, 101
—on the future of the Trojan women, 57
—ransomed, 64
—redeems Hektor's body, 61, 62, 120n.29
Prier, Raymond, 39
prizes
—in marriage contest, 87
—at Patroklos' funeral games, 55, 117n.61

probata, 50, 51
procreation. *See* reproduction
production, artisanal vs. domestic, 50
Prokne, 87, 97, 120n.27, 131n.62
Prometheus, 38, 44, 124n.106
prostitution, and spinning, 121n.47
Protagoras (Plato), 44
purse, male, 32, 121n.48
Pylades, 92, 106, 108

Rabinowitz, Nancy Sorkin, 2
ransom, 59, 60–61, 127n.29
reciprocity, 1
—balanced, 14, 58–59, 62, 126n.25
—crises of, in *Iliad*, 56, 57–63
—failed, between husband and wife,
    32, 77
—generalized, 62, 111
—and gifts, 12–13
—negative, 14, 44
—in Penelope-Odysseus marriage, 20
—perverted, 8
—and sibling relations, 2
—Redfield, James M., 115n.25
reproduction
—alternative models of, 89, 94, 103, 104,
    124n.97
—male anxiety about, 39
The Republic (Plato), 51
robes
—without armholes, 79, 80
—Hekabe's, made by Sidonian women,
    119n.18
—*himatia kai chrysia*, 121n.43
—poisoned, Deianeira's, 1, 77,
    130nn.39–40

sack of Troy, by Herakles, 63–64
Sacks, Karen, 11
sacred sister, 95
Sahlins, M. D., 12, 13, 58, 59
sailing. *See* seafaring
sailmaking, 14, 25
Samaraka Maroons, 116n.47
Samoa, brother-sister relationship in, 95
Sanday, Peggy Reeves, 14
scepter of Agamemnon, 36–37
Scheid-Tissinier, Évelyne, 71

Schuwalow Painter, gift scenes by, 30, *31*, *32*, 121n.45
Schwimmer, Erik, 18
seafaring and trade, 129n.20
—as bad idea, in Hesiod, 48, 49
Seaford, Richard, 1, 4, 36, 51, 56
seal, 80, 83, 108
—of Agamemnon, 133n.32
seduction
—opportunities for outside the *oikos*, 118n.10
—signed by male handling of chest/basket, 32
Segal, Charles, 82
self-sufficiency. *See autarkeia*
sēmanterion, 80, 83
Semonides of Amorgos, 23, 45, 54, 118n.7
Seven against Thebes, expedition of, 30
Seven Sages, tripod of, 7, 33–35
sexual dimorphism, societies characterized by, 1
sexuality
—anxiety over women's, 84
—"explosive," in Herakles' and Deianeira's houshold, 130n.42
—threatening behavior, and women's work, 84
shamelessness, 55
shell valuables (*vagyu'ua*), in *kula* trade, 9, 15, 16
sibling intimacy, 4
—Melpa dream of, 101, 102, 104
—in Sophocles's Theban Cycle, 109
siblings, 4, 91–112
—and fantasy of marriage avoidance, 10, 101, 109
—half-sibling marriages, 114n.11
—and reciprocity, 2
—relationship exempt from fear of divided loyalties, 5
silver bowl, Menelaos's, 17, 72, 111, 122n.64
sister exchange, 20
sisters, 12. *See also* brother-sister pairs
—classificatory, 20
—and fantasy of avoidable exchange, 5, 10
—power of, and status, 95
—rights of, in kin-corporate societies, 11

Sophocles, 132n.5
—*Antigone*, 92–95
—*Elektra*, 105, 108
—*Eurypalos*, 128n.14
—*Tereus*, 87
—*Trachiniai*, 5, 68, 81–86
Sparta, women as landowners in, 21
spear of Pelops, 108
spheres of exchange, ranked, 15
sphragis, 80, 83, 108
—of Agamemnon, 133n.32
spinning, 25
—associated with prostitution, 121n.47
—vs. weaving, 119n.18
—as women's work, 14
status
—and Homeric war, 126n.16
—male vs. female, 22
Stesichoros, 34
stolos, 82
Strathern, Andrew, 101
Strathern, Marilyn, 18
Strife/Discord. *See* Eris
suicide, 85–86, 130n.49, 131n.55
sungenēs, 88, 101
supplication, 59
suspicion, and exogamy, 2
Sussman, Linda S., 118n.7
sword, Deianeira's suicide by, 85–86, 130n.49, 131n.55

Tantalos, 87, 126n.11
taonga exchange system, Maori, 15
technai, 44
technology, and the Prometheus myth, 124n.106
tekmēria, 108
—of Elektra, in *Choephoroi*, 133n.32
tektōn, 81, 130n.27
Telamon, 64, 101
Telemachos, 22
—guest-gifts to, 17, 71–72, 75, 122n.71, 127n.4
Tereus, 131n.62
textiles
—ambiguous and deadly, 130n.40
—benign use of, between brothers and sisters, 96

—circulation of, 1
—as female wealth, 16
—as gifts to brother, 10
—given to Odysseus by Arete, 127n.4
—as *keimēlia*, 50
—male slaves engaged in making of, 119n.16
—as male wealth among Samaraka Maroons, 116n.47
—as means of communication, 101
—as means of deceit, 40–41
—and metal, combined, in Medea's gifts, 77
—offered to Artemis Brauronia, 120n.37
—production of, as women's work, 14, 23, 25, 81, 126n.9
—as ranked wealth, 17
—in ransom of Hektor's body, 120n.29
—vs. metal wealth, 29, 71–72
—as women's work, 23, 25, 81, 126n.9
Thales, 34, 121n.53
thauma idesthai, 39
theft, 77
—and adultery, 120n.37
Theseus, 88, 104
Thetis, 59, 63
—and Achilles' armor, 126n.26
thuraioi, 100
Thyestes, 1, 30, 37, 87, 107, 108, 122n.69
tokens of recognition, 108, 133n.33
trading
—Achilles engaged in, 126n.26
—Hesiod skeptical of, 48, 49
—*Odyssey's* ambivalence about, 49
—and the sea, 129n.20
tripod
—as prize, 55, 117n.61
—of the Seven Sages, 7, 34, 35, 121n.53
—as transgendered wealth, 116n.44
Trobriand Islanders, 15, 16
—high female status among, 103
—textile distributions on brother's behalf, 95
Trojan horse, 62, 64
Trojan War, myths of, 34, 38
—commodification of women in, 5
—and crises of reciprocity, 56, 57–63
—first sack of Troy, 63–64

—seduction of Helen as cause of, 34
—value of a woman at Troy, 53–57
Tros, 64, 128n.13
two-handled cup
—as funeral-games prize, 55
—Menelaos', 17, 72, 111, 122n.64

uterus, Pandora's jar as, 43, 123n.78

vagyu'ua. See shell valuables
valuables. *See agalmata*
value
—cattle as measure of, 126n.10
—mythic idea of (Gernet), 7
van Wees, Hans, 9
vase paintings, Attic, 3
—women and gifts depicted on, 30–35, 122n.57, 122nn.59–60
veil
—Andromache's, 122n.57
—as noose, 85
—thrown by Zeus over goddess of Underworld, 123n.80
—used to ransom Podarkes, 101
—as woman's status marker, 26
Vernant, J. P., 38, 44, 47, 87, 114n.6, 122n.74, 123nn.78,85, 124nn.101,108, 132n.22
violence, 77
—and negative reciprocity, 14

Wagner-Hasel, Beate, 115n.18
walking stick, 121n.49
war, Homeric, impetus for, 126n.16
wealth
—amassed through having more children, 43
—competitive destruction of, 115n.27
—gendered, 16–19, 29, 94, 117n.50 (*see also* female wealth; male wealth)
—loss of, through women's infidelity, 3
—of the *oikos* (*see* household possessions)
—ranked, 15–16, 17
weaving
—by Deianeira, 130n.39
—equated with speech, 119n.23
—and exposure of sexual crimes, 120n.27

weaving (*continued*)
—in Freud's genital-deficiency theory, 116n.37
—in Hesiod, 43, 124n.95
—low prestige of, 116n.42
—and lying, 40–41
—in the Pandora myth, 18
—Penelope's "loom trick," 26–28, 120n.25
—vs. spinning, 119n.18
—as tokens, 107–108
—as women's work, 14, 25–28
Weiner, Annette, 12, 95, 100, 101, 102
Westbrook, Raymond, 75
wife
—connection with natal family, 12, 96, 115n.25
—exogamic, suspicion of, 2
—fidelity of, 8, 74
—in India, absorbed into husband's family, 115nn.22–23
—necessarily imported from outside the *oikos*, 52
—reproductive potential of, 43
—as resident alien, 87
—as woman's primary identity, 22
Wilson, Donna, 60
Wohl, Victoria, 2, 82
women
—acquired by purchase or capture, in the *Odyssey*, 65
—as *agalmata*, 7, 114n.4
—agency (*see* agency, women's)
—anxieties about, 20, 21
—as both gifts and givers, 1, 90, 91
—in brother-sister pairs (*see* brother-sister alliances)
—*charis* of daughters, 111
—as dangerous gifts, 38–45
—enslavement of, 56
—*epiklēroi* as domestic tyrants, 10
—as funeral-games prizes, 55, 117n.61
—and gifts, as dangerous mix, 1, 66
—in Hesiod, 36–47, 38–45
—illicit circulation of, 8
—Klytemnestra's perversion of role of, 80
—means of suicide, 85

—and natal family, 11
—as objects of exchange, 5, 7, 20–21, 55, 56, 92, 111, 117n.61, 121–122n.54
—ongoing relationship with natal family, 12
—and pottery manufacture, 119n.17
—powers of the sister, and status, 95, 102
—as proletariat, 116n.32
—property ownership by, 21, 24–25
—as propitiatory victims, 58
—reproductive powers feared, 124n.97
—in rural India, 115nn.22–23
—in Semonides, 45–46
—sexual dangers of, 84
—and textile production, 14
—treachery of, in exchange relations, 66, 69–76
—value of, in the *Iliad*, 65
—wars over access to fertility of, 126n.16
—wealth of (*see* dowry; female wealth)
women's work, 49, 125–126n.9
—Klytemnestra's perversion of, 81
—in the *Odyssey*, 65
—plaiting and weaving of natural materials, 119n.19
—and sexually threatening behavior, 84
wool-working, 32
Works and Days (Hesiod), 37
—*oikos* self-sufficient in, 48
—Pandora story in, 40–42
—self-sufficiency of the *oikos* in, 49, 51

xenia, 58, 62–63, 64, 110–111
Xenophon, 23, 47, 50, 114n.6, 118n.7, 125n.9

Zeitlin, Froma, 74, 118n.6, 124nn.96,97,102, 125n.2, 133n.28
Zeus, 37, 38, 59
—fathers Herakles, 99
—gives compensation for Ganymede, 70, 128nn.12–13
—incestuous marriage of, 100
—motive in fathering Helen, 125n.4
—throws veil over goddess of Underworld, 123n.80
zonē, 26, 119n.19

Milton Keynes UK
Ingram Content Group UK Ltd.
UKHW011821150724
445436UK00019B/243